THE MIRROR

A Political History

By the same author

*

Fiction

A TRIAL OF LOVE
WHO GOES HOME
A DREAM OF TREASON
THE HAPPY ONES
A CALL ON KUPRIN
THE MINISTER
THE FRATRICIDES
THE PRIME MINISTER'S DAUGHTER
SHARK ISLAND

Non-Fiction

PRODUCTION FOR VICTORY NOT PROFIT
HOW RUSSIA PREPARED
FRANCE: THE BIRTH OF THE FOURTH REPUBLIC
BEN GURION: A POLITICAL BIOGRAPHY

CECIL HARMSWORTH KING

CHAIRMAN OF THE INTERNATIONAL PUBLISHING CORPORATION

THE MIRROR

A Political History

BY

MAURICE EDELMAN

Illustrated

HAMISH HAMILTON

LONDON

First published in Great Britain, 1966
by Hamish Hamilton Ltd
90 *Great Russell Street London WC*1

Printed in Great Britain by
Western Printing Services Ltd, Bristol

Contents

Illustrations

Acknowledgements

MY PRIME SOURCE in writing this book has been the *Daily Mirror* itself with its back numbers from 1904 to the present day. Among the literary references listed in the bibliography, *Publish and be Damned* and *At Your Peril* by Hugh Cudlipp have been invaluable for his record of the newspaper's development.

For the *Mirror*'s contemporary history, I have had the benefit of conversations, among many others, with Cecil King, Hugh Cudlipp, Sidney Jacobson, John Beavan, the late Herbert Morrison, Ted Castle, Sir William Connor (Cassandra), Alan Fairclough, Matthew Coady, L. A. Lee Howard, Bill Greig and Ellis Birk, all of whom have been closely connected with the *Mirror* at some time in the last thirty years.

I should also like to thank Tom Read, chief and invaluable assistant in my research, together with my secretary, Elinor Kitching, who dealt so patiently with the typing of my manuscript and who investigated, assembled and checked its substance. I am much indebted, too, to Gwen Goddard for her help in retyping this work, and Sonia Abrams for reading and checking the text.

Introduction: The First Thirty Years

THE HISTORY of the *Daily Mirror* is the history of our times. From 1903 till the early 1930s, it reflected in its class-structure an Edwardian society, stratified, self-confident, self-satisfied, hierarchical, crystallized in its values and traditionalist in its politics. After 1934, it expressed the social revolution of the twentieth century. H. G. Bartholomew, Hugh Cudlipp and William Connor (Cassandra), found a language and style through which they made articulate the hopes and demands of a dissatisfied electorate who were beginning to challenge the old values of Britain's Imperial twilight; Cecil King, nephew of its founder Alfred Harmsworth, later Lord Northcliffe, gave them inspiration and a creative framework. From 1926, when King joined the *Mirror*, he was to give the paper political theme and significance, decisive in its importance in the General Elections of 1945 and the post-war years.

The genius of the *Daily Mirror* was that it spontaneously attuned itself to the aspirations of its age. It was vulgar. It spoke for the crowd. At critical times it became the voice of the people, never more so than when Hitler held Europe by the throat and the appeasers were on their knees in supplication. Irreverent and earthy, the *Mirror* found the words for the fighters and workers, for their wives and families, for a whole social class which had emerged from rejection to find itself all-important in Britain's life-and-death struggle.

When the *Mirror* was put on the conveyor belts of the Standard works in Coventry in the 1945 Election, its headline, 'Vote for Him', was a summons to fashion a Britain for the men returning from the wars. The *Mirror* helped to save the old Britain; it helped to fashion the new. It had no ideology; it wasn't the agent of any Party, not even of the Labour Party it supported in 1945; it had a British pragmatism, a common-sense prejudice in favour of jobs, homes and security for ordinary people.

In the thirty years from 1934 to 1964, a silent revolution transformed the established order. Aristocratic authority withered, the trade unions took political power, and the aeroplane and rocket ended Britain's insulation. Recognizing these realities, the *Mirror* acted as a Public Conscience, quickening the public opinion which was to bring about this change.

In the tradition of Northcliffe, the quality of the *Mirror* has been to generate excitement. Page one became the stimulant and page two the prescription. In bold, terse language, the *Mirror* in its leaders told its readers what they thought, and the same day in the pubs and clubs its readers told each other how the *Mirror* agreed with their opinions. The *Mirror* led public opinion by always appearing to march in step with it, and almost always marching half a step ahead.

Generally speaking, the paper has been an advocate rather than a preacher. Those who dislike its brashness and those who admire its forthrightness agree on one thing—the *Mirror* is a unique phenomenon of the twentieth century, not only in its journalistic formula but also in the particular influence it has exercised. No newspaper has the right to decide Government policy. That ultimately is the function of the electorate. But a newspaper has not only a right but a duty to comment on the conduct of governments and to recommend principles of good government. That is the job of a free press in a democratic society.

The *Mirror*, dedicated to entertainment and enlightenment made easy in the form of capsule information, bright pictures, chit-chat correspondence and comic strips, has nevertheless been for thirty years a potent influence in Britain's political life. Beneath its frivolities, there is a solid core of responsibility. That is why within the era from Northcliffe to King, the weight of political achievement lies with the successor rather than with the innovator. Northcliffe invented a style of journalism for mass circulation which King continued. But Northcliffe, despite or because of his egocentricity, had little political success. The *Mirror*, developing its own personality in the last thirty years, always recognized the frontier between press and government; it never tried as Northcliffe did to encroach on government; yet following Northcliffe's principle, it never allowed itself to become its instrument. A reforming newspaper, it began its life by reforming itself—a process which thirty years later it was to repeat.

*

Northcliffe founded the *Daily Mirror* in 1903 as 'a daily newspaper for gentlewomen.' Within three months the prototype turned out to be a failure. It was Northcliffe's only commercial failure in journalism, and his misjudgment can be explained psychologically as springing from *pietas* towards his mother Geraldine rather than as a miscalculation about the market for gentlewomen readers.

Northcliffe was a man of passionate family loyalty, attached to his mother (who was to survive him) with a neurotic intensity. During the First World War on his way to New York, he wrote to her:

'We were in what is considered the danger zone for two and a half days but the passengers took very little notice of it. . . . Wouldn't I like to start straight back to my darling Mum, submarines or not. . . . My love to everyone I love, and most for my darling mother who is in my thoughts a thousand times a day.'

From Washington on June 14th, 1917, he wrote:

'I begin my work as at home at about six o'clock. It is very hot at that hour and I miss my cool room at Poynters which I can see vividly as I write, and I miss my darling, darling Mother. . . .'

He was then fifty-two.

The eldest of fourteen children, Northcliffe, the 'devoted first-born' with his handsome head and Napoleonic forelock, claimed a particular place in his mother's affections, and his last wish was to be buried as near her as possible. The 'old lady of Totteridge' where he provided her with a home had, in turn, a special authority over her son. (Its most striking expression was in 1921 during the Irish negotiations when Northcliffe as proprietor of *The Times* cabled the paper from Japan, ordering 'absolutely no further concessions Irish.' This disturbed his mother, who cabled him in turn:

'Alfred, I will not have Ulster coerced.'

She followed it with another message,

'Alfred—I cannot make up my mind which of your two principal papers is the more vulgar this morning.'

After this stern censure, *The Times* softened its mood.)

In 1903 Alfred Harmsworth, as Northcliffe then was, produced a paper designed to eschew vulgarity. As a guarantee of this, ladies were to write it. The nineteenth-century trend towards equality of the sexes, underlined by Ibsen and the emancipated women socialists, had resulted paradoxically in a female separatism. Harmsworth had learnt that a body called the Women's International Progressive

Union had met in the office of W. T. Stead, editor of the *Westminster Gazette*, to plan a paper for women by women. Harmsworth liked the idea and got in first. Thus, in his diary of 1st November, 1903, he was able to note,

'Came down to Mirror office (at 2, Carmelite Street) found Kennedy Jones in full swing, and after the usual pangs of childbirth produced the first copy at 9.50 p.m. It looks a promising child, but time will tell whether we are on a winner or not.'

Despite his Welsh surname, Kennedy Jones, known in Fleet Street as K.J., was a Scotsman born in Glasgow. It was he who had been responsible for arranging the sale of the *Evening News* for £25,000 to Harmsworth, and thus starting his chain of success. Jones, himself, had begun his career as a newspaper boy, and had starved in Fleet Street; but when he buttoned his fortunes to those of Harmsworth his place in the new journalism of the twentieth century was made. Rough, brutal and sardonic, he was also an expert in the mechanics of journalism. Like many other Fleet Street successes, he was disliked but respected.

His favourite recipe was 'crime, love, money and food,' and although Alfred Harmsworth was to frown on his crudeness, he recognized that K.J. knew how to make newspapers sell. Jones midwifed the new paper with £100,000 spent in publicity, including a gift scheme of gilt and enamel mirrors. On its first day, the *Mirror*'s circulation was 276,000—a gratifying figure that didn't last.

The atmosphere in the *Mirror* office at this time, according to a surviving eyewitness, was of 'a French farce, except that all the ladies were plain. Under the strain of parturition, many swooned away happily to be revived in a setting of chintz curtains, dainty looking-glasses, and Queen Anne chairs.' Harmsworth, with his gallant view of gentlewomen, found this a suitable frame for the *Mirror*, though he was slightly disturbed by their dresses, austere and reinforced by what he called, 'manly collars and cuffs.'

Within a few days Harmsworth saw that this tough exterior wasn't a substitute for efficiency. The circulation wasn't falling; it was diving. K.J. had become a grim onlooker as the women did their best. In the first issue, under the title of 'Our Venture,' Harmsworth had written,

'It may be asked why, if this provision for feminine interests is so urgently needed as the immense demand for the *Daily Mirror* indicates, has it never been supplied before? Partly because it was never necessary, and partly because it was never possible. It was unnecessary, because the freedom, the education, the aims of women have only recently become wide enough to demand serious provision on so large and organized a scale; it was impossible, because it is only now that increased breadth in interests makes it possible for me to find the large staff of cultivated, able and experienced women necessary for the conduct of a suitable newspaper.'

That was the intention, but the performance was far different. In a Napoleonic weekend purge, Harmsworth replaced the editor, Mary Howarth, formerly in charge of the *Daily Mail* women's features, by Hamilton Fyfe, who had been working on the *Morning Advertiser*, the old and robust journal of the publicans and brewers. The scene that followed was, as Fyfe himself put it, like 'the drowning of kittens.' Almost all the women, who till then had spent their time turning out dainty prose, were sacked. The boudoirs disappeared, and tobacco smoke and bellowing laughter filled the offices, replacing lavender water and tinkling tea-cups. And not a moment too soon, for the circulation had reached a low point of 24,801. The *Mirror* was losing £3,000 a week, and was to lose a total of £100,000 before Harmsworth found a formula for recovering the public's interest.

According to Hamilton Fyfe, Harmsworth sat staring at the paper, shaking his head and asking over and over again, 'What's gone wrong?' Finally, he gave his verdict. 'It's taught me that women can't write and don't want to read.'

Kennedy Jones, meanwhile, acted as a censor of *double-entendres*, after an actor and actress at Drury Lane, who got married at matinée time but didn't have time to go away for their honeymoon, were reported by the *Mirror*, in a tail-piece to their self-denial, as 'taking part in the usual performance in the evening.'

The paper continued to sag, and at the beginning of 1904 Harmsworth came to the conclusion that what it required wasn't reform but revolution. The *Mirror* should reflect images. It should be a *picture* paper for men as well as women.

On January 2nd, 1904, the first photographs appeared in its pages. They were virile images. The Russo-Japanese war was brewing, and the *Mirror*'s front page had a studio portrait of Admiral Tora Ijuin, who commanded a Japanese naval squadron; there was also a two-column picture of Japanese sailors at gun-drill on board a man-of-war.

Harmsworth demonstrated with these two historic pictures that a successful journal, to be topical, must carry tomorrow's agenda.

So he began the task of changing the moribund women's newspaper into a picture paper that would dramatically reflect current events and gratify curiosity. On January 26th, 1904, he completely transformed the paper, altering its name briefly to the *Daily Illustrated Mirror*, and reducing its price to ½*d*., 'the first halfpenny daily illustrated publication in the history of journalism,' and henceforward officially described as 'a paper for men and women.' By February 27th, with the circulation rapidly rising, the proprietor was able to publish a jubilant article called, 'How I Dropped £100,000 on the *Mirror*.'

'Owing to much good luck and many loyal co-workers,' he wrote, 'the *Daily Mirror* is, up to the present, the only journalistic failure with which I have been associated. But the *Daily Illustrated Mirror* which has replaced it is certainly one of the simplest journalistic successes with which I have been associated.

'Disaster may often be changed to triumph by alteration in tactics. The faculty of knowing when you are beaten is much more valuable than the faculty of thinking you are not beaten when you are. I had for many years a theory that a daily newspaper for women was in urgent request, and I started one. The belief cost me £100,000. I found out that I was beaten. Women don't want a daily paper of their own.

'It was another instance of the failures made by a mere man in diagnosing women's needs. Some people say that a woman never really knows what she wants. It is certain she knew what she didn't want. She didn't want the *Daily Mirror*.'

'I then changed the price to a halfpenny, and filled it full of photographs and pictures to see how that would do.'

'It did.'

The reorganization meant a change in printing machinery, the setting up of rapid working engraving plant, improvements in halftone stereotype, and the training of a staff of news photographers at a time when press photography was novel and the photographers themselves were called artists.

Harmsworth knew that people were interested in power. Power was his own overriding preoccupation, and within his own field of journalism he allied power to professionalism. In the wider field of politics and public achievement he had the impatience and the curiosity of a talented amateur, but his prejudices and interests coincided with those of millions of ordinary people who were to become his readers.

The early photographs published in the *Mirror* were concerned with power, and men of power. Among them were pictures of the funeral of Admiral Keppel, the Father of the Fleet, a portrait of the famous barrister Rufus Isaacs, a photograph of the new Pope and a pioneer picture of M. and Mme. Curie, whose discovery of radium was then claiming the attention of the world. At that time too Harmsworth introduced to the paper the cartoons of W. K. Haselden, which were to prefigure the strip cartoons of later years, and to attune the public's eye to the evocative outline drawing.

But what decided the success of the *Mirror* was an invention by Arkas Sapt, formerly editor of one of Alfred Harmsworth's publications, *Home Sweet Home*, with which the proprietor had hoped to popularise Bible reading. Sapt himself was by no means a pious man; his chief interest was printing, his chief characteristic improvidence. Constantly in debt and pursued by duns, he would take refuge in station cloakrooms and send a parcel ticket to his colleagues asking them to get him out.

Harold Harmsworth complained to his brother about Sapt's 'eccentric notions,' and wanted to have him sacked for Bohemianism. But Alfred refused. Sapt told him that he could fill a daily newspaper with photographs printed on high speed rotary presses. The idea was as revolutionary in picture journalism as the invention of gunpowder for war. The *Daily Graphic*, then the chief picture paper, still relied on woodcuts and line drawing for illustration, only occasionally using half-tones and printing about 11,000 copies an hour. Sapt claimed that he could treble the speed of printing on an ordinary Hoe press. His first pictures were messy. The ink for retouching was unsuitable. But soon his presses were roaring away printing clear and exciting news pictures in the form designed to remain constant for nearly thirty years. Within a month the *Mirror*'s circulation had risen sevenfold.

Sapt himself commuted for a few hundred pounds his arrangements for commission on the *Mirror*'s sales, thus losing a fortune.

On March 23rd, 1904, the paper appeared with its first all-photographic front page, which henceforward was to determine its style. Ten days later Harmsworth, having realized the intense interest of the British public in royalty, published a whole page of pictures of the Royal children, Prince Henry in a frock, the Prince of Wales, Prince Albert and Princess Mary in sailor suits on ponies. Now the *Mirror* formula was beginning to take shape.

Harmsworth's method was to identify in photographs the key figures of the day, and to leave the rest to the reader's imagination. On the front page of May 9th, 1904, for example, there were four pictures—a photograph of Sir William Harcourt, the Liberal statesman, two photographs of the principals in a sensational French treason spy story, and a composite picture consisting of a map and photograph of Colonel Younghusband, who was missing in Tibet. The leader page also had the characteristic form which it was to retain for thirty years—a Haselden cartoon, letters, gossip, and a striking leader on the Russo-Japanese war, dramatically headed, '? ? ?'

*

At the end of January, 1905, the *Daily Mirror*, in a remarkable logistical exercise moved from Carmelite Street, where its companion paper the *Daily Mail* was born, to 12, Whitefriars Street. In twenty-four hours, three hundred men manhandled the whole *Daily Mirror* machinery—printing, telephones, desks, photographs, stereotyping plant, a total weight of 70,000 tons—from its old site to the new. Drama was the characteristic of a paper already firmly established as a national excitement.

The paper, now registered in the ownership of Pictorial Newspapers, Ltd., belonged to the *Daily Mail* Publishing Co. Ltd., (27,393 shares), Alfred Harmsworth (10,800 shares), Kennedy Jones (2,500), Harold Harmsworth (1,000), Leicester Harmsworth (750). Harold Harmsworth took over the financial and business control, while a short, fat journalist, called Alexander Kenealy, son of the barrister who defended the Tichborne claimant, was in charge of editorial policy, later displacing Hamilton Fyfe. Fyfe was more robust than the ladies before him; but his taste for *belles-lettres* wasn't what the *Mirror* wanted.

Though Fyfe continued to write leaders till 1907, Kenealy took over the editorship in that year and introduced some Transatlantic slam-and-bash, novel in British journalism and distasteful to Harmsworth himself. In 1911, the proprietor was moved to protest. Taking evasive action, Kenealy replied:

'I quite agree with your letter about the bad taste and ignorance of some of the things that appear in the *Daily Mirror*. I have been trying to stop them. Highly educated men, I find, as a rule have no sense of news. They always want to write about ancient Rome or what happened to Jupiter. They regard the death of King Edward as unimportant because it is recent. We have Oxford men here and Eton men. None of them can write gramatically (sic) or spell, and they are woefully ignorant of anything that has happened since 42 B.C.

'I heard one of our Eton young men asking a Board School office boy who hadn't an "H" to his name, who "this man Chamberlain" was. The office boy told him. The Eton man has not been with us for some time.'

Since 1911 there have indeed been few Old Etonians on the staff of the *Mirror*.

Kenealy had been trained by Hearst in the United States. Whatever this meant in terms of picture stealing and infringement of privacy, Kenealy successfully gratified the public curiosity and taste for fun by a series of newspaper stunts which characterized the age of the Press lords.

No one is greatly interested in an acrobat who turns twenty-four consecutive somersaults. But if he does the same thing leaping from an aeroplane with a message to the Prime Minister between his teeth on behalf of old age pensioners, the public interest grows. Already in June, 1904, the *Daily Mirror* organized a 26,000-mile non-stop motor run in order to demonstrate the progress in this embryonic method of travel. On June 22nd a twenty-horse power Talbot driven by a Mr. D. M. Weigal set out from the *Mirror* on its way to Perth and back twice, then on to Portsmouth before completing its course at the *Daily Mirror* offices. Enormous crowds watched the start and finish of this one-car rally. It was a stunt, but it stimulated a widespread interest in the motor-car as a practical form of travel.

A month later, the *Mirror* offered a hundred guinea prize for the first person to swim the Channel. These were the first of a whole series of imaginative competitions and promotions. Beauty competitions for women were interspersed with beauty competitions for babies. The *Mirror* took the Crystal Palace for a Gala Day to which the only admission fee was a cut-out coupon. Within a year the *Mirror*'s Days, like a Royal Garden Party, had to be spread over three days. Empire Day, not yet born, would have nothing on the vast celebrations of the *Daily Mirror*, which became great social jamborees. At Clacton alone in 1908, 10,000 people assembled to celebrate *Daily Mirror* Day.

The strength of the *Mirror* personality as Alfred Harmsworth was building it in those days, was that it commanded public attention by a judicious mixture of gimmick and solid achievement. As its circulation grew so public men were more and more eager to use its columns; Harmsworth for his part was glad to give his paper the prestige of acting as their platform. The 'exclusive' was born. In August, 1905, the *Mirror* obtained an exclusive interview with Lord Minto when he was unexpectedly appointed to follow Curzon as Viceroy of India. A month later, when Serge Witte, the Russian Minister, returned from the Russo-Japanese Peace Conference in the United States, he gave an 'exclusive' to the *Mirror*, partly because of the remarkable photographs which the *Mirror* had published of Port Arthur during its disastrous siege by the Japanese.

The circulation in that year was 350,000 a day, and Harmsworth, now Baron Northcliffe after his elevation by A. J. Balfour, encouraged the enterprise of his circulation department in distributing the paper by unorthodox means which were themselves an advertisement, as when the French and British fleets met at Spithead, and a special motor boat service was organized to carry the paper to readers on the warships. This practical ingenuity was reinforced by more serious experiments in communications. In 1910, the *Mirror* organized the earliest radio experiments from an aircraft, and characteristically chose an actor, Robert Loraine, who was also an airman, to experiment in sending Morse code messages from the air over Salisbury plain to a ground receiver. Loraine, who was acting in a London theatre at the time, would drive down from the theatre after the matinée, and return to London in time for his evening performance.

As a parallel to these experiments, the *Mirror* became the first English newspaper to exchange radio messages with a journalist in a motor-car. This enthusiasm for innovation was characteristic of Northcliffe, who liked to link publicity with social service. In May, 1912, when the inhabitants of St. Kilda, the island in the Outer Hebrides, were having a bad time because of the weather and food shortages, the *Mirror* sent them supplies and set up a complete radio station.

The *Mirror*'s readers liked these public-spirited activities. The paper constantly gave the impression, a justified one more often than not, of being ahead of its day in identifying what was important for the life of the community. The stuff it sold was excitement, and the public liked it.

Yet Northcliffe always regarded the *Mirror* as a sort of bastard child which he protected without pride. His chief interests remained the *Daily Mail*, which he had founded in 1896, and *The Times*, of which he gained control in 1908. It was through these papers that he sought to exert political power. His campaigns for a strong navy, for a military *entente* with France, for an understanding with the USA and, during the war, for the organization of munitions supply, though this involved criticizing the sacrosanct Lord Kitchener, and for compulsory food rationing, were all eventually won—but in the face of constant personal defeat at the hand of the political leaders. His strength was as an opinion-former; his weakness was as a politician.

He could have had little inkling of the manner in which the *Mirror*, his disregarded though brawling brat, was to mature thirty years later as an opinion-former of the new *demos*.

Some months before the Great War broke out, Northcliffe decided to drop his interest in the *Mirror*, and in January, 1914, sold his shares to his brother Harold. The change of ownership was a watershed in the *Mirror*'s development, barely perceptible at first, but gradually becoming clearer as Rothermere, primarily a business man, imposed his own crude personality on the paper. Northcliffe himself was above all a journalist, and on his death, *The Times*, despite his quarrels with his subordinates on the paper, acknowledged it with respect.

The Times History wrote of him,

'The creator of *Answers* (1888), *Comic Cuts* (1890), *Sunday Companion* (1894), *Home Chat* (1895), the *Daily Mail* (1896), and the *Daily Mirror* (1903), the restorer of the *Evening News*, and the saviour of *The Times*, was unquestionably the greatest popular journalist of his time. To begin with, his technical capacities ranged widely. He had performed all the work of the editorial, advertising or layout man, and knew the uses and costs of copy, type, ink, paper and binding.'

It added this obituary note.

'Alfred Charles William Viscount Northcliffe knew that he could have won 'success' at far less effort and at almost no risk if he had adopted for the *Daily Mail*, the *Evening News*, or the *Weekly Dispatch* the formula of the nineteenth century Sunday scandal-sheet.

Crime and pornography were, are, and will remain the easiest way to the largest circulation in the world. That would not mean success to him. Also he could have adopted the latest New York methods of news-selecting, sensationalizing and display. He never allowed that sort of thing in the *Daily Mail* or the *Evening News*. From the first, Northcliffe had too much honesty, too much self-respect, too great an esteem for journalism and too much concern for his staff to choose either of these short ways to fortune. A proprietor's capacity to write will always set limits to the policy of stealing other men's ideas as a means of making money. Northcliffe was not an illiterate proprietor. He began as a writer, always liked writing, and was writing within six weeks of his death. . . . Alfred Harmsworth was a journalist at the age of sixteen, a proprietor at twenty-two, a baronet at thirty-eight, a baron at forty, and a viscount at fifty. The supreme popular journalist was a failure in everything else.'

Yet, despite his failure in personal relationships, especially towards the end of his life when he developed a megalomania physically morbid in its origin, Northcliffe dedicated himself to wide and generous public causes. As *The Times* History says:

'It took Northcliffe to make politicians respect newspapers as a discipline for those apt to forget pledges, evade decisions, or conceal facts. In 1914 to advocate in the *Daily Mail* such an unpopular measure as conscription was to take a risk from which Ministers flinched. His campaigns against Haldane, Kitchener, Asquith and Lloyd George were paralleled only by Barnes' philippic against Brougham and Althorp, and Delane's attacks on Crimean inefficiency. The man had no lack of moral courage. He did nothing for money, though his native ability attracted millions and gave him the power to bestow fortunes on all his principal colleagues. The history of his popular newspapers, when written, will form the fittest monument to him and his genius. He needs to be appreciated as the journalistic pioneer of motor travel, air travel, daylight saving and the numbering and registering of motor-cars, not to mention such diversions as gardening competitions, Ideal Home exhibitions and many more. The *Daily Mail*, the *Evening News*, the *Weekly Dispatch*, which he vitalized, and the *Daily Mirror*, which he founded and made over to Rothermere, were his greatest achievements, and every detail of their making and their progress stimulated their creator to fresh creations.'

Already in 1912, however, his interest in personal power was symptomatized by the narcissism of his self-descriptions. His nicknames, 'The Napoleon of the Press,' and 'The Demon of Fleet Street,' were self-applied titles which he popularized. He tried on Napoleon's hat and commented, 'It fits!' He signed letters 'Lord Vigour and Venom.' He enjoyed the power of money with a practical cynicism. He enjoyed having knights on *The Times* to jump to his command, at the same time as he recognized the snobbery of titles for *The Times*' middle-class readers. He enjoyed the tycoon's pleasure of dominating his employees by making them feel insecure.

In politics, he tried to frighten governments; and his campaigns against Lloyd George, Curzon and the war-time coalition were obsessive and sustained. The origin of his dislike may well have been Lloyd George's spurning of him as a would-be delegate to the 1918 Paris Peace Conference. But his campaign against Lloyd George was in his own mind as much a public and patriotic cause as it was a private vendetta.

Lloyd George wrote in *The Truth About the Peace Treaties* after Northcliffe's death:

'When the 1918 election was impending I had the luck—good or bad—to have an unmendable break in my relations with Lord Northcliffe. They were always precarious. He wielded great power as the proprietor of the most widely-read daily paper and also as the owner of the most influential journal in the kingdom. He was inclined to exercise and to demonstrate that power. When he did so most politicians bowed their heads. He was one of the most outstanding figures of his generation. He was far and away the most redoubtable figure of all the Press barons of my time. He created the popular daily, and the more other journals scoffed at it and the populace derided it at every political gathering of all parties, the more popular it became. . . . He owed no allegiance to any party, so that every genuine party man deplored his paper. Most of them bought it and read what was in it and then damned it.'

Lloyd George could afford to be generous to Northcliffe because the December elections of 1918 were to provide a triumph for him and a crushing defeat for Northcliffe.

Northcliffe was a newspaperman, Rothermere an accountant. But the Harmsworth brothers were allies in the fight against the politicians, a situation which blended into the later Rothermere-Beaverbrook alliance.

In November, 1917, Rothermere, now the established owner of

the *Daily Mirror* and the *Sunday Pictorial*, was appointed Air Minister. His period of office was an unhappy one, troubled by both personal and public misfortune. Two of his sons, Harold and Vere, were killed in the war, the second dying of wounds in February, 1918, a month before Rothermere resigned, his health broken by private grief. In the same month Beaverbrook became a member of Lloyd George's Cabinet, nominally as Chancellor of the Duchy of Lancaster, but actually as Minister of Information, a new Department which was violently resisted by the Old Guard in the Government, who objected to the entry of what they regarded as an upstart press peer into the Cabinet. In the face of opposition from Balfour, the Cecil family and Austen Chamberlain, Beaverbrook attached Northcliffe to himself as Director of Propaganda in Enemy Countries, and gave his friend Rudyard Kipling an information job at home. Of the joint performance of Northcliffe and Beaverbrook, Ludendorff was to write in his post-war memoirs:

'We were hypnotized by the enemy propaganda as a rabbit is by a snake. It was exceptionally clever and conceived on a great scale. . . . In the neutral countries we were subject to a sort of moral blockade.'

In 1914 the ownership of the *Mirror* changed, but not its journalistic policy. Kenealy died in 1915, and he was succeeded by an American friend, Ed Flynn.

The emphasis remained on pictures, and the only difference was that now the public's curiosity about the drama of Continental assassinations and public disasters became more personal. Everyone wanted to know the circumstances in which their husband or father or brother was fighting. The *Mirror* in turn became the most popular paper in the trenches because it carried portraits of home. Just as in peace-time the motor boats sold copies of the *Mirror* to the sailors at Spithead, so during the war the distributors, chiefly children, came regularly up to the reserve lines within a mile and a quarter of the German trenches to sell the paper to the troops. The *Mirror*'s complete service of war correspondents and photographers, who had gained experience in two Balkan wars and in Tripoli during the Italian-Turkish war, dispersed to France and Belgium to record the great drama of war. There were *Mirror* photographers at Ostend when the Germans swept down the coast. They photographed the early attacks on Antwerp and the Naval Division's attempt to support the city, and finally the retreat from Mons. At home the *Mirror* photographers took remarkable pictures of a daylight raid over

London in 1917, showing twenty Gothas in the air at the same time. By the end of the war, the *Mirror* was at a pinnacle of success as a popular picture paper, and one with decided political views.

But Rothermere's capacity for political misjudgment of men and policies was in direct ratio to his capacity to accumulate power as a newspaper owner. Seldom in history has time been able to provide such abundant proof of error. In 1915, Rothermere founded the *Sunday Pictorial*, and made the classic humbug Horatio Bottomley one of its leading writers. Week after week Bottomley harangued its growing readership on God, patriotism, and the need for a non-stop drive to Berlin. On July 25th Rothermere, irked by the Government's indifference to his pressures, wrote in the *Sunday Pictorial*:

'Although we are not short of leaders of men, we do not sufficiently employ them. Take the case of Mr. Horatio Bottomley, whose tonicsome utterances in this journal give inspiration and comfort to the most lugubrious souls. Mr. Bottomley exercises an enormous influence with his pen and voice. Are recruits wanted? He gets them. Is there a strike to settle? He can pour oil on troubled waters. Is there a cause to plead? He pleads it successfully. . . . Yet his great talents are most exercized "unofficially"! He is a force in the State. His services should be utilized more and more by the Government.'

Rothermere failed to get Bottomley into the Government. After the war, with a similar arrogance, he flung the *Mirror* into the anti-waste, anti-Government campaign which was to become for him a morbid obsession. He accused the Government of 'squandermania' —a term of abuse which he distributed recklessly.

On October 4th, 1920, he attacked the idea of a Health Scheme, and followed it two months later with an apocalyptic article called 'Has the Day of Reckoning Come?'

'The House of Commons,' he wrote, 'must listen to the irresistible cry of the people. How shall it help us that our arms were carried to victory, if the fevered Squandermania which followed success in the field drags us down to national bankruptcy?'

He detailed the dangers.

'Why,' he asked 'do we still spend £1,563 upon "King's Plates" for race meetings in Ireland? Can we now afford to subscribe £5,000 a year to an institution called the Empire Parliamentary Association? Ought we to pay £1,000 annually to the Universities because they no longer print certain almanacs?

'Is the Petroleum Department necessary? Does the nation know that the Ministry of National Service is so far from being buried that £10,000 is being allotted to it this year?'

The *Mirror* had now decided to divide Members of Parliament into the waste M.P.s and the anti-waste M.P.s. In a threatening article entitled, 'Hoaxing the Public', it attacked those Members who it claimed, 'were squealing because the newspapers were publishing their names and telling the public how they voted.'

'Do they think,' the article went on, 'the division lists are a monopoly of the Official Reports? Do they want to return to the dark and evil days when the Press was not allowed to describe or to report the proceedings of Parliament?

'No wonder some of them are angry. There are dozens of Members of Parliament who have gone to their constituencies and have made pretentious speeches in favour of economy, after which they have returned to Westminster and voted for one squandering Estimate after another.'

Richard Jennings, later to become the radical voice of the *Mirror*, wrote an article called 'Women Voters and Waste M.P.s: The Housewife's Protest against Squandermania.'

Among Members of Parliament, there was a growing resistance to Rothermere's bullying, but Rothermere and Northcliffe were impenitent. 'Anti-Waste Campaign: Protests in the Commons,' said the *Mirror*'s headlines. 'Members wanted Lord Rothermere and Lord Northcliffe to appear at the Bar of the House. But on the recommendation of the Speaker, a motion by Colonel Archer-Shee to call attention to certain newspaper articles relating to the conduct of certain M.P.s was withdrawn.'

In the meantime, Rothermere had decided to back Sir Thomas Polson as an anti-waste candidate in a Dover bye-election, and as a prelude the *Mirror* attacked those supporters of the Government who had refused to be bullied. Austen Chamberlain described the *Mirror*'s criticism as 'ignorant and irresponsible,' and lumped the *Daily Mail* and the *Mirror* together as 'unworthy critics.' The *Mirror* replied that there was 'no proprietory relationship between the *Daily Mail* and the *Daily Mirror*. Lord Rothermere has no interest in the *Daily Mail* and Lord Northcliffe none in the *Daily Mirror*.'

By the beginning of 1921, the campaign to back Polson was in full swing, and among the articles which the *Daily Mirror* published was one by Horatio Bottomley, M.P., entitled 'Dover's Chance to Make History.' Polson claimed that he was standing as an 'independent anti-waste candidate, the friend of every working man, and every working woman, the friend of the farmer and farm-worker and of the great middle-classes who have been so hard-hit by the squander-mania of the present Government.' The following day the *Mirror*'s front page said, 'The Eyes of the Country are on Dover Today.' With a certified circulation larger than that of any other daily newspaper, the *Mirror* also carried a photograph of Sir Thomas Polson with Bottomley, raising his hat to the crowd.

On January 14th, Rothermere made his point. Colonel Sir Thomas Polson, the anti-waste candidate, defeated the Hon. J. J. Astor, the Unionist candidate, by 3,130 votes. Polson's first announcement was that he wanted to abolish the Ministries of Shipping, Munitions, Food and Health. Rothermere was triumphant. The *Mirror*'s campaign had made a significant inroad into the Government's policy. Encouraged by this success, he went on to join forces with Beaverbrook.

After the Armistice Beaverbrook had supported Lloyd George briefly, but their relationship had soon cooled and Beaverbrook began his campaign to make Bonar Law Prime Minister in his place. Bonar Law left the Cabinet in 1921, and in October 1922 the Conservatives, now led by Bonar Law and Stanley Baldwin, decided to break the Coalition. At the General Election that followed, the Conservatives won with a majority of 71. Although Lloyd George supposedly fell because he backed the wrong horse in the Graeco-Turkish war, he was in fact defeated because the public, with the inspiration of the Rothermere–Beaverbrook press, no longer trusted him.

But Bonar Law, already dying of cancer, didn't live to enjoy his victory, and in May, 1923, Baldwin, for whom Beaverbrook had obtained his first political promotion as Joint Financial Secretary to the Treasury under Bonar Law, was appointed his successor, much to the disappointment of Lord Curzon, the ex-Viceroy and Foreign Secretary or, as Beaverbrook called him, 'His Royal Pomp.'

Some months later the vendetta began between Beaverbrook and Baldwin. Beaverbrook hated Baldwin on two counts; he accused him of disloyalty to Bonar Law, and of having sold out British interests over the American Loan. Baldwin, a patient man, put up with Beaverbrook's gibes for a long time, but eventually he turned on his tormentor, and in an interview with *The People*, then a Conservative weekly, attacked Churchill, Austen Chamberlain and Lord

Birkenhead, whom he believed to be conspiring with Beaverbrook and Rothermere. But his most withering contempt was reserved for the two Press Lords.

'I care not what they say or think,' he said. 'They are both men I would not have in my house. I do not respect them.'

The General Strike of May, 1926 brought a short armistice in the battle of the Press Lords and Parliament, but it could not produce a fundamental reconciliation between them and Baldwin. Nor did the foundation of a United Empire Party by Beaverbrook and Rothermere do anything to endear them to the Conservative leader. They called it a crusade. He called it a vendetta. Their purpose, they claimed, was to reinvigorate the Tory Party. Baldwin saw it as an attempt to destroy it. Rothermere himself in 1929 urged the Tory party to throw Baldwin out and appoint Beaverbrook in his place, reforming the House of Lords to make it possible for peers to be elected to the Commons. The net result of this wrangle was that the United Empire Party campaign split the Tories and helped the Labour Party to win the Election of 1929.

But the climax of the Press Lords versus Parliament battle took place at a meeting in Caxton Hall in June, 1930, when Baldwin said, 'There is nothing more curious in modern evolution than the effects of enormous fortune rapidly made and the control of newspapers of your own.'

After referring to Hearst, Rothermere and Beaverbrook, he continued:

'Here is a letter from Lord Rothermere. "I cannot make it too abundantly clear," he writes, "that under no circumstances whatsoever will I support Mr. Baldwin unless I know exactly what his policy is going to be, unless I have complete guarantees that such policy will be carried out if his Party achieves office, and unless I am acquainted with the names of at least eight or ten of his most prominent colleagues in the next Ministry." '

Then Baldwin continued, amid tremendous applause,

'A more preposterous and insolent demand was never made on the leader of any political party. I repudiate it with contempt, and I will fight that attempt at domination to the end.'

Rothermere wriggled. On July 3rd, the *Mirror*, in an editorial called 'Who Shall be in the Cabinet?' claimed that there were precedents for the names of the prospective Cabinet to be announced by the Party leader in advance of a general election. It called in evidence the views of constitutional authorities like Lord Haldane to sustain this case. It also said of Baldwin's refusal to discuss the names of his prospective Cabinet:

'To appoint such men in privacy, and then to foist them upon the public after an election is grossly to abuse a power not conferred upon leaders by the law and custom of our constitution.'

All of this was part of an unremitting attack on Baldwin for his Safety First policies. But Baldwin's fighting speech was what the Tory party needed, and what the Commons as a whole wanted, because that same night when he entered the Chamber, both sides of the House rose and cheered. Baldwin asked for a vote of confidence from his party, and got it by 462 votes to 116.

The last salvo in this battle which, though unedifying, was concerned with an important question of principle about the place of the press in public life, came in Baldwin's speech on behalf of Duff Cooper when he stood for election in the St. George's constituency of Westminster against a Beaverbrook and Rothermere candidate. The *Daily Mail* had made a savage personal attack on Baldwin, and he replied:

'I have one observation to make about that. The article is signed, "Editor, *Daily Mail*." I have no idea of the name of that gentleman. I would only observe that he is well qualified for the post which he holds. The first part of that statement is a lie, and the second part of that statement by its implication is untrue. The paragraph itself could only have been written by a cad. I have consulted a very high legal authority, and I am advised that an action for libel would lie. I shall not move in the matter and for this reason: I should get an apology and heavy damages. The first is of no value, and the second I would not touch with a bargepole. What the proprietorship of these pages is aiming at is power, and power without responsibility—the prerogative of the harlot throughout the ages.'

These were to become famous words, quoted and re-quoted in every debate on the press that followed.

The United Empire Party contested five bye-elections, and returned one candidate. It lived and died a newspaper stunt.

Shortly afterwards, in 1931, the economic crisis broke over Britain, and a Coalition Government was formed by MacDonald with Baldwin's support. At the General Election MacDonald and Baldwin won an overwhelming victory, and for the time being, the Press Lords' feud abated.

The *Mirror*'s Rothermere period ended formally in 1931, when he finally disposed of his interest in the paper to individual shareholders. By this time the *Mirror*'s circulation had begun to stagnate at the low level of 800,000 to which it had slowly dropped. Its policies, a product of Rothermere's own reactionary and melancholy character, were equally stagnant. The traditional programme of the Tory party decayed at his touch. More and more his sympathies had turned to Fascism, and it was no accident that in 1930 he adopted in his papers a vigorous campaign for the revision of the Treaty of Trianon. He was a popular figure in the Hungary of Admiral Horthy, especially among the ultra-Right Wing *revanchistes*. When he visited Hungary, his carriage was detached from the horses and he was drawn in triumphal procession through the streets of Budapest. At one stage, there was even a movement to make him King of Hungary, a proposal to which Rothermere prudently gave no countenance.

Later on he was to visit Hitler, and to return with an assurance to the British public that Hitler was 'simple and unaffected and obviously sincere. . . . There is no man living whose promise given in regard to something of real moment I would sooner take,' though in his later years he came to recognize that the face of Fascism which he had admired so unreservedly was only a mask for its decomposed features.

With such a misjudgment, the Rothermere era of the *Mirror* came to an end. The spectre of revolution and alarms like the Zinoviev letter were no longer adequate to stampede the mass of the British people into fear of the rising Labour Party. The middle classes were seeking a new place in society. And the formulae of free insurance, competitions and gift schemes which had jollied along the *Mirror*'s circulation were no longer able to support it. The *Mirror*, like the nation itself, was in need of a change.

CHAPTER I

The Nazis: the Early Years

THE HITLER REVOLUTION didn't burst on the British public. It arrived dimly at the beginning of the 1930s; and only towards the end of the decade did its outline become clear. In an age when civil aircraft had not yet familiarized the middle classes with exotic travel, only foreign affairs specialists took note of the rise of the National Socialist Government, the hypnotic influence of Adolf Hitler, its leader, and the significance of far-off places with names like Brno and Memel. The famous men of contemporary German history were Hindenburg and Ludendorff, the respected Field-Marshals of the defeated Imperial Army. In their old age they represented the picture of a Germany dignified despite its humiliation, and protecting its conservative values against Bolshevist revolution. Even Ludendorff, playing in his senility with ideas of Wotan and Nordic mysticism, seemed like an archetypal Teutonic figure, already prehistoric when Tacitus wrote *Germania*. Hindenburg, the revered President, was the solemn repository of the nation's traditional values. With his granite face, his orderly moustache and his soldier's carriage, he was the incarnation of Germany's cherished past. But Hitler's dedicated purpose was to reject the past.

Appointed Chancellor on January 30th, 1933, Hitler crushed all opposition within six weeks. The whole administration fell under Nazi control; a Government-directed boycott of Jews was introduced; and the universities, the Bar and the Civil Service were purged of anti-Nazi elements.

If the phenomenon of applied anti-semitism was the first symptom of Nazism to impinge on the Western mind, it was because official and overt anti-semitism as state policy was novel. The anti-semitism of the Tsarist regime had been familiar to the British public before the First World War; it had been denounced by Christian leaders; and its effects had been felt in the West through the refugees who had found asylum in Britain and the U.S.A. But the Tsarist persecutions had always either been denied or rationalized in political terms. The most extreme Court anti-semite had never justified anti-semitism in racial terms. The most rabid clerical persecutor of Russia's Jews had always offered his victims the escape of conversion to Christianity. What was revolutionary in Hitler's anti-semitism, apart from the fact that he made it public policy, was his attribution to the Jews of original racial sin. Condemned to it and trapped within it, no Jew, according to the Nazi verdict, could ever escape. This denial of the rights of human personality was a negation of Christian belief, and therefore an element in a revolution against the Christian basis of Western civilization. It was the factor which eventually sent millions of Jews to the gas-chambers with the acquiescence of those Germans who had accepted that Jews had no human, let alone civil, rights. In 1933 there were few people, outside Germany, who could conceive that in the progressive twentieth century Germany's leaders could be publicly moved by any other principles than those of reason or accepted Christian tradition. And if the contrary could be proved from *Mein Kampf*, the *bien-pensants* were unwilling to believe it. The persecution of the Jews in 1933 had a curiosity value. There were few who recognized its longer-term significance as a token of Nazi intentions.

The characteristic, indeed, of the early 1930s was the unwillingness of the British Press to believe in the reality of the monster which was beginning to take shape in front of its eyes. The first inhibiting reason was the widespread belief among liberals and conservatives alike that the Treaty of Versailles was unfair to Germany. Accompanying it was a sense of guilt. Thus each breach by Hitler of the Treaty's various clauses produced an ambivalent reaction among British politicians and informed onlookers. In one scale, apprehension tinged with admiration for his audacity; in the other, a sense of relief at being purged of an old burden on the Western conscience.

The Times summed up its own position in these words on June 28th, 1933.

'Europe in fact is placed in the dilemma of having to refuse to force what reason suggests should at least in part be conceded, or else of yielding to extremism what earlier was refused to moderation.'

That was the basis of *The Times*' policy, from which it did not recede until the spring of 1939. As the *History of The Times* puts it:

'For six years the paper saw no reason why an action that was justified by ethics and politics before January, 1933, should be held to be falsified by the events of the 30th of that month.'

It was to ignore totally the nature of Hitler and Nazism, and the purposes for which they acted. The political concessions of appeasement to a potential friend were, as events were to show, of a totally different kind from political concessions made to an enemy who was to use the concessions for the destruction of those who made them.

The most compelling reason why leading British politicians and journalists refused to believe in the enormity of the Nazi programme was fear. To accept the consequences of Nazism was to accept the probability, if not the certainty, that Germany could only be contained by force. Neither the Right nor the Left in Britain wanted war. And the pacifist Left didn't even want to arm. The paradox of the Left was that while it was prepared to support collective military and economic action of the kind expressed by the Peace Ballot organized by the League of Nations Union, it was not prepared to provide the arms or make the economic sacrifice necessary to sustain such action.

British attitudes to the Nazis in the early 1930s can only roughly be differentiated as those of appeasers and anti-appeasers. The differences were rather between those who hoped that Hitler would achieve his national aims without injuring Britain's interests, and those who recognized that his aims were fundamentally hostile to Britain. Within these broad differences, there were variants of disapproval of Hitler's methods as well as his aims. After January 30th, 1933, hope was merely the shield of fear. From that date onwards, Hitler was a dominant European figure whose speeches were studied with the same care by political students searching for assurances of peace as theologians practise when they seek promises of life everlasting in the Bible.

The persecution of the Jews during Hitler's first year was condemned by *The Times*, the *Manchester Guardian* and the *Daily Telegraph*. But laws that protect vice give vice respectability. The Nazis made anti-semitism respectable in Germany and fashionable abroad. On October 4th, 1933, the *Manchester Guardian* wrote:

'We have repeatedly heard in our own columns of "the other side": of the undue preponderance of Jews in the professions, of the many foreign Jews who flocked in after the war, of the Jews involved in this and that "scandal". Were it all true, which it is not, how would it justify the relentless grinding down of the Jewish race, which lives in Germany, so far as it lives, as all private and public reports show, in misery and terror?'

Rothermere's *Evening News*, on the other hand, showed less sympathy with anti-Nazi protest. The day before it had written in a leading article on a meeting at the Albert Hall addressed by Professor Einstein with the support of Sir William Beveridge, Sir Austen Chamberlain and the Bishop of Exeter,

'The lecture is a piece of alien agitation on British soil; its promoters ask nothing better than that it shall make bad blood between this country and Germany. . . . Intelligent and patriotic people will stay carefully away . . . not because they necessarily approve of everything done under the Hitler regime but because "fair play" as they see it, means allowing the Germans to run their own country in their own way exactly as we demand the right to run our country in our own way. It will be time for British agitation when British interests are assailed.'

A few months later, on March 21st, 1934, Rothermere recommended in the *Daily Mail* that Germany be given back Tanganyika, the Cameroons and Togoland. As he explained,

'Though this proposal may not be popular, I am convinced that it is wise. We cannot expect a nation of "he-men" like the Germans to sit forever with folded arms under the provocations and stupidities of the Treaty of Versailles. . . . To deny this mighty nation, conspicuous for its organizing ability and scientific achievements, a share in the work of developing backward regions of the world is preposterous.'

On June 30th, 1934, the Nazi 'he-men' carried out the blood-bath in which General Schleicher, Roehm and the Storm Troopers were massacred at Hitler's personal initiative—the charge, homosexuality and treason.

The *Mirror* commented on Hitler's purge in two searing editorials, 'The Iron Hand in Germany,' and 'What is Happening in Germany?' On July 3rd, the *Mirror* wrote,

'Calm and order secured by political massacre is . . . apt to be the hushed lull before further storm.

'The theory of the totalitarian state and of despotism (a theory as old as the history of mankind) is confronted by this practical difficulty—that no despotism can be run without support, without a backing. The moment the backing begins to waver in its loyalty it has to be violently destroyed, not, as in England, by General Elections, but by machine guns.

'There is again—we have been told—calm and order. For how long? And (most serious question of all) how long before internal dissension seeks to conceal itself by directing the gunfire, not upon "treasonable" Germans, but upon the "enemies of Germany" across her frontiers?'

Rothermere himself wasn't interested in appeasement. What he offered Hitler, Mussolini and Oswald Mosley in Britain was active support. On July 10th, 1933, he said in the *Daily Mail*:

'I urge all British young men and women to study closely the progress of this Nazi régime in Germany. They must not be misled by the misrepresentations of its opponents. The most spiteful detractors of the Nazis are to be found in precisely the same sections of the British public and press as are most vehement in their praises of the Soviet regime in Russia.

'They have started a clamorous campaign of denunciation against what they call "Nazi atrocities" which, as anyone who visits Germany quickly discovers for himself, consist merely of a few isolated acts of violence such as are inevitable among a nation half as big again as ours, but which have been generalized, multiplied and exaggerated to give the impression that Nazi rule is a bloodthirsty tyranny.'

Then came an apologia for Hitler's anti-semitism.

'The German nation, moreover, was rapidly falling under the control of its alien elements. In the last days of the pre-Hitler régime there were twenty times as many Jewish Government officials in Germany as had existed before the war. Israelites of international attachments were insinuating themselves into key positions in the German administrative machine. Three German Ministers only had direct relations with the Press, but in each case the official responsible for conveying news and interpreting policy to the public was a Jew.'

By January 22nd, 1934, he was urging in a special article as an outside contributor to the *Mirror*, 'Give the Blackshirts a Helping Hand.'

'Timid alarmists all this week have been whimpering that the rapid growth in numbers of the British Blackshirts is preparing the way for a system of rulership by means of steel whips and concentration camps.

'Very few of these panic-mongers have any personal knowledge of the countries that are already under Blackshirt government. The notion that a permanent reign of terror exists there has been evolved entirely from their own morbid imaginations, fed by sensational propaganda from opponents of the party now in power.

'As a purely British organization, the Blackshirts will respect those principles of tolerance which are traditional in British politics. They have no prejudice either of class or race. Their recruits are drawn from all social grades and every political party.'

There followed a list of Blackshirt headquarters where prospective Fascists could enrol.

'Hurrah for the Blackshirts' was Rothermere's follow-up article. 'Young men,' it ended, 'may join the British Union of Fascists by writing to the Headquarters, King's Road, Chelsea, London, S.W.'

His support of Mosley wasn't a flash in the pan. On May 2nd he urged his readers to rally to Mosley, who had 'set the whole country thinking, talking, hoping,' by his 'magnificent speeches' and who was the country's only chance of salvation 'from a socialist dictatorship.'

Throughout 1934 from his *Daily Mail* prophecy on January 25th, that 'The Blackshirts will stop war' to his eulogy, 'Germany on her Feet again'—'We and the Germans are blood kindred' and 'Herr Hitler neither drinks, smokes nor eats meat'—he backed the Nazis, claiming that 'nearly all the news regarding the Nazi régime published even in our most responsible journals is pure moonshine.'

It was fortunate for the *Mirror* and the nation that Rothermere had ended his journalistic overlordship of the *Mirror* in 1931, although he wrote occasional articles like the one already quoted. In a letter to John Cowley, then *Mirror* chairman, he had written:

'Referring to our conversation this morning, I wish you to understand most clearly that, in future, the *Mirror* and *Sunday Pictorial* businesses are entirely under your and your colleagues' control.

'As my responsibility I am reserving for myself the Associated Newspaper Company, Northcliffe Newspaper Company and the *Daily Mail* Trust. This is sufficient for a man of my age.'

Thus, apart from an occasional intervention, the *Mirror* was spared Rothermere's influence in favour of fascism and Hitler's Germany, which he was to spread in the *Daily Mail* as late as 1937, when he published his article, 'An Anglo-German Pact Means

Peace,' underlining the terms of that pact with a picture of himself standing shoulder to shoulder with Hitler.

By 1934, the *Mirror* had reached a low point in circulation—just over 700,000—which proved that it had lost contact with its public. Its editor, Leigh Brownlee, who had taken over from Alexander Campbell in 1931 and was to occupy that position for three years, was an ex-schoolmaster and an Oxford 'blue.' But his enthusiasm for cricket and the space he gave to sport couldn't hold the *Mirror*'s readership. In the depression years of enforced leisure, the public wanted a pep-pill, not a sedative. It wanted a paper it could talk to and hear from, a paper with a personality. The public, working-class and unemployed, didn't want to look into or overhear the private world discussions of the middle classes, or gawk at great figures like Lord Birkenhead and John Galsworthy, who straddled the *Mirror*'s feature pages. The newspaper reading public wanted to participate.

H. G. Bartholomew, the down-to-earth, self-taught, editorial director who had joined the paper almost at its birth, recognized this. He saw that in the first instance the *Mirror* would have to make a more direct impact on its public. The shouting age needed shouting headlines. And so he ushered in his revolution with banner headlines in November, 1934, when he transformed the paper with the use of heavy black type. It set the *Mirror*'s style apart from its competitors. It was as direct an approach as a handshake. The public responded, and the circulation began to rise. The straightforward, simple and well-written editorials by W. M., dealing with critical questions of international affairs towards which hitherto the British had the insular detachment of spectators were in tune with the new style, and were undoubtedly one of the elements in the *Mirror*'s new attraction.

'W.M.' was the pseudonym of Richard Jennings, who joined the *Mirror* in 1904, and stayed with it till he retired through ill-health in 1942. The son of L. J. Jennings, M.P. (a former editor of the *New York Times* and later a leader-writer on *The Times*), he had both politics and journalism in his blood. With his spectacles and his tall thin frame, Jennings might seem to have been more suited to be a *littérateur* than a pungent editorialist. His appearance did not, however, belie his tastes or even his function. The aesthetic young man who joined the paper when it was designed as a journal for gentlewomen became one of the most famous book-collectors of his day.

Within his limited scope as literary editor of the *Mirror* in 1913, he published distinguished verse, including the first poems of Edith Sitwell. Northcliffe appreciated his scholarship. For a time he employed Jennings on both the *Mirror* and *The Times*. As a change from the knockabout world of the *Mirror*, Jennings also wrote for the *Times Literary Supplement*, the *Spectator* and *Time and Tide*.

Jennings had Socialist sympathies from his Oxford days, and his pseudonym 'W.M.' was supposed by his colleagues to derive from William Morris. The synthesis of aesthetics and mild socialism expressed his general aspirations. In his private bachelor life as well as in his office, Jennings disliked noise, disorder and loutishness. It explains why, although he had for years written bland and belles-lettristic leaders in the traditional manner of the English essayists, commenting with a gentle detachment on the national scene, except for an occasional hatchet-job like his article on Squandermania for Rothermere, the arrival of Nazism transformed his life and gave a new authority to his writing.

Nazism, with its braying crowds, its jackboots, and its indecent exposure was alien and abhorrent to Jennings. For nearly ten years, his leaders gained in power, so that eventually he became the most quoted and the most hated British journalist in Nazi political circles. Yet his talent could not have flourished had it not grown within the atmosphere of the *Mirror* and the men who were transforming it. It was the atmosphere of a British and radical resistance to the advance of Facism and Nazism. Inside the *Mirror* it wasn't called anti-Fascism. That was a specific doctrinal term of the Left. The *Mirror*'s theme was simply that Britain didn't want to be kicked around. It appealed to everyone except Britain's domestic fascists and those who didn't want to be nasty to Hitler in case he became even nastier than he was.

W.M.'s direct and lucid style was of cardinal importance in the *Mirror*'s self-appointed task of explaining to its readership the nature of the Nazi animal as it emerged through the miasma of propaganda, so different from the picture of the Nazi knight, glistening in his armour as seen in the hallucinatory, self-deceiving, self-induced visions of the future appeasers.

The methods of Nazism soon revealed themselves. On July 27th, 1934, the Austrian Nazis, inspired from the Reich, murdered Dr. Dollfuss, the Austrian Chancellor. The *Mirror* recognized that international gangsterism—it was the first to use the phrase—was a stage on the road to war.

'Hitler's sympathies with the Austrian Nazis are known,' it said. 'However, his first few lessons in responsible diplomacy may have taught him to modify them. Can he control his own gang?

'We can only hope that behind each vapouring Dictator, whose own life is threatened by the hatreds his violence has inspired, are men who will at least attempt to understand the *international* complications that may follow from nationalist outrage. The hope is faint, like the last faint words of the dying Dollfuss, "I only wanted peace." '

Von Papen, whose secretary had been murdered in the June 30th, purge, was sent as Minister to Austria in a cynical cover-up of Hitler's complicity in the murder. The *Mirror* commented in its leader of July 28th,

'A knowing man, anxious to save his own skin in these days, would however be wise not to rely on protestations of friendship from a dictator.

'You never know. There's always a revolver in the drawer and a machine-gun outside the council chamber.'

Hitler's strength was that he could present himself to two great mass interests as a saviour—to the unemployed German workers as a bulwark against capitalism, especially Jewish capitalism, and to the middle classes, from the post-war *declassés* to the property owners, as a champion against Communism. He gave pride to the humiliated and protection to the insecure. He knew that fear is more powerful than love in moving masses. He dominated Germany by fear; and then used the aggressiveness which is the counterpart of fear to dominate Europe. On August 3rd, 1934, just over a year after Hitler had become Chancellor, Hindenburg died; an hour later, Hitler succeeded him as President, took a personal oath of loyalty from the Army as leader of the German Reich and people, and thus, with the foundations of his domestic policy laid, began the second stage of his dynamic career—the stage of outside expansion which was to make Europe tremble.

The *Mirror* had little doubt about the character of the new President. In a trenchant summary on August 7th which stood out in contrast with the politeness of the general press, the *Mirror* said,

'After the old Junker, stern and stalwart, the typical Prussian, comes the hysterical Austrian, with his megalomania, based on an acute inferiority complex, his neurasthenia, his oratorical brilliance, his inexperience in the government of a great people. He is now President as well as Chancellor. He is all and everything—in appearance.

'The next few months will show what substance of power lies behind the passionate gestures and flaming words of Germany's *ersatz* hero—Hindenburg's "substitute." '

Lord Rothermere, quick to give the Nazis the benefit of any doubts, promptly published in the *Daily Mail* an interview with Hitler in which the Führer protested his devotion to peace. The *Mirror* was sceptical. The interview in the *Mail* was, it acknowledged, remarkable. But, it added, 'some of us remember an equally remarkable interview which the ex-Kaiser gave to the *Daily Telegraph* in 1908. That was about six years before the biggest war in history.'

In Hitler's case, the time-lag between peace-loving protestations and military aggression was five years.

The hopes originally entertained by the *Mirror* that the traditional conservative elements might contain Hitler gradually ebbed away as Hitler demonstrated his mastery over the German working class, the middle class and the Junker class. He united them all against a mythical encirclement. He excited the claustrophobia from which the Germans felt they had to break out. Treating non-Germans with contempt and insolence, he created among his fellow-Germans delusions of grandeur supported by a massive rearmament programme which kept them busy. He revived concepts which the civilized world had long rejected as primitive tribalism—the doctrine of the super-race and the master-people—and made them the doctrine of a national faith. And while creating a theology and a theocracy with his own apotheosis, he also established in the methodical German manner an unprecedented Government machine of dictatorship and control. Seen from the outside, Nazi Germany was a stable country daily growing in power, which had accommodated itself to Hitler's supremacy.

A year after Hitler succeeded Hindenburg, the democracies had resigned themselves to the fact that the Treaty of Versailles wasn't worth the bones of a British guardsman or a French *poilu*. The pictures of Nazi soldiers in marching order, the anonymous faces under steel helmets, the glint of light on cold, naked bayonets, the sinister bombers and the promise of other, unknown death-dealing machines rolling through clouds of poison gas, frightened the

British as much as the French. It is idle to deny what pride in the past has rejected, that Hitler succeeded in the 1930s because he terrorized the British as well as the Poles and the French, men, women and children alike. To most people surrender, especially of the interests of others, was preferable to an ugly death. Bullies aren't necessarily cowards, but they are quick to sense the smell of fear. First came Hitler's demand for a Saar plebiscite. On the eve of the poll, the *Mirror* wrote:

'Whoever may gain as a result of tomorrow's vote in the Saar, the defeated can expect small mercy.'

On January 16th, 1935, under the headline, 'The Saar Goes Back to Germany,' the *Mirror* thanked the officials of the League of Nations who had supervised the plebiscite, and then washed its hands of the matter with the words, 'The rest is no longer our affair.'

In March, the *Mirror* still tried to take a detached British view about German belligerence. Hitler, in defiance of the Treaty of Versailles, introduced conscription. The *Mirror* recorded:

'The Versailles Treaty is a dead letter.'

This was indeed the prevailing mood in Britain, and one which the press both inspired and echoed. *The Times* wrote on March 25th, 1935,

'Clauses of the Treaty of Versailles which were long known to be regarded as intolerable by the vanquished country have now been openly defied. They cannot of course be regarded as legally annulled by any unilateral action, but they have in fact been rendered inoperative; and it becomes the part of statesmanship and common sense to arrange for their formal disappearance under the best conditions possible.'

The *Mirror* acknowledged that an arms race had begun, but somehow or other it still clung to the hope that 'after the reverberations of the *hochs* and *heils* and joy-bells has died away,' Germany might be willing to make some constructive effort in the interest of European security.

At this stage, the *Mirror* tried to play down any idea that a crisis had arisen between Britain and Germany. 'W.M.' took the traditional liberal view that the Treaty of Versailles was an unjust imposition. When Hitler called it a *Diktat*, few ILP-ers would have disagreed. 'Is it a Crisis?' asked the *Mirror*. And 'W.M.' replied:

'No great and populous nation can be permanently kept in subjection to the terms of a vindictive peace treaty. The thing could only be done by permanent armed occupation of that people's territory. Or by massacre—as with the Armenians.

'The German people exist. When they strove to fulfill the terms of the Treaty, they existed miserably. It is mere humbug, therefore, to reproach them for defying the Treaty—if they can. We shall get nearer a hope for peace if we recognize these realities.'

Yet even in this comprehending mood, the *Mirror* had no doubt about the danger of German rearmament. 'Her armaments are a danger,' it said, 'particularly in view of the collective or herd hysteria of her people.'

The *Mirror*, like many others, was still searching in 1935 for the most favourable interpretation of Hitler's actions. On September 16th, it spread over the front page the story of the Nuremberg Decrees which degraded the Jews to the status of State-subjects, removed their citizenship and forbade them to contract marriages or have extra-marital intercourse with Aryans. But the editor's perception of the importance of this particular development in applied Nazism made little impact on 'W.M.' He wrote that Hitler's Nuremberg speech was short, and referred to Memel. He also referred to Hitler's avowed intention 'to injure none while tolerating injury from none.' The significance of the major injustice done to the Jews either escaped him or seemed secondary to his more general anxieties about Hitler, who had spoken of his wish to play a part in 'the concert of nations.'

'The terrified audience,' said 'W.M.', wishes that it could escape from the fracas and get on with its own business in peace of mind.'

The mood of 1935 was to 'forget all about the war'—the war being the Great War. There was, as *The Times* History puts it, writing of that newspaper's policy, 'an invincible disposition in the paramount quarters of the office, though not in the Berlin agency,' to make the paper acquiesce in German professions.

That was the mood in which the Nazis tried to split Britain and France in order to destroy each.

But there was little chance of the peace of mind which the *Mirror* had referred to in the last quarter of 1935. Mussolini invaded Abyssinia on October 3rd. The day before the Labour Party Conference at Brighton enthusiastically voted for sanctions against Italy. The *Daily Herald* had commented, 'Sanctions, certain and overwhelming sanctions, mean peace.' The *Mirror* sounded a warning.

Had not the Labour Party consistently voted against rearmament? How could sanctions be applied without adequate arms?

'The Labour policy', as Anthony Eden put it in a later Parliamentary debate, 'is a policy of threats, insults and perorations.'

The *Mirror* agreed.

That didn't mean it shared any of Rothermere's old tenderness for Mussolini. While seeking to keep Britain out of a Mediterranean war, the *Mirror* denounced the 'brawling dictator,' and after the decision by the League of Nations to apply petrol sanctions against Italy, urged that any peace terms should not be an act of appeasement to the aggressor. The *Mirror* opposed a threat of sanctions which were based either on bluff or on a refusal to accept the consequences of ineffective sanctions. At the same time, it reacted indignantly to the Hoare-Laval Pact for the ending of the Abyssinian war at the expense of its victim, Abyssinia.

'We are not ourselves ardent sanctionists,' said the *Mirror* on December 20th, 1935. 'But there is an enormous difference between a doubt about the wisdom or efficacy of reprisals against a warmonger, and the bland acceptance of that warmonger as victor in advance of the event.'

By 1935, the *Mirror* was well aware of the danger of the Nazi-Fascist axis. Yet it still clung to the hope that somehow or other reason would prevail even among the German and Italian leaders, and that they would draw back from the gulf of a general war. The *Mirror* certainly did not share the illusions of the eminent Britons whom Hitler received and harangued on his peaceful intentions.

In 1936, Lord Lothian wrote to Anthony Eden:

'I believe that if we assist Germany to escape from encirclement to a position of balance in Europe, there is a good chance of the twenty-five years peace of which Hitler spoke. British public opinion, with its traditional sagacity, feels that Germany has not yet had justice.'

Appeasement in 1936 was no more than the much-canvassed view that an Anglo-German *rapprochement* was desirable. This was the theme of Joachim von Ribbentrop when he became Ambassador to London on October 30th, 1936. The British public received him coldly. But he had valuable connections among those who held the levers of power. He had, after all, accompanied Lloyd George on his visit to Hitler in September, when the British statesman, accepting a signed photograph from the Nazi said, in a voice warbling with emotion, 'You are the greatest living German.' Lord Londonderry was an old friend—Ribbentrop called him Charlie; they both agreed that Communism was the enemy. At Cliveden, the natural ally of Britain seemed Germany, not France; and the outspoken anti-Germanism of Vansittart, the Permanent Under-Secretary of State at the Foreign Office, was treated by the Astors and their intimates as more of an obstacle to European peace than Hitler's own programme of domination set out in *Mein Kampf*. The mood of the proto-appeasers can be summed up in the words of Tom Jones, the Deputy Secretary to the Cabinet and an assiduous attendant at Cliveden, who travelled with Lloyd George on his visit to Hitler, and concluded after tea, 'Hitler doesn't seek war with us. He seeks our friendship. If we fail him he will turn to Italy and we shall be sorry to have refused him.'

Jones himself records in his *Diary with Letters, 1931–1950*, that when asked by Baldwin what we should do about the pro-French Sir Eric Phipps, Ambassador to Germany till 1937, Jones replied, 'He should be replaced by a man . . . able . . . to enter with sympathetic interest into Hitler's aspirations.'

During his first three years of power, Hitler had no lack of British pilgrims eager to pay him homage as head of state. Among the most attentive was Lord Lothian himself who, on January 31st, 1935, wrote to *The Times*, 'The central fact today is that Germany doesn't want war and is prepared to renounce it absolutely as a method of settling her disputes with her neighbours.' Lothian had no doubt that Hitler had saved Germany in 1933. He believed that Germany's destiny was to save Europe from Communism for the rest of the century.

This was a belief which the *Mirror* didn't entirely share, and when on February 29th, 1936, it published the scoop of an exclusive interview with Hitler, beginning with the words 'Let's be friends. I appeal to reason in international affairs,' the *Mirror*'s comment was a reference to *Mein Kampf*. And yet, with a determined longing to see some merit in the blackmailer's offers, the *Mirror* spoke of the interview as 'a glow of Spring sunshine upon the wintry scene of European confusion.' Hitler spoke of Franco-German reconciliation. But, asked the *Mirror* doubtfully, does not *Mein Kampf* 'abound in bellicose and vengeful references to France?'

Only a week after Hitler gave his pacific interview to the *Mirror*, he marched into the Rhineland, tearing up the provisions of the

Treaty of Versailles and of the Locarno Pact which Germany had voluntarily signed. Hitler accompanied his march with an offer of twenty-five-year peace pacts with his neighbours.

In the face of this, *The Times*, on July 6th, 1936, four months after Hitler's reoccupation of the Rhineland, found itself able to say:

'As for Germany, British opinion is determined, in spite of many setbacks, to come to close grips with Herr Hitler's peace offer as representing the best immediate hope of the stabilization of Western Europe. It may prove to be a vain hope. Certainly German methods of the last last few years (or indeed of the last few days) have not been calculated to foster it.'

The *Mirror*, meanwhile, still under the influence of Hitler's lying interview, gave his twenty-five year Peace Plan its support. This was, indeed, a sudden descent in the *Mirror*'s judgment, the nadir of its political sagacity. 'It Must not be War,' shouted its headlines. 'Hitler's Peace Plan Should Succeed.' And then, standing fair play on its head, it added, 'But French Premier has Refused to Negotiate.' The aggrieved French had indeed to accept the *fait accompli.*

Then, in a blustering editorial on March 9th, the *Mirror* said:

'We refuse to believe that the latest bold blow aimed by Hitler against the moribund Treaty of Versailles provides the slightest excuse for talk about imminent war; or about more sanctions, this time against Germany; or about obsolete pacts and fatuous commitments to which the people of this country have never given their consent.

'Who will be caught again by lying twaddle about war to end war, and about our sacred honour and our solemn oath? The futile pacts and obsolete treaties may lie in pieces wherever Hitler or anybody else has thrown them. Better flimsy fragments of imbecile documents on the ground than millions of rotting bodies of young men!

'The latest week-end crisis does *not* mean war—for us. Enough said, and plainly said. . . .

'Confronted by facts and by the obvious failure of any of these treaties and pacts to fulfil their peaceful aims, we had all ceased to believe in them long ago. Paradoxically, it may be said that those who openly defy them are, perhaps, bringing us, henceforward, no nearer war than those who persist in regarding them as unalterable. Hitler's is only one more exposure of their utter inadequacy to meet the new situation in Europe.

'The time has ended for the making of further pacts, guarantees, agreements, understandings and whatnots in defence of an impossible system, which seeks to perpetuate the ludicrous settlement of the revengeful post-war years. Those arrangements still divide Europe into watertight compartments of victors and vanquished, the satiated and the rebellious. Statesmen talk about "our" signature here, there and all over the world. Whose signature is it? Not that collectively of the millions who would perish in another war. The signature merely of a few muddled and terrified politicians.'

These were contemptible words, and March 1936 was an unhappy month for the *Mirror*'s political judgment. Its editorials kept returning to the theme that Britain should try to reason with Hitler, that it should keep clear of European alliances and that it might even act as an honest broker between France and Germany. By the end of March, 'W.M.' became lyrical.

'Nature is already in a merry mood. The daffodils and the primroses are out and the lambs are skipping in the sun. . . . What does the world and his wife want? Merely to get on with their work and play.'

The Abyssinian War had ended with the annexation of the Abyssinian Empire by Mussolini. Sad but a fact, was the attitude of the *Mirror*. It was glad that Socialist malcontents and a few sincere religious leaders had not had their way and 'brought about a general catastrophe.' The *Mirror* believed that 'a new phase in Europe' was about to begin, and 'that peace might yet be reconstructed on a more confident basis.'

Before the summer was over, the hungry noises of the wolfish dictators recovering from the meals that had gorged them made the *Mirror* put aside its pastoral pipe. By July, the Spanish Civil War had begun, and with it the Fascist intervention in the Western Mediterranean. In the Commons, a debate on defence took place, and Churchill made the first of his monitory speeches. The *Mirror* shook its head, and said:

'Once more it is Mr. Churchill's perhaps not distasteful duty to ginger up our rearming Government in the House of Commons yesterday afternoon.

'He imparted an alarmist atmosphere to the proceedings.

'He can claim credit for having drawn Mr. Baldwin's somnambulist attention to the huge, the inexplicable armaments of Germany. He speaks with authority, as one long closely concerned with the technicalities of war. Thus yesterday we seemed, indeed, back in the dark war age—with Mr. Churchill again demanding his state of emergency and clamouring for a deputation to confer with the Prime Minister.

'It is depressing to have to admit it. But Mr. Churchill is right.'

The next three years were to prove exactly how right Churchill was; and the *Mirror*, independently, joined him in his challenge to the nation's complacency.

CHAPTER II

'Bart' and the Common Touch

If the century of the common man had been looking for a representative in 1934, Harry Guy Bartholomew, appointed in that year as editorial director of the *Daily Mirror* and later to become chairman of the *Mirror* Group, would have been an ideal choice. Though the 'Establishment' was still an object of reverence, 'Bart', as everyone called him, was against it. Long before the aristocracy and its imitators in Britain recognized that their authority was crumbling, Bart spontaneously pointed out to the millions of working-class and lower middle-class readers of the *Mirror* that they mattered, that many of the old accepted and snobbish values were bunk, that stuffed prigs should not be taken at their self-assessment, and that you didn't have to be a public school man to have worthwhile views.

Bart's own background was humble and somewhat Dickensian. His father was a clerk in the City, a struggling Bob Cratchit, his mother a teacher of singing. Born in 1878, Bart grew up in the heyday of Victorian power and social stratification. His schooling was elementary and perfunctory, and all his life he found it hard to express himself in discussion or on paper. He almost never wrote letters in his own hand, and his private file of correspondence at the *Mirror* consisted of refusals to invitations. What he lacked in verbal articulacy, however, he made up for in a visual acuteness. He interpreted ideas as an artist. Indeed, for a short time, he studied at the Slade School of Art, and his first job was as a cartoonist.

He joined the *Mirror* in 1904, two months after it was founded; at the time it was selling 25,000 copies daily. When he left it, its circulation was 4,350,000. This was a collective achievement, stimulated by others as well as by Bart. But he set a tone which was taken up by the *Mirror*'s full orchestra.

Cassandra wrote of him, 'He never, as far as I could see, came to a decision by the normal process of reason or logic.'

He was a tough man, 'hard as nails and soft as butter.'

But toughness was the dominant note struck by this short, white-haired Cheerybles whose appearance contradicted his character. Towards the end of his life, he consciously raised his standards of living in order not to leave an undue inheritance to his surviving family; he didn't believe in inherited privilege. The basis of all his actions, despite the apparent absence of rationale, was careful, forward-looking calculation. Thus, when he joined the Canadian Air Force rather than the British Services, his intention, as he explained to his adopted son, was to make sure that when the war was over he would be among the overseas units which would have priority in demobilisation.

He had achieved distinction on the paper early, first as assistant art editor to Hannen Swaffer and later, at the age of twenty-five, as a director of the *Mirror*. He was a courageous man, eager for action, and after being turned down as a volunteer to fly—his eyesight was bad—he became a war photographer with a commission. Some of his photographs of men going 'over the top' can be seen in the Imperial War Museum. His personal experience under fire became his own standard of what a photographer should risk to get the picture. Earthquakes, wars, revolutions—the whole range of public and private catastrophe was the *Mirror* photographer's parish.

As enterprising and extrovert as he was in this sphere, Bart was shy and withdrawn in his social life. He had almost no personal friends. Though he regularly visited El Vino's, the wine bar in Fleet Street, he usually drank apart with Jennings, the company's secretary. Bart detested pretentiousness. He especially hated the lushness of smart hotels, and when, late in life, to please his wife he lived for a time in a luxury hotel, he couldn't bring himself willingly to use the scented public lifts; whenever he could he used the staff lift. On one occasion, when he stayed at the best hotel in Manchester, he was asked by his adopted son how he would like to spend the evening. 'Shooting rats in the basement,' Bart replied. And that, indeed, is how the two Bartholomews, armed with a borrowed air-pistol, spent their evening in Manchester.

His democratic tastes were instinctive. His sympathies were radical. 'He was no Keir Hardie,' Cassandra said of him, 'but he dearly loved a dead Tory.' That is overstating the case; what Bart wanted was death to the snobbery, the mumbo-jumbo, the self-importance and the arrogance of the upper classes of the 1930s. And if all that couldn't go without taking their owners with them, that was too bad. What Bart despised most of all was incompetence and muddle. Much of the *Mirror*'s criticism of Governments from 1934 onwards was of their fumbling rather than of their wickedness.

To the extent that he had any politics, Bart was a reformer; but as a press man he was a revolutionary. Early in his career at the *Mirror*, he arranged for special trains to bring the paper exclusive photographs; later he used charter aircraft. He was a mechanic who enjoyed using his hands. One of his successful interests was in developing a technique of sending photographs by telegraphic cable. With the help of an assistant named Macfarlane, he invented the Bartlane process, based on earlier German experiments, with which he succeeded in sending the first telegraphed pictures across the Atlantic—photographs of the Shamrock's race for the America's Cup. Some of his practical work was less successful. Thus, he destroyed the *Mirror*'s complete library of four million photographs and press cuttings, substituting for it a microfilm system which was laborious to operate and cumbersome to use. Yet, for all this, Hugh Cudlipp has recorded that 'Bart saved the *Mirror*' when in 1934 it had gone into a decline with a loss of circulation that threatened its life. Pictures and sport weren't enough. What readers wanted was transformation, not amendment.

For at least five years Bart and Cecil King, then the advertising director of the *Mirror*, had been interested in the tabloid style of the New York *Daily Mirror* and the New York *Daily News*. In 1934, with the advice of an American advertising agency, J. Walter Thompson, and with the enthusiastic urging of Cecil King, Bart decided to switch to a tabloid form for the *Mirror*. The old Northcliffe formula of the telegraphic sentence was revived with a modern layout. The leader gave the paper voice and identity. Above all, Bart's own personality was instinctively attuned to the earthy mood of the potential mass readership. The cartoons appealed to those who wanted simple, unsophisticated pleasures. The heroes and heroines of the strip cartoons—Jane, Belinda, Buck Ryan, Patsy, Jumpy and Garth—fed the fantasies of power, loveableness, mystery and charm shared by men and women alike. They fitted in with the *Mirror*'s central theme—irreverence for the sacred cows of the pre-war establishment. Bart's great achievement was to give the common man a swagger, and to make him feel that the *Mirror* and a whole family of beautiful, prepotent and all-knowing strip characters were his friends and cronies.

In 1935, the boldness of the *Mirror*'s new line was reinforced by the arrival at the *Mirror* of a twenty-one-year-old Welshman, Hugh Kinsman Cudlipp, who had answered an advertisement in the *Daily Telegraph* inserted by Bart for a 'bright assistant features editor with ideas, able to take charge.' At the time, Cudlipp was working on the *Sunday Chronicle*, but, as he was to prove very quickly, he had ideas and was able to take charge. He got the job, appointed by the features editor, Basil D. Nicholson, a hard-drinking, eccentric but challenging journalist. Nicholson had joined the paper in 1935, and although he had immediately made an impact by his technical skill with strip cartoons, he habitually clashed with Bartholomew, who resented Nicholson's lack of awe in his presence. Nicholson took a cynical view both of the intelligence and the interests of most people, including Bartholomew's. He believed that what concerned them was their own appetites and the misfortunes of their neighbours. He also thought that the average person preferred to be directed rather than to think. His conclusion was that a diet of strip cartoons was what a mass readership needed. He was right to the extent that 'strips' were a highly acceptable element in the *Mirror*. But it wasn't enough.

Bartholomew's crudeness was spontaneous; Nicholson's was highly sophisticated. The two men quarrelled constantly, and six months after Nicholson appointed Cudlipp, he himself was sacked in favour of the younger man, though not without leaving him a legacy of the *Mirror*'s feature style and a tradition of rows with the editorial director.

'It's *Mirror* teamwork that counts,' said Cudlipp many years later in an interview with the journal *Stet*. But in *Publish and Be Damned* he gave a more subtle definition of the nature of team work.

'No successful newspaper has been generated by team work,' he wrote. 'Northcliffe knew it. Beaverbrook knows it.' So did the staff at the *Mirror* during the Bartholomew revolution. 'The world's largest circulation, and the second, third and even the nineteenth are directly the product of internecine warfare, departmental unarmed combat—or, to be polite in front of the customers, a headlong clash of ideals, techniques and ambitions.'

Cudlipp, who was later to be called 'unquestionably the finest journalist in the country' by Cecil King, generated excitement. John

Cowley, the company's sedate and elderly chairman, was often to be outraged—though for different reasons than Bartholomew—by Cudlipp's bold, brash journalism.

'Bossy wife gets husband's goat—he wants a vamp at 40,' was too much for the survivors from the Northcliffe era. Under Cudlipp's direction, the feature department plunged into the heart of mankind's common denominator—love. And observing that love is a preoccupation of the married as well as the unmarried, the *Mirror* called in love consultants like Miss Dorothy Dix to guide its readers on questions like, 'Should married couples have separate holidays?' and 'How many cocktails are too many?' The *Mirror* became a school of manners, a *carte du tendre*, a guide to every sentimental problem. It bothered about a society wider than ever before. And it enjoyed being rude. When Hore-Belisha, one of the *Mirror*'s favourite sons for a short time, was Minister of Transport, the *Mirror*, to underline the slaughter on the roads, published a picture of him laughing with the caption, 'What's he got to laugh about?' The *Mirror* pulled no punches.

One of Cudlipp's chief journalistic discoveries was the need for reassurance hidden away among the private fantasies of most people, coupled with a curiosity about the anxieties and fantasies of others. 'Am I normal?' is a standard question among the sensitive who find their *id* struggling with their *super-ego*. The *Mirror*'s letter columns were cathartic. Have you a personal problem? Write to the *Mirror*.

'This may sound silly,' wrote one reader, 'but I want to know whether I should keep my eyes open or closed when I kiss my boy friend. Most of the time, my boy friend has his eyes closed, and I don't know what to do myself.'

Another reader asked,

'Am I unreasonable? I have been married for twelve years, and have a family, and my husband recently asked me to be intimate with him on the back seat of our car. This happened in the heart of the country, and I agreed. I am now worried because I am sure this is very wrong. Please help me.'

The letters were at once a relief to the writers, a detached amusement for the readers, and a reassurance to all that the *Mirror* understood, that the *Mirror* could be told everything, and that in its confessional, as accessible as a priest's stall or a psychiatrist's couch, the troubled could find repose.

Like Bart, Cudlipp was a man of the people. It was the quality which linked them to each other, while provoking their bitterest clashes. Cudlipp, who was born in Cardiff in 1913, the son of a commercial traveller, left school at fourteen and started his journalistic life as a junior reporter on the somewhat obscure *Penarth News*. He moved up rapidly. At fifteen, he was a reporter on the Cardiff *Evening Express*, at sixteen a reporter on the Manchester *Evening Chronicle*, at seventeen a reporter in Blackpool, at eighteen a sub-editor on the *Evening Chronicle*, at nineteen features editor of the *Sunday Chronicle* in London, and at twenty-one features editor of the *Daily Mirror*. As with his two brothers, Percy, at one time editor of the *Daily Herald*, and Reginald, who became editor of the *News of the World*, journalism was with Cudlipp a passion, a profession and a built-in part of daily life.

Hugh Cudlipp's strength as a journalist was, like Bartholomew's, irreverence. When the popular press was under attack in Parliament, Cudlipp said in a speech to the Commonwealth Press Union that some of its critics were 'the Fifth Column of their own profession.' Then he turned on the venerable *Times*, once the property and totem of the *Mirror*'s founder.

'*The Times* is the zealous and self-appointed leader of this movement for ritualistic suicide,' Cudlipp said. 'But for some indiscernible though no doubt lofty reasons, it appears to cherish the illusion that while the rest of the press lie around in the macabre postures displayed by the victims of a mammoth hara-kiri, the quality papers will survive the disembowelling. I would remind Sir William Haley that a self-inflicted wound in the stomach can be as fatal as a stab in the back.

'*The Times* has not merely thrown open the rolling acres of its correspondence columns to any Tom, Dick and Harry—and particularly Lord Tom, Sir Dick and Mr. Harry, OBE—who wanted to attack the popular press. It did so in spite of what transpired to be (in the words of the *Manchester Guardian*) "flimsy evidence." It can scarce forbear to allow one year to slip by without itself indulging in the sport of lecturing and hectoring from its self-built pedestal the rest of the press.'

This was powerful irreverence. With Bart, irreverence was an instinct. With Cudlipp, it was conscious criticism. Britain in the 1930s was still a conservative society based on accepted ideas. Certain institutions like the throne and the social order were beyond challenge in what was regarded as good company and its representative organs. The Establishment existed, and the generation of grammar-school boys who penetrated the older universities and emerged as critics and self-confident satirists, hadn't yet appeared. The *Mirror* was a precursor in puncturing the Establishment. Its weapon wasn't satire but common sense. And its success was due in varying measure to the quadrumvirate of Bart, Cudlipp, William Connor (Cassandra) and Cecil King.

Cassandra joined the *Mirror* on the same day—August Bank Holiday, 1935—as Hugh Cudlipp. The son of an Irish father and a Scottish mother, himself born at Muswell Hill in North London, William Connor went to elementary school and later tried, after a period of private coaching, to get into the Navy. He failed to do so because of his poor eyesight. His nature was belligerent, and the aggressiveness that the Navy was deprived of found a home first when he worked as a copywriter for J. Walter Thompson and later, more permanently, when he joined the *Daily Mirror*.

The six years that he spent as a copywriter for J. Walter Thompson determined the whole personal style of the Cassandra column which he began shortly after he joined the *Mirror*. The expletive slogans, the imperative mood, the polished-up barrack room style, all made a dramatic impact. No subject of popular interest was too remote from Cassandra's concern. From love—'How old were you when you were first kissed?'—to military affairs—'We in Britain don't need a big army, but we need a good one'—Cassandra was the *Mirror*'s stand-by in slashing out an image of immense popular appeal.

Not only that; Cassandra regularly visited Germany, and reported in the 1930s to an indifferent Britain that Germany was ready for war. He wrote of Hitler on April 1st, 1938;

'Before this visit to Germany I always had a sneaking feeling that there was a strong undercurrent of opposition to Hitler.

'I am now certain that I was wrong.

'I know now that this man has the absolute unswerving confidence of the people.

'They will do anything for him.

'They worship him.

'They regard him as a god.

'Do not let us deceive ourselves in this country that Hitler may soon be dislodged by enemies within his own frontiers.

'Germans regard him as the greatest figure in their history.

'Better and greater than Bismarck.

'Infinitely superior to Frederick the Great.'

Cassandra's instinctive reaction to power was to challenge it. He reinforced the conscious radicalism of Cudlipp and the spontaneous anti-Establishment attitude of Bart with his own brand of non-conformism. He was against the power of the tycoon, whether political or financial. Yet even when he had shown some sympathy with the anti-Versailles feelings of the German people, he could never acquiesce in the authoritarian humbug of Hitler and Mussolini, even before they declared themselves at their worst. His rough, violent style expressed the rebellious mood of the submerged classes of the 1930s. Not surprisingly, he became for millions of *Mirror* readers an articulate spokesman.

By contrast with his three colleagues, Cecil King was the uncommon man among common men. Six foot four in height, he was literally a towering figure who dominated his environment.

Born on February 20th, 1901, he was the second and only surviving son of Sir Lucas White King of the Indian Civil Service and an Orientalist, and Geraldine, sister of Alfred Harmsworth, later to become Lord Northcliffe. His own middle name was a pious tribute to his mother's respect for her brother. Unlike Bartholomew and Cudlipp, King grew up in an upper-class tradition which took him to school at Winchester and later to Christchurch, Oxford. Above all, however, he grew up in the aura of his uncle's genius, which worked over the whole family.

King always viewed Northcliffe with admiration, but with unillusioned eyes. Cash and kinship were mingled in Northcliffe's philanthrophy, and he had a special interest in his nephews and nieces.

Thus, he wrote to King's mother on 15th January, 1892:

'My dearest sister—When I got home to Maida Vale last night, I found the cheerful news of the safe arrival of a little niece. . . . The baby arrived on the very best financial day in the history of the family . . . with lots of love to all three, my dearest sister, Yours devotedly, Alfred.'

But out of his own income of £200,000 a year, Northcliffe gave his sister an allowance of £2,000 only, sent to her in monthly instalments and with intermittent threats to cut it off.

As a boy, King often used to go and stay with his grandmother, Geraldine Mary Harmsworth, where he regularly saw Northcliffe and witnessed his devotion to his mother. King has recalled that at the age of four, when Northcliffe became a peer, he gave him a gold sovereign. 'That,' he says, 'made a great impression.' The impression wore off somewhat when Northcliffe's will was proved. Out of the £6 million that Northcliffe left, Cecil King got £500.

But it wasn't money alone that, in his youth, impressed King about Northcliffe's success. It was his capacity to understand popular taste and to respond to it. It was also Northcliffe's recognition that a newspaper was an instrument of power. Even if Northcliffe failed as a press politician, King saw that the instrument of the press which he wielded was a powerful one which could be used for the public good. Pragmatic in his approach and remote from ideologies, King nevertheless felt that the function of a newspaper was to promote and sustain worthwhile causes, and by 1934, the time of the Bartholomew revolution, he was already using his influence consciously to make the *Mirror* an instrument of public opinion, designed to affect Government policy. What Bart did by instinct and Cudlipp by a common-sense judgment, King achieved by a sophisticated, trained intellect which married theory with action.

Northcliffe's part in the first quarter of the century was to challenge governments. His forward-looking mind, which could already in 1910 recognize the value of aeroplanes both for peace and war, was a challenge to his age. King's challenge was in the field of society rather than of mechanics. Though brought up in an upper-class tradition, he was still a man of radical instincts with an atavistic recollection of the fact that his maternal grandfather was originally a struggling schoolteacher. Yet, like Hugh Gaitskell, his fellow-Wykehamist, King had a sense of outrage at the social inequalities which he witnessed in the second quarter of the century. 'I am really interested,' he said in a BBC interview on August 27th, 1964, 'deep down, in the underdog. I will do anything I can through my newspapers to see that the underdog of whatever kind gets a break . . . I feel that those who are poor and ignorant should be less poor, less ignorant. I have a great feeling for coloured people, who I think have been very badly treated by our country in the past. . . . I think the elderly and old in this country get a raw deal . . . they are not properly provided for.'

No one could say that this was a complex political philosophy. Yet it is basic in the radical philosophy which seeks to transform society in the interests of social justice.

In 1926, King joined the advertising department of the *Daily Mirror* from the *Daily Mail* after a year's training on the Glasgow *Record*. When he became a director in 1929, his interests were already too large to be contained merely by the advertising department. Too detached and too intolerant of human foibles to become a politician, he nevertheless was profoundly interested in politics, the system by which society is organized. After arriving at the *Mirror*, he rapidly interested himself not only in administration but also in formulating editorial policy and in acting as a kind of ambassador in government circles where his own personality, his impressive family connections and the circulation of the Mirror carried great influence. Politics, King recognized, are something which concern even those who dislike politicians.

In the critical mid-1930s, he was nominally fifth in the office hierarchy, after John Cowley, chairman, W. D. Roome, general manager, who had been a director since 1904, J. Lovell, finance, and Bartholomew, editorial. But King was obliged to involve himself in the paper's editorial resurrection. He felt that he couldn't sell advertising for a paper whose sale fell below its claims and lacked a positive personality directed towards a specific readership. At the same time, he was the only director who had a genuine interest in politics and an understanding of politicians. In the 1930s, the groundswell of radical opinion among the submerged working classes was already beginning on a national scale. The intellectuals of the Fabian Society and the *New Statesman* and the Communist intellectuals of the older universities who wrote proletarian prose in the *Daily Worker* or poetry of socialist realism in obscure periodicals, made hardly any impact on the mass electorate. Rich in manifestoes, the radical movement in Britain was destitute of a popular journal.

Without King's intervention and his political influence on Bartholomew, the *Mirror* might well have remained a ragbag of Right Wing attitudes, lingering on from the Rothermere dispensation. King took the amorphous potentialities of the paper and translated them into political power. Far more effectively than any of the press lords of the old establishment, he was to make a newspaper a decisive electoral factor.

King was interested in clear exposition. That is why, despite the difference between his background and that of Cudlipp and Bartholomew, he found a common denominator with them in making the *Mirror* the paper of the ordinary man, interested in his day-to-day living and the affairs which determine it. His natural ally in this was Cudlipp, the young and exuberant ideas man who was also absorbed by the political revolution which was going on in Britain. He was less sympathetic towards Bart. Bartholomew viewed with suspicion and some resentment the brilliant Harmsworth intruder who, according to his own prejudices, should have been merely the beneficiary of nepotism, but who surmounted all the disadvantages in the eyes of himself and his colleagues, of family membership, by proving to have inherited the flair, talent and enterprise of his uncle, while adding talents of his own.

Between Bart and King there was, within their dedication to the *Mirror*, a fundamental clash of personality which was to last till the final battle when Bart was outvoted from the *Mirror* board, and King took over the chairmanship. Bart, who had worked his way up from the ground-roots of journalism, resented what seemed to him the gate-crashing of the tall young Wykehamist with his Northcliffian good looks and his intellectual, withdrawn manner. One of Bart's great hatreds was privilege; and he treated the arrival of King at the *Mirror* as an exercise in favouritism. Only really at ease with a few tough, hard-swearing cronies, Bart had nothing in common socially with the remote and, in his eyes, lordly King.

Bart's strength was, in a way, a product of his weakness. Angry with the social 'haves'—to use the language of those days—he spoke for the under-privileged, the 'have-nots.' Sometimes in his dealings with his colleagues, Bart's attachment to his grievances made him insufferable. He liked to feel himself embattled; he enjoyed the idea that the world was against him. For example, in an eccentric act of minority identification, he declared of himself to Philip Zec, the *Mirror*'s cartoonist in the 1940s, that he was a Jew. There was no truth in the claim.

And so in the late 1930s when Britain faced a crisis which only brave new minds could overcome, the *Mirror* had spokesmen capable of saying 'No' to tradition and to accepted modes of thought. They transformed the *Mirror* into a tabloid with a political message and gave a voice to the common man. But it was an edited voice, modulated and determined by a group of resolute journalists with 'a banner strong enough to blow against the wind.' In France, the mood of the nation was pleasure-seeking, egotistical and defeatist. In Britain, the mood might have been similar, except that defeatism was tempered by a belief in the Channel and the armour of Empire.

But Britain's fate might well have been that of France had it not been for those who rejected the apathy and the neurosis of their age.

Then in the midst of an era when men were lacerating each other in civil war, when millions were hungering in mass unemployment and Essen's factories were working night and day on Hitler's war preparations, the world was diverted by a theme fit for a Viennese operetta—the king who fell for a commoner, a divorcée, an American. The awe of kingship still stifled the British public, and for the most part those who heard the rumours of a royal romance, as it was prettily called, were either incredulous or aghast.

The *Mirror* didn't take this attitude. Always 'ready to intrude into private joy,' in Cudlipp's words, it regarded the royal drama as a fit subject for its general concern with those whom love puts in various dilemmas. When is the right date to kiss? Should one clock-off early to keep a date? Should women over forty have children? Should kings contract morganatic marriages? Should love come before duty? Turning its face away from large issues, the nation focussed its attention in 1936 on King Edward's love-problems.

There was, however, a major political and constitutional question. If the king were to abdicate his duties in favour of love, could the monarchy survive?

CHAPTER III

'Tell us the Facts, Mr. Baldwin' : An Interlude

THE CONFLICT BETWEEN love and duty had long been a preoccupation of the *Mirror*; it was one of the themes which its readers and writers were always ready to discuss. Now it had become the tragi-comic subject of what was to be a national debate about a national institution.

Ever since 1935 when Edward VIII first met Mrs. Wallis Warfield Simpson, there had been talk in fashionable circles of his infatuation with the divorced and remarried American. In 1936, at the time of King George V's death, their relationship was being gossiped about not only on the periphery of the Court and among the aristocracy, but in the American popular press as well. In the *Mirror* office, Cudlipp was regularly supplied from the New York office with cuttings from the Hearst newspapers which stated categorically that the new King and Mrs. Simpson were, in their terms, 'making woo,' and that there was 'suppressed rage in the Royal household.'

For his part, Edward VIII was determined that his relationship with Mrs. Simpson should be treated as a private matter, and that if possible it shouldn't get into the papers. This wish, so often experienced by private citizens, who rightly or wrongly object to their names being bandied about in unfavourable circumstances, met with understanding and sympathy from the newspaper proprietors, chief among them Lord Beaverbrook who had first heard from Percy Cudlipp, brother of Hugh Cudlipp and editor of the *Evening Standard*, that Mrs. Simpson was suing for divorce at Ipswich Assizes on the grounds of her husband's adultery.

'What had stayed their (the British press's) hand,' Edward wrote later, 'was Fleet Street's long-standing reticence where the privacy of the Royal Family was concerned. There is nothing servile in this tradition. . . . It is founded on the premise that if the exalted position of the monarchy is to be preserved in the face of the encroaching cynicism of modern life, it must be held above carping and criticism.'

In fact, the reticence had been carefully organized. The King had sent for Lord Beaverbrook to come to the Palace on October 16th 'to protect Wallis from sensational publicity,' in Britain. With the cooperation of Esmond Harmsworth, the present Lord Rothermere, who was then President of the Newspaper Proprietors' Association, Beaverbrook arranged for the divorce story to be tucked out of sight, without being related to the King's affairs.

In November, Lord Beaverbrook was on the Bremen on his way to Arizona, where he was going to take a cure for his asthma, when he received a radio message from the King asking him to come back and give him further advice. A few days later, on the 20th, Beaverbrook, who had hesitated to return, was lunching with Joseph Patterson, owner of the *New York Daily News*, when he received a telephone call from the King, setting out to the reluctant newspaper proprietor his hopes and plans for a morganatic marriage. Beaverbrook promised to return at once, and left New York on the homeward-bound Bremen. The *New York Daily News* preserved an unusual discretion, and on the 26th November Beaverbrook arrived at Southampton and motored from there to the King's country house, Fort Belvedere, where they had a long and confidential talk in which Beaverbrook tried to dissuade the King from making the stark choice between abdication or marriage.

But the press was approaching a dilemma of conscience. Quite apart from the fact that a Mr. John Smith would have been treated with self-righteous indignation by any news editor whom he asked to throw out a personal news item, was it proper for newspapers to suppress a story which clearly was of great constitutional importance?

On November 13th, Alexander Hardinge, the King's new private secretary, had written to him, after a consultation with Geoffrey Dawson, the editor of *The Times*:

'Sir—With my humble duty.

'As Your Majesty's Private Secretary, I feel it my duty to bring to your notice the following facts which have come to my knowledge and which I *know* to be accurate.

1. The silence of the British Press on the subject of Your Majesty's friendship with Mrs. Simpson is *not* going to be maintained. It is probably only a matter of days before the outburst begins. Judging

by the letters from British subjects living in foreign countries where the Press has been outspoken, the effect will be calamitous.

2. The Prime Minister and senior members of the Government are meeting today to discuss what action should be taken to deal with the serious situation which is developing. As Your Majesty no doubt knows, the resignation of the Government—an eventuality which can by no means be excluded—would result in Your Majesty having to find someone else capable of forming a Government which would receive the support of the present House of Commons. I have reason to know that, in view of the feeling prevalent among members of the House of Commons of all parties, this is hardly within the bounds of possibility. The only alternative remaining is a dissolution and a general election in which Your Majesty's personal affairs would be the chief issue, and I cannot help feeling that even those who would sympathize with Your Majesty as an individual would deeply resent the damage which would inevitably be done to the Crown—the corner-stone on which the whole Empire rests.

'If Your Majesty will permit me to say so, there is only one step which holds out any prospect of avoiding this dangerous situation, and that is for Mrs. Simpson to go abroad *without further delay*—and I would *beg* Your Majesty to give this proposal your earnest consideration before the position has become irretrievable. Owing to the changing attitude of the Press, the matter has become one of great urgency.

'I have the honour . . . Alexander Hardinge.'

In the meantime, the press was becoming restless under the constant flow of information and innuendo which was crossing the Atlantic from the United States. The King had seen the Prime Minister on November 16th, and at 10.30 in the evening Baldwin had asked the editor of the *Times* to visit him at the House of Commons. Baldwin said then that the King had decided to marry Mrs. Simpson, and to abdicate if necessary. He (Baldwin) hoped that the press would not comment on the matter, as such comment might weaken his influence with the Sovereign.

The precipitating effect of press publicity on the growing crisis appeared on Monday, November 23rd, when the *Daily Mail*, indicating its sympathies with the King, contrasted his concern for the unemployed when in South Wales with the indifference of the Government. *The Times* was indignant at this involvement of the

Crown with government. 'The King's constitutional position,' it said, 'is above and apart from party politics, and those who cherish the institution of the monarchy will always strive to keep it so.'

By now, Beaverbrook had been recalled by the King and the division between the King and his supporters and the traditional Establishment began to deepen. For three months *The Times*, which had known of Edward's liaison, had been silent. Suddenly the accumulating interest of press and public was heightened on December 1st, by the Bishop of Bradford, the Right Reverend A. W. F. Blunt, who, in an address to the Diocesan Conference, regretted that the King hadn't shown 'more political awareness of the need for Divine guidance in the discharge of his high office.' What the Bishop meant was that the King didn't go to church regularly. But the *Yorkshire Post* used the occasion to say the next day, 'Dr. Blunt must have had good reason for so pointed a remark. Most people are by this time aware that a great deal of rumour has been published of late in the more sensational American newspapers.'

The *Manchester Guardian* referred explicitly to a controversial issue having arisen between the King and the government. The London press still remained silent.

Meanwhile, however, the Cabinet had held a special meeting at which Baldwin disclosed that the King had asked him to consult the Dominions on the question of a morganatic marriage. Baldwin himself dismissed the possibility. The alternative was whether Mrs. Simpson should be the King's wife and Queen, or whether, if the King insisted on marriage in the face of Cabinet opposition, he should abdicate. The Cabinet accepted that the only choice, if the King persisted, was abdication.

Dr. Blunt's admonition to the King about his churchgoing practices set the smouldering public discussion aflame. The Prime Minister, the Archbishop of Canterbury and Geoffrey Dawson, editor of *The Times*, had already been in close consultation. By December 3rd, Fleet Street was bursting to 'break' the story of the Cabinet's decision and of Baldwin's discussion with the King. Beaverbrook telephoned the Palace to inform Edward that the so-called 'King's party' was about to collapse. The King asked Beaverbrook what he intended to say in the *Express*.

'Sir,' Beaverbrook answered, 'the *Express* will, with the other newspapers, report the facts. It is our duty to do so.'

The King then went on to ask what Beaverbrook's position would be. The attitude of the press was the inassessable which the King had to calculate in making his decision. Beaverbrook replied:

'Baldwin has seized the initiative. You can be sure that from this moment he will exploit his advantage to the full. The facts about to be revealed to the public will shock and stun. Inevitably its first reaction will be hostile to you and sympathetic to him—the pro-Government press will see to that. If the flow of adverse opinion is to be halted and reversed, then you must allow your friends to counter hard, and at once.'

Beaverbrook made it clear to the King that Baldwin, backed by the Established Church, Geoffrey Dawson of *The Times* and what he called the 'pro-Government press' would undoubtedly win the day unless his own newspapers and those of other 'friendly groups' could strike back vigorously. Beaverbrook was all in favour of making a strong case that there was nothing wrong in the King marrying a woman who had divorced her husband. The King was reluctant, but on Thursday, December 3rd, he was to receive a shock.

'Publicity,' he has written in his memoirs, 'was part of my heritage, and I was never so naïve as to suppose that my romance was a tender shoot to be protected from the prying curiosity of the press. But what stared at me from the newspapers that were brought to my room on Thursday morning really shocked me. Could this be the King or was I some common felon? The Press creates; the Press destroys. All my life I had been the passive clay which it had enthusiastically worked into the hackneyed image of a Prince Charming. Now it had whirled around, and was bent upon demolishing the natural man who had been there all the time.'

The shock occurred when Mrs. Simpson entered his drawing-room with a London picture newspaper in her hand.

'Have you seen this?' she asked.

'Yes,' the King replied. 'It's too bad.'

'The world,' he has said, 'can hold few worse shocks for a sensitive woman than to come without warning upon her own grossly magnified countenance upon the front page of a sensational newspaper.'

The 'sensational newspaper' was, naturally, the *Mirror*. Mrs. Simpson's reaction to its story was to say:

'It isn't only that they are attacking you personally, or me. They are attacking the King.'

There is a moment when the most reticent of newspapers—and

the *Mirror* certainly wasn't that—can no longer restrain its impatience to publish a story when it is in possession of the facts, whatever may be the occult influences which inhibit it. Besides, the *Mirror* might have been scooped by a rival. Bartholomew was not a man to be held back. On the night of December 2nd when the two first editions had gone to press, he decided to publish the story of the dilemma which the King's wish to marry had produced for the nation. The headline story read:

'The King Wants to Marry Mrs. Simpson: Cabinet Advises "No".'

The *Mirror* was the first newspaper to break the self-imposed veto on references to Mrs. Simpson herself. *The Times* leader of December 3rd entitled 'King and Monarchy' contained an account of the American press campaign, and admitted its fundamental truth. But Mrs. Simpson was not referred to. *The Times* was concerned with constitutional principle, and made it clear that in a trial of strength between monarchy and government, it would be on the side of government. Other newspapers took a similar view, and the *News Chronicle* summed up the matter by saying that while the King might choose his wife, Parliament chooses the Queen and regulates the succession.

The *Mirror*, on the other hand, took an ultra-Royalist view which in a curious way was congruent with an ultra-democratic view. The King was the King; he should be respected as such; but he was also a man who was entitled to marry the woman of his choice like any other man. Mrs. Simpson had misjudged the mood and the intention of the *Mirror*. Its object was to back the King.

In this, the *Mirror* was fundamentally out of tune with public opinion, whereas Baldwin, whose political fortunes at the time were at a low ebb, handled the Royal issue with such skill that he raised himself, within a fortnight, to quote Churchill's words in *The Gathering Storm*, 'from the depths to the pinnacle.' Baldwin understood the fundamental puritanism of the British public and its resentment of openly expressed happiness.

In the Labour Party itself, there was far less support for the King than might have been expected from the 'progressive' attitudes towards sexual freedom which many of its members proclaimed. Hugh Dalton, one of Labour's leaders, was at the time the guest of Attlee's Parliamentary Private Secretary, Arthur Jenkins, at Pontypool, a depressed area in Wales, where not long before on a famous tour the King had said, in connection with its hardships, 'Something must be done.' But even here he found that the unemployed 'brought their disapproval from the chapels.' The women were even bitterer than the men in their objections to the King marrying a twice-married divorcée. And a commoner, at that! Royal 'misalliances' had not yet become popular.

Contrary to Edward's belief, his conduct was disapproved in wide circles. There were rumours on the Left that through the influence of his American friends he had undue sympathies with Nazi Germany. He had spoken disparagingly of the League of Nations. In June, 1935, he had addressed the British Legion and proposed that a deputation of ex-Servicemen should go to Nazi Germany on a friendship mission. On top of it all, Prince Charming seemed to have turned into a middle-aged playboy.

'Every time I dipped into the bran-tub of provincial opinion,' said Dalton, 'I pulled out a puritan.'

However sentimental it was about Edward, the *Mirror* was anything but puritanical. Having rejected many other sexual taboos and euphemisms it saw the King's dilemma in plain human terms. He wanted to marry: so why not? It was a political weakness of the *Mirror* during this crisis that it had no intimate connections with the main centres of power—the Cabinet and the Palace—where the decisions were being made. Its judgments were inspirational rather than well-informed, and only much later was it to remedy this lack. Yet its constant theme till the abdication was a plea for time and patience. While *The Times* was issuing final notices, the allegedly impetuous *Mirror* was pleading for delay. In this the *Mirror* found itself allied with the *Daily Express* and the *Daily Mail.*

'No Government,' said the *Daily Express*, 'can stand in the King's way if he is resolved to walk that way. . . . Let the King give his decision to the people, and let him give the reasons for it too.'

The *Daily Mail* said, 'Abdication is out of the question, because its possibilities of mischief are endless. The effect on the Empire would be calamitous.'

The respectable Liberal *News Chronicle* came out strongly in favour of morganatic marriage. This was a particular surprise to Baldwin, who hoped that the organ of Liberal Nonconformity would unhesitatingly support the rigid Establishment view. Edward himself made an assessment of the weight of newspaper opinion for and

CECIL KING WITH THE RT. HON. HAROLD MACMILLAN, M.P. (THEN PRIME MINISTER), 1962

CECIL KING WITH DR. HASTINGS BANDA, NOW PRIME MINISTER OF MALAWI, 1960

WANTED!

FOR MURDER . . . FOR KIDNAPPING . . . FOR THEFT AND FOR ARSON

[illegible] full face by habitual scowl. Rarely smiles. [illegible] screams like a child.

ADOLF HITLER

ALIAS

Adolf Schicklegruber, Adolf Hittler or Hidler

Last heard of in Berlin, September 3, 1939. Aged fifty, height 5ft. 8½in., dark hair, frequently brushes one lock over left forehead. Blue eyes. Sallow complexion, stout build, weighs about 11st. 3lb. Suffering from acute monomania, with periodic fits of melancholia. Frequently bursts into tears when crossed. Harsh, guttural voice, and has a habit of raising right hand to shoulder level. DANGEROUS!

Profile from a recent photograph. Black moustache. Jowl inclines to fatness. Wide nostrils. Deep-set, menacing eyes.

FOR MURDER Wanted for the murder of over a thousand of his fellow countrymen on the night of the Blood Bath, June 30, 1934. Wanted for the murder of countless political opponents in concentration camps.

He is indicted for the murder of Jews, Germans, Austrians, Czechs, Spaniards and Poles. He is now urgently wanted for homicide against citizens of the British Empire.

Hitler is a gunman who shoots to kill. He acts first and talks afterwards.

No appeals to sentiment can move him. This gangster, surrounded by armed bandits, is a natural killer. The reward for his apprehension, dead or alive, is the peace of mankind.

FOR KIDNAPPING Wanted for the kidnapping of Dr. Kurt Schuschnigg, late Chancellor of Austria. Wanted for the kidnapping of Pastor Niemoller, a heroic martyr who was not afraid to put God before Hitler. Wanted for the attempted kidnapping of Dr. Benes, late President of Czechoslovakia. The kidnapping tendencies of this established criminal are marked and violent. The symptoms before an attempt are threats, blackmail and ultimatums. He offers his victims the alternatives of complete surrender or timeless incarceration in the horrors of concentration camps.

FOR THEFT Wanted for the larceny of eighty millions of Czech gold in March, 1939. Wanted for the armed robbery of material resources of the Czech State. Wanted for the stealing of Memelland. Wanted for robbing mankind of peace, of humanity, and for the attempted assault on civilisation itself. This dangerous lunatic masks his raids by spurious appeals to honour, to patriotism and to duty. At the moment when his protestations of peace and friendship are at their most vehement, he is most likely to commit his smash and grab.

His tactics are known and easily recognised. But Europe has already been wrecked and plundered by the depredations of this armed thug who smashes in without scruple.

FOR ARSON Wanted as the incendiary who started the Reichstag fire on the night of February 27, 1933. This crime was the key point, and the starting signal for a series of outrages and brutalities that are unsurpassed in the records of criminal degenerates. As a direct and immediate result of this calculated act of arson, an innocent dupe, Van der Lubbe, was murdered in cold blood. But as an indirect outcome of this carefully-planned offence, Europe itself is ablaze. The fires that this man has kindled cannot be extinguished until he himself is apprehended—dead or alive!

THIS RECKLESS CRIMINAL IS WANTED—DEAD OR ALIVE!

WANTED! THE MIRROR'S FRONT PAGE, SEPTEMBER 3RD, 1939

against him at the time. He estimated that of an aggregate circulation of 21 million among newspapers which took up a position in the matter, 8½ million supported the Government, and 12½ million supported him. He has since said that because of his constitutional position, he did not want to take advantage of this preponderance of favourable opinion within a divided country.

There is, however, something entirely artificial in this type of referendum by newspaper circulation. Apart from the fact of overlapping readership, editorial policy is in the first instance shaped by probably less than a hundred people in Fleet Street, who then try to lead the public opinion they fashion.

On December 5th, Cassandra weighed in with a full-page article called 'I Accuse!'

'I am writing,' he said, 'about what I regard as the biggest put-up job of all time.

'I accuse leaders of the Church of England of placing our King in a position from which it is almost impossible to retreat.

'I accuse the Prime Minister and his Government of manoeuvring with smooth and matchless guile to a desperate situation where humiliation is the only answer.'

The article went on to attack the hypocrisy of what Cassandra called 'the sorry pageant of adultery and divorce' in the aristocracy, which accompanied the condemnation by that self-same social class of the King's projected marriage to the twice-divorced Mrs. Simpson, and was ardent in its support of the royal right to self-determination.

But editorially, the *Mirror* was more cautious. Its three determinative leaders, written by Jennings at Cecil King's suggestion, were sympathetic to the King's position, but never partisan and always soberly concerned with the national interest. On December 7th, the *Mirror* wrote:

' "I plead for time and patience; I pray that time and tolerance will not be denied." '

'So Mr. Winston Churchill in a statement published during this weekend.

'The first point in this lamentable crisis is surely clear.

'We all wish we could see light. We all deplore the interruption to grave public business involved in the prolongation of this debate. We hope it will soon be settled. But it must be fairly settled. To ask for a few days of careful deliberation is not to ask for weeks.

'Now the public is by no means sure that a sort of ultimatum—a negative ultimatum—has not been presented to the King.'

'The general feeling is that there should be no atmosphere of hustle.

'No hurry. Time and patience.'

Seeking information, as always, it asked in a front-page spread, 'What 45,000,000 Demand to Know.' It had already demanded, 'Tell Us the Facts, Mr. Baldwin.' Now it asked, 'Is the British Cabinet sure beyond doubt that the abdication of Edward VIII would not strike a terrible blow at the greatest institution in the world—our monarchy—and thereby cause irreparable harm?'

The next day, after Baldwin had made a statement confirming to Parliament that a morganatic marriage would be unacceptable, the *Mirror* struck a judicious balance of sympathy between the King in his romantic and constitutional dilemma and Baldwin in his dilemma of respect for the King and concern for the institution of monarchy.

'We feel very deeply, then, for the King in his personal suffering.

'We feel also for the King's Minister and particularly for the Prime Minister.

'Mr. Baldwin's position in this matter has been one of extreme delicacy and difficulty.

'We all realize that this crisis has descended upon a Government already harassed by grave difficulties in the field of foreign policy; while, from the constitutional point of view, the Prime Minister (whatever his personal feelings) has to take account of the opinions of his colleagues in the Cabinet, of Parliament and of the great world of English-speaking peoples beyond this country.

'In this time of strain for all concerned we may be sure that it is the desire of no public man, who has proved his worth in public service, deliberately to put difficulties in the way of a clear solution of the problem.'

At last, on December 9th, the *Mirror* decided that it could not assume the role of King's Champion in an issue—'a hard issue, as are all conflicts between public duty and private feeling'—where the *Mirror*'s own ultimate concern was with the interest of the people. It had recognized its earlier misjudgment. On December 11th, it recorded that Edward VIII would bid a radio farewell to the nation that same night. In smaller type, it added, 'London Cheers George VI.'

Its human sympathies had lain with Edward VIII; but the

Mirror's duties as an instrument of public opinion lay with the constitution. 'We must unite around the new King,' said its leader on December 11th. It spoke of the sense of dismay which would overwhelm all English-speaking peoples on that day. Great harm had been done. Britain's social stability in a common respect for the Crown had been one of the few fixed points in a world visibly convulsed by political experiments and wild adventurers. For a moment, it had seemed that even these foundations had been shaken. But, said the *Mirror*, the foundations would have to be restored.

'We must rally round the King's successor. His task is tremendous We believe he will face it bravely.

'It is for him to unite us all again, with a high sense of public duty, which may in time efface the painful memory of these days of humiliation, anxiety and grief.'

Personal grief had indeed to be overcome. In the convulsions of the previous fortnight, the external menace had been forgotten. But no sooner had the dismay of the abdication disappeared than the muttering, growling anxiety about resurgent German militarism returned.

CHAPTER IV

The 'Mirror' against Appeasement: A Counterpoint to 'The Times'

IN A LEADING article in *The Times* of October 28th, 1937, Geoffrey Dawson, the editor, wrote:

'There is little sympathy here with the view, which has sometimes seemed to prevail on the Continent, that the proper way to treat Germany is to ring her about with vigilant allied states, sometimes masquerading as the League of Nations. . . . She has broken these limits here and there already—broken them by methods which are creditable neither to herself nor to the rest of the world—and every article of statesmanship suggests that a halt should be called to a process which must otherwise lead inevitably to war and to the downfall of civilization in the West. Let us at least be clear at what point a stand should be made, and let us make a supreme effort, so far as Great Britain is concerned, to do what is possible for appeasement before that point is reached.'

As editor of *The Times* from 1912 to 1919 under Northcliffe's direction, Dawson, whose apprenticeship to power had begun when he was Private Secretary to Lord Milner, High Commissioner in South Africa at the beginning of the century, had learnt at an early stage how newspapers could affect public policy. When he was recalled to the editorship in 1922 after the interregnum of Wickham Steed, he confirmed the position of *The Times* as a national institution, closely bound with Throne, Church and the Tory Party. Educated at Eton and Magdalen, a fellow of All Souls and a Yorkshireman, sprung from the squirearchy, he was an anchorman of tradition. His stocky physique and his energetic and lucid but obstinate mind spoke of his origins. His feeling for tradition found personal expression in an unshakeable attachment to his chosen leaders and friends—Milner, Baldwin, Chamberlain and Halifax. He believed in the hereditary principle and in the merit assembled in the aristocracy, the middle-class gentry and what *The Times* History has called 'their ennobled offspring.'

As for the *demos* knocking at the doors of power, he regarded it as an irrelevancy to be brushed away. He had no friendships with Labour leaders; their governments were accidents in the transmission of authority. He preferred the received idea to the innovation; the subfusc to the flamboyant; the Germans to the French. The only grace that he could find in a Labour Minister was in Lord Snowden's hostility to France; but even that couldn't reconcile him to Labour's upstart pretensions.

Between Dawson and the men who ran the *Mirror* in the 1930s there could not have been a greater gap. With an Olympian serenity and a Gadarene determination, Dawson drove his readers towards appeasement.

Appeasement—that was the innocent word which was to win such notoriety within a few months. Dawson relied heavily on the views of his governmental friends Baldwin, Chamberlain and Halifax, whose political analysis he preferred to the detailed reports of his own correspondents. In a curious act of vanity which was to have a lamentable effect on Britain's future, Dawson had suppressed the position of foreign editor in 1929. His own qualifications for this highly specialized job were negligible. He knew none of the leading European statesmen; he hadn't read any recent European political history; and he knew no foreign languages.

Dawson also had a mystical belief in his own instinct about British public opinion. But the guidance which he received from both his advisers and his intuition failed to serve the long-term interests of Britain. By every means in his power, Dawson tried not to wound Hitler's susceptibilities, and in a particularly revealing letter to the acting Berlin correspondent in May 1937, shortly after Chamberlain had been made Prime Minister in place of Stanley Baldwin, he wrote with pained surprise after some Nazi criticism of *The Times* in Berlin:

'It would interest me greatly to know precisely what it is in *The Times* that has produced this antagonism in Germany. I did my utmost, night after night, to keep out of the paper anything that might hurt their susceptibilities.'

He ended the letter:

'I have always been convinced that the peace of the world depends more than anything else on our getting into reasonable relations with Germany.'

Dawson's faith in Hitler's reasonableness survived the expulsion from Berlin of *The Times* correspondent on August 19th, 1937. The Nazis clearly feared *The Times* correspondent more than they feared Dawson's 'leaders'.

When Hitler met Dawson's friend Halifax in Obersalzburg on November 19th, 1937, and complained of 'malignant criticism' in the British press, his aim was to muzzle the British press and to throttle its protest.

The *Mirror*'s reply to Hitler's complaint was to become even more outspoken in its comment. It condemned Fascist 'frightfulness' in Spain—'the word that became familiar when the Germans entered Belgium a quarter of a century ago.' It condemned criticism in the City of the National Defence Contribution introduced by Chamberlain. On November 25th, when Hitler's headquarters had already become a terminus for dozens of official and unofficial busybodies offering him their brands of homage, the *Mirror* declared firmly:

'What really lies behind these feverish attempts on the part of the British Government to 'get in touch' with Germany; to placate Germany; to get Herr Hitler into a nicer mood; to ask him what he wants, and whether he will promise to keep quiet if he gets it?

'Would it not be better to try for peace, not by yielding, in separate talks, with blackmailers whose object is to isolate us; but never to move without full consultation with those who stand by us today as they stood by us—or we by them—in the last convulsion of Europe?'

And again, at the end of the leader, the *Mirror* sounded its tocsin warning which history was to justify against the failure of British statesmen to treat *Mein Kampf* as a programme.

'Today it is vitally important that we should not drop France for Germany. For Herr Hitler long ago explained that it would be good to separate us.

'We shall be fools if we don't remember his "plan." It is all in his unreadable book.'

*

The *Mirror* Group as a whole had already crystallized its position on the question of appeasement at the beginning of 1938: it was against it. Early in that year Cecil King, then editorial director of the *Sunday Pictorial*, invited Hugh Cudlipp to join the paper as its editor. The *Pictorial*, whose circulation had fallen from approximately two and a half million in 1925 to just over a million and a quarter in 1937, had begun to waste away because its outlook no longer corresponded with the public mood. It had an out-dated, extreme right-wing policy, and entertained its readers with domestic trivia. King was determined that the paper should deal with major social and political questions. As Cudlipp has written in *At Your Peril*, it developed a social conscience of a type that had not appeared in its pages before.

The *Sunday Pictorial* became a crusading paper which lost nothing of the sensational tradition which had been the success formula of the *Mirror*. Between 1937 when King enlisted his new team, and 1940 when Cudlipp left to join the army, the sale of the paper rose by nearly half a million. After the war, its total circulation touched five million. Week after week Cudlipp, the *porte-parole* of Cecil King, wrote pungent articles on politics. When Bartholomew, who hadn't taken kindly to Cudlipp's departure from the *Daily Mirror*, complained about his writing under his own name, Cudlipp took the pseudonym of Charles Wilberforce. The *Pictorial*'s political articles began to probe the inadequacies of Britain's defences. It consistently exposed the fiction of a harmless Hitler put out by the Nazis' friends in Britain. The anti-German, pro-French, unpopular Lord Vansittart, Permanent Under Secretary at the Foreign Office, was a friend of both King and Cudlipp, and in the choice between his views and those of the appeasers, the *Pictorial* came out strongly in favour of Vansittart. Thus in 1938, despite the clash of personalities between Bartholomew on the one side and King and Cudlipp on the other, the *Pictorial* and the *Mirror* were solidly united in their opposition to Hitler.

On February 20th, Hitler made a speech lasting nearly three hours, which the *Mirror* described as 'a rambling, interminable speech of Nazi self-glorification. Sneers at democracy, attacks on Jews and Christians with Bibles. Ending with talk of Germany's love of peace.'

On the same day Anthony Eden, who had disagreed with the inaction of the Cabinet in face of the increasing Nazi menace, resigned, refusing to substitute for his own broad League of Nations policy the plan for talks with the dictators which *The Times* had been urging, and which Halifax, his successor, and Chamberlain favoured. Now the *Mirror* reinforced its previous stand.

'The Prime Minister,' it said, 'may feel happier. But does Britain? Mr. Eden is young and courageous. He is sincere and decisive. He refused to see Europe at the mercy of gangsters who seize what they want and keep what they can.

'So he has resigned. With him go the loyal good wishes of millions of British men and women. Mr. Chamberlain will be wise to remember that.

'And now what is Mr. Chamberlain going to do? Will he and the rest of his colleagues now go, hats in hand, to Mussolini and say: "We yield everything. We ask nothing. We recognize your conquests. We beg you to help us against Germany."

'Will the British Government speak thus?

'If so, what will be the reaction of the British public?

'We doubt if they will acquiesce. We doubt if they will submit to Mussolini's terms. They will not approve of a big loan to Italy. They will not believe that the situation is so desperate that we have to kowtow to one dictator in the hope of controlling another.'

The following day it added:

'From Abyssinia to Austria, by way of the tortured wastes of nearly ruined Spain—the same story: broken agreements, broken faith, broken promises.

'For Eden it has gone far enough; Mr. Chamberlain hopes to try again.

'That is the difference between them.'

At the same time the *Mirror* took a swipe at *The Times*, which had now emerged as the standard-bearer of appeasement.

'Are we worrying you with the crisis?' the *Mirror* asked. 'If so, take consolation in Aunty's Cosy Corner from yesterday's *Times*.

'The eldest of the Shiver Sisters held, in a priceless leader, that Mr. Eden and the Prime Minister differ without disagreement. No change, therefore, in foreign policy. No quarrel. Just a tiff.

'On with the Shiver Ballet.'

The Shiver Sisters was a reference to a Low cartoon showing *The Times*, Lady Astor, Garvin of the *Observer* and Lord Lothian, wearing newspapers as *tutus*, dancing a ballet in front of a gramophone playing a record of Nazi foreign policy, with Goebbels conducting.

The new Foreign Secretary, Halifax, was a member of the Imperial Conservatives among whom Geoffrey Dawson himself had moved for many years. Contacts between *The Times* and the Government were tightened. The pro-German lobby was in the ascendant. On March 10th, Geoffrey Dawson and his deputy Barrington-Ward attended Ribbentrop's farewell reception at the German Embassy. The following day Hitler marched into Austria.

A little shocked by this, *The Times* agreed the following day that something ought to be done about air-raid precautions. But the *Mirror* now came out with an insistence that force should be met by force.

'The situation in Europe,' it said on March 14th, 'is much graver than it was before the gangsters seized helpless Austria. But it is the same situation.

'Germany is strong. Austria was weak. Germany therefore annexes Austria. Perfectly simple.

'Nobody but a nincompoop can have believed, after Hitler's brutal dismissal of Schuschnigg a few days ago, that he would allow Schuschnigg to defy him.

'The first step was the ultimatum. The next was the invasion. There was never an earthly chance that Austria would be allowed to parley, to vote or to decide for herself.

'Years and years ago—long before he secured power—Hitler told the whole world what he intended to do with power when he got it.'

Again the *Mirror* returned to Hitler and *Mein Kampf*.

'Let us do him justice. He has never concealed his aims. They are all written in his book, the new Bible of Germany, written by Germany's new deity.

'Step by step—watching his opportunity—he fulfils those aims. We have no excuse for ignorance concerning them.

'To ignore them is as futile and foolish as it would be for a householder to open the door to a burglar who had been obliging enough to announce his visit and the exact amount of property he intended to steal.

'Why, then, talk of talks with the burglar? Gangsters are not disarmed by talk.'

The *Mirror* proposed, therefore, a three-point plan—for National Service, for a National Government and for united military command with France.

'Arm, arm, arm,' it said in its leader on March 15th. It urged that in an age of mechanized warfare the best technicians should be recruited. Muddling through wouldn't be good enough if war came. It repeated its demand for some form of National Service.

'We must arm, arm and arm—with the best brains in the country to direct us.'

Meanwhile, the Nazis had begun to move troops along the Czechoslovakian frontier. On May 28th, Hitler had announced his 'unalterable decision' to smash Czechoslovakia by military action in the near future. Yet on June 3rd, *The Times* still preserved an optimistic pro-German tone.

'Rigid application of the principle of self-determination everywhere,' it said, 'is obviously impracticable; but if the rectification of an injustice left by the Treaty of Versailles *should be made* the Sudeten Germans have an undoubted case.'

The conclusion of the editorial, however, was a decisive act of appeasement and was to have far-reaching consequences not only on British policies but also on Hitler's attitude.

'It is easily intelligible,' *The Times* said, 'that the Czech Government might not willingly agree to a plebiscite likely to result in a demand for the transfer of the Sudetens and the loss of their territory for the Republic. Nevertheless if they could see their way to it, and to granting a similar choice to the other minorities, Hungarian and Polish, the rulers of Czechoslovakia might in the long run be the gainers in having a homogeneous and contented people, still more numerous than the populations of Belgium and Holland, and twice as numerous as those of Denmark or Switzerland. If it was an injustice that these minorities should have been included in the new Republic, that injustice would be removed; and the neighbouring States which take a racial interest in their kinsmen would have to look after them themselves and would lose any sort of claim to interfere in the affairs of Czechoslovakia. It would be a drastic remedy for the present unrest, but something drastic may be needed.'

The *Mirror* rejected *The Times*' appeasing posture, which, whether ingenuous or disingenuous, was foolish. It kept recurring to its own theme that Hitler had set out his programme in *Mein Kampf* and intended to carry it out. As early as March 16th, in an editorial, 'Now for a Real Foreign Policy,' it had said.

'While Herr von Ribbentrop, the German Foreign Minister, was cajoling his friends in English "upper-class" society, while Frau von Ribbentrop was giving the last of her pretty parties, Hitler was advancing upon Austria. "Keep the English chattering while I act. Then laugh at them." '

'Hitler believes in action; we in words. Hitler has a foreign policy. We apparently have none. What is Hitler's foreign policy?

'It is all in his book which should be made compulsory reading for all British Prime Ministers. He has announced his aims.

'After he has gained the rest of Eastern Europe and terrorized the already panic-stricken nations of the Little Entente—what next?

'Next, the destruction of France. Here is the relevant passage from the book:

' "There must be full clarity on one thing: the deadly enemy of the German people now is and remains France."

'How is France to be destroyed?

'By isolation; then by attack.'

The attitudes of *The Times* towards France and Germany must, however, be seen in the context of its general anti-Soviet position. In 1938 any proposed policy of military alliance with the Russians *ipso facto* belonged to the Left. Respectable Right Wing opinion in Britain about Soviet affairs was being shaped for the most part by the Riga correspondent of *The Times*, R. O. G. Urch, whose reporting suffered both from a lack of political detachment and an excessive geographical remoteness. His correspondence was dogmatic, second-hand, and may well have been affected by his earlier imprisonment by the Bolsheviks. The *Mirror* on March 18th was, therefore, making a bold proposal when it said:

'The situation is far too serious for the few remaining democracies in Europe to drift on and apart—engaged in their domestic quarrels.

'We ought to get together without delay.

'Yesterday came, to the non-aggressive Powers, an invitation from M. Litvinoff, Russian Commissar for Foreign Affairs.

'An invitation to meet and discuss the plight into which we have been plunged by the fatal policy of refusing help to our friends and trying to make friends with our enemies who openly scorn our advances.

'We plead most earnestly with the British Government to accept this offer without delay. The united democratic front! Let us aim at that—before it is too late. It may be too late for Spain.'

Throughout the summer, the crisis mounted. Hitler's intention of keeping the Czechs anxious and distraught was amply fulfilled. It was in this atmosphere that on August 31st, 1938, *The Times*' diplomatic correspondent announced that Hitler's pacific professions were 'trusted' in London. The Runciman Mission set off at the end of July. Runciman himself learnt in detail the views of the German princelings in the Sudetenland and the Nazi Czechs elsewhere.

Everywhere he showed understanding—of the dislike of the Sudeten Germans for the Jews in Czechoslovakia, whom he described, according to Geoffrey Peto, his secretary, as 'not comparable with British Jews', and of the general fear of the Bolshevik influence in Czechoslovakia.

The Runciman Mission was a failure, not only because of Runciman's personal inadequacy, but also because of Chamberlain's fixed intention to work out a solution with the Germans which he then could oblige the Czechs to accept.

For its own part, *The Times*, through the person of Barrington-Ward, remained convinced that what Hitler wanted to do was not so much to dismember Czechoslovakia as to force her to break her alliance with France and Russia. On September 5th, the paper appeared with a leader, 'Negotiations Continue,' in which it returned to its own recommendation that 'it might be worthwhile for the Czechoslovak Government to consider whether they should exclude altogether the project, which has found favour in some quarters, of making Czechoslovakia a more homogeneous State by the secession of that fringe of alien populations who are contiguous to the nation with which they are united by race. In any case the wishes of the population concerned would seem to be regarded as permanent, and the advantages to Czechoslovakis of becoming a homogeneous State might conceivably outweigh the obvious disadvantages of losing the Sudeten German districts of the borderland.'

The reference to the cession of the Sudeten German districts was entirely Dawson's, inserted in the absence of any specialist advice. If the Prime Minister and the Foreign Secretary had both acquiesced, it still would have represented an act of conceit and an abuse of *The Times*' power and prestige.

The effect of the leader was dramatic, casting the Czechs into the deepest dejection, and rousing even Runciman to protest against *The Times*' adventurous speculations.

Dawson had recommended a grovelling act of surrender to the Nazis. On the afternoon of September 7th, after Jan Masaryk, the Czechoslovakian Minister in London, had called at the Foreign Office, the Foreign Secretary issued a statement that the proposal in *The Times* did not represent the views of the Government.

The *Mirror*, opposed to further surrender, had few doubts that the moment of decision was approaching. In Paris it reported Daladier as saying, 'As soon as German troops cross the Czechoslovakian frontier, France mobilises and fights.' And on September 14th, it tolled out the solemn warning:

'If France fights, Britain fights. That is the official attitude on the situation that emerges after Hitler's speech at Nuremberg.

'It is the issue every man and woman in Britain must face.'

In Downing Street, emergency talks were taking place. At six o'clock the Premier talked with the chiefs of the fighting forces. At eight o'clock the Inner Cabinet—the Premier, Lord Halifax, Sir John Simon and Sir Samuel Hoare—met. They left at eleven o'clock. Lord Halifax went to the Foreign Office and left at midnight. They were joined by the Service Ministers—Sir Thomas Inskip (Defence), Sir Kingsley Wood (Air), Mr. Hore-Belisha (War), and Mr. Duff Cooper (Navy).

The suggestion was made of general mobilization. *The Times* had begun to back away from the door which it had flung open. On September 9th, it had already said:

'It is really grotesque that so much righteous indignation should be expended on the mere suggestion, which has frequently been made in these columns before, that a revision of boundaries should not be excluded entirely from the list of possible approaches to a settlement. It is not a solution for which anyone is likely to feel enthusiasm.'

Having used its influence for a settlement which it now claimed that no one was likely to feel enthusiasm for, *The Times* had begun tactfully to play down its own recommendation. The *Mirror* by contrast was blunt, courageous and unequivocal. On September 14th, it said:

'We are still on the edge of catastrophe. The maniacal vanity of one man may at any moment plunge the world into the abyss. No illusion is possible. For the Nazi technique is wellknown. It is this:

'To refuse all offers of compromise. To stimulate acts of violence and oppression against "poor," persecuted, miserable, tortured Germans. Then to march.

'Invasion from within! It was tried upon Austria. It succeeded. It succeeded because the world wants peace. It is being tried again in Czechoslovakia. It will not immediately succeed this time because Czechoslovakia will fight.

'We hope, we pray, that the blackmailers know this. And that they know something more. Which is that Russia will support Czechoslovakia; that France will fight. Lastly, that we stand by France.

'Those are the facts, if maniacs can see them. There is still time.

'Remember the wobblings of 1914. Remember the fumblings of poor Grey. In 1938 the British Government is firm—at last. If France moves, the British Commonwealth moves with France.'

Nor did the *Mirror* retreat the following day when Hitler continued to challenge Czechoslovakia. No one wanted war. The *Mirror*'s postbag was full of suggestions for a settlement, some arguable and plausible, some fantastic and impossible. Most of the suggestions recommended joint declarations by Britain, France and Russia. Yet the *Mirror* recognized that even such a declaration of solidarity would only be received with what it called, "ravings and insults." In contrast to *The Times* which still addressed the Nazis with the politeness of a suppliant, the *Mirror* spoke of Goering's 'loutish bellowings' and Hitler's 'Satanic purpose of making war inevitable.'

While the *Mirror* was writing thus, *The Times* on September 14th published an article entitled 'Back to Prague.' implying that Hitler in his violent speech on the last day of the Nuremberg Conference (September 12th) had 'left the door open for negotiations.' The article was in anticipation of Chamberlain's visit to Berchtesgaden, which took place on September 15th, and from which he returned with information that Czechoslovakia was disintegrating now and was certainly not worth a war. Such was the nature of Hitler's 'negotiations' with Chamberlain.

To give its readers a first-hand account of the war situation, the *Mirror* sent Cassandra to Berlin, Prague and on a ten-day assignment. He reported the danger on September 15th in a page of heated prose entitled 'hell's Poker Party,' which said:

'France has fooled around with it (bluff). Czechoslovakia has feared to use it, but Germany has staked all upon the biggest gamble that could be pitched. Will Britain fight?

'Yes, says Chamberlain!

'Yes, says Simon!

'Yes, says Daladier!

'Yes, says Benes!

'But Ribbentrop answers No! No!'

Yet despite the determination expressed by the *Mirror* that Britain 'would not indefinitely be kicked around,' there still was a great yearning for peace in Britain, a great fear of the unknown catastrophes which war could bring. When Chamberlain came back from Berchtesgaden, the *Mirror* published a plaintive editorial called 'Back Already!' But apart from disappointment that the flight had not yielded more concrete results, it tried to seek comfort from 'two small results.' Chamberlain's visit had given the world proof of Britain's anxiety to preserve peace, and had also 'advertised to the German people the close interest felt by the British Government in the Eastern European turmoil.'

By September 17th, however, the *Mirror*'s impatience with the hypocrisy of Hitler in Czechoslovakia broke out again.

'Let us call Hitler's bluff,' it said, 'by inviting him to take back into Germany itself the German populations of Czechoslovakia. If he is not ready to accept a proposal for the migration of populations, then we will know what lies behind the Sudeten humbug.'

The *Mirror*'s passionate sympathy with the Czechoslovaks led it into an excessive optimism.

'How long?' asked its editorial on September 19th, 'How much time have we left in which to save or to destroy the future of Europe and of democracy?

'Ask Hitler.

'The pace of his somnambulistic blackmail quickens. His demands have risen steadily since we heard his raving voice at Nuremberg.

'It was (vaguely) "self-determination" then. It became "plebiscite" next. It was "secession" after that. Early this morning it was, apparently, secession without plebiscite. What now? It may be the lightning stroke.

'Hitler's position within Czechoslovakia is visibly weakening.

'Thanks to the magnificent courage, moderation and tactical skill of President Benes, the ugly Nazi thrust at Czechoslovakia has been parried. The idiotic Henlein has skipped into Germany. There is evidence that those Sudeten "martyrs" who don't want to be martyred in a war are retreating from the extreme position thrust upon them by Hitler, through Henlein.'

The situation was in fact deteriorating. At Godesberg, Hitler's demands had been harsher, more offensive and bullying than before. He wanted to get inside the fortifications of Czechoslovakia, and it was quite clear that if the Czechs did not yield, he intended to march. Now trenches were being dug in Regent's Park and in Hyde Park. The *Mirror* urged men to join the territorials or the A.R.P. It called on housewives to fill larders, to grow potatoes and vegetables, to meet the crisis and to meet it armed and unafraid. 'Make Britain Strong!' it urged. It reminded the country that Hitler was unappeasable. And it summed up its attitude to the Hitler terror in these words.

'The world has a choice of the end of this terror, or terror without end.'

The *Mirror* knew that Hitler was blackmailing Europe. While others were ready to offer him danegeld, the *Mirror* raised on September 21st the question of the price of peace. When Chamberlain had his second interview with Hitler at Bad Godesberg, the *Mirror*, without exaggerating the dangers, pointed out the futility of yielding to blackmail. It was echoing the words of Churchill and Eden, who in speeches on September 21st declared that the sacrifice of Czechoslovakia to the Nazis would lead only to catastrophe. Churchill said:

'If peace is to be preserved on a lasting basis, it can only be by combination by all powers whose convictions and vital interests are opposed to Nazi domination.'

And Eden said:

'If the truth continues to be ignored there can be no escape from that final calamity which it is the supreme task of statesmanship to avert.'

Once again, on September 22nd, the *Mirror* drew attention to Hitler's *Mein Kampf* and quoted this sentence from it:

'We must be absolutely clear that France is the inexorable enemy of the German nation.'

That, it said, was the true view which Chamberlain should bear in mind at Bad Godesberg, not the beautiful view of the Rhine but the ugly view of Hitler's future intentions.

What the *Mirror* called 'heil-Hitlerite organs of the British press' were still claiming that the question between Britain and Hitler was merely a question of certain minorities in Czechoslovakia. Robustly the *Mirror* said in its editorial, 'Last Chance' on September 24th, that what we were now concerned with was 'Hitler's next move towards the conquest (without fighting) of the sinews of war in Eastern Europe. So that he may fight the West.'

'We believe,' the *Mirror* concluded, 'that a firm resistance to threats may even now save us from a real war with weapons. But it is the last chance.'

On September 26th, the *Mirror* campaigned for the recall of Parliament.

'Call Parliament now,' it said. 'Parliament is the voice of the people and it is time for the people's voice to be heard.

'That voice will strengthen the resolution of the Government.

'The whole nation will fight if there is war. It is therefore time to put the issues of peace or war before the nation as a whole.

'Call the representatives of the nation without a day's further delay!

'Call Parliament now.'

Then, on September 28th, while Chamberlain was at the House of Commons reporting on his visit to Hitler, a note from the Nazi dictator inviting him to Munich was handed to him, together with the information that Mussolini and Daladier would also be there. When he reported this to the House, Members, tense and anxious from the feeling of the imminence of war, rose to their feet in enthusiasm, waving their order papers, while strangers in the Gallery, contrary to standing orders, cheered. This sense of relief was echoed in the country. In the social columns of the *Mirror*, Ivor Lambe, the gossip columnist, solemnly reported that people who had lately given up dressing for dinner had now resumed their black ties. Instead of the horror of bombs raining on a defenceless population, a benign and untroubled sky would greet a people who had never thought to see 'bright morning again.'

'On to Munich' was the title (to which history was to give new overtones) of *The Times*' leader which gave unqualified praise to the Prime Minister. 'Where Sir Edward Grey failed, Mr. Chamberlain has, for the moment, succeeded,' it wrote on September 29th. Some days later it was to defend Chamberlain against the charge that he had callously sacrificed a small and democratic people to the overbearing might of undemocratic Germany. 'That,' it states, 'was facile and false.'

There were, of course, dissenters. Duff Cooper resigned; Churchill himself failed to share in the general enthusiasm. The *Mirror* was sceptical. When Chamberlain had flown to Berchtesgarden, it said of him, that he had 'flown on wings of hope, blown on a breeze of public gratitude.' The *Mirror* said it wanted peace. On the other hand it couldn't believe that peace worth a moment's security could come if Britain gave up one after another the strategic points which would be of supreme importance if she had to fight. 'On to Munich,' said *The Times*, with an unconscious emphasis on the name which was to become synonymous with appeasement, humiliation and defeat.

The *Mirror* didn't pull its punches.

'At Heston airport on Saturday,' it said, 'the Prime Minister urged "all concerned" to continue their efforts towards peace.

'Cheers greeted that appeal.

' "All concerned!"

'May we ask whether the phrase includes Hitler with his dwarf Goebbels' infamous propaganda of streaming lies? Does it include the pale spy Ribbentrop, so recently the darling of a treacherous upper-crust riff-raff in this country?

'It is for the Nazis to slow down the war march time-table; for them to call off the war of propagandist lies; for them to begin the peace efforts that the rest of us (except bawling Musso) are continuing.'

Hitler had given the Czechs an ultimatum to surrender by October 1st. The Germans, the Italians and the Hungarians were beginning to mobilise. On September 28th, the King issued a Royal Proclamation calling up naval reservists and the *Mirror* carried a front-page spread, 'Every man and woman must act,' and called on 25,000 women to join the Women's Auxiliary Territorial Service. Chamberlain on September 27th had told the nation in a broadcast that he had done 'all that one man can do' to stop 'this horrible, fantastic and incredible thing'—a world war about 'a quarrel in a faraway country between people of whom we know nothing.'

That was the general line, prompted by all the appeasers of the day. The *Mirror* warned its readers against the bogusness of the argument.

'We know enough,' it said, 'to be sure that this is not a quarrel about Czechoslovakia.

'We know that it is, in essence, a quarrel between the man who rules a vastly powerful nation and the rest of the world, which will not be "dominated by the fear of force."

'Under such domination the life of people who believe in liberty would not be worth living.'

On September 29th, the scrawny Chamberlain arrived in Munich. 'Dig! Enrol! Be Ready!' the front page of the *Mirror* warned. And in an editorial which supported Chamberlain's mission, it said:

'With Chamberlain goes the iron support of our people—a people that in defence of liberty and sanity has keyed itself to the dreadful brink of war without flinching.

'We have called the criminal bluff of the Third Reich. And their Leader knows it.

'Let them remember that this time the Nazi Whip can be cracked no more.

'The lamps of Europe are alight again. But we shall never forget that one reckless man was about to snuff them into the darkness of death.

'For a thousand years the invader has been held from these shores —all the might and courage of Great Britain must go to prove that today, as ever, we stand unchanged.'

The following day, like almost the whole nation, the *Mirror* greeted the Munich settlement with what it called, 'immense relief.' Yet while Chamberlain waved his piece of paper with a claim 'It is peace,' the *Mirror* continued to utter its warnings.

'We are still in darkness,' it said, 'encouraged by a gleam that may be either a false dawn or real daylight. Go on steadily without a moment's hesitation. Intensify all defensive precautions. Do not reckon upon anything but the hope that, if we stand firm, we may win peace. Firmness is the only way of winning it.'

The *Mirror* overrated the value of Chamberlain's visit. 'The personality of a democratic leader,' it said, 'has managed to impose itself upon a nation taught to believe that democracy is dying through its own "bloodthirstiness."'

Yet even in the relief and optimism of its leaders, the sense of doom that Hitler's ultimatum had left still persisted. Chamberlain had spoken of 'peace in our time.' But the sacrifice of Czechoslovakia had only left guilt and apprehension.

'The Czechs came over to us and fought on our side in the "great" war,' said the *Mirror*. 'We own our brief respite to the humiliation and prospective ruin of a gallant people.'

It praised Duff Cooper, First Lord of the Admiralty, who had had the courage to resign his high post by way of protest. It praised Leo Amery and Harold Nicolson, who had offered their own warning against Munich. 'Spare a thought of gratitude for them,' said the *Mirror*.

Once the aspirin of Munich wore off, the pain returned. On October 5th the *Mirror*, summing up the threat to Europe by Hitler, ended its editorial with its recurrent theme, 'Make Britain Strong.'

Churchill spoke in the Commons debate on Munich, and in the *Mirror*'s words, 'flayed the Government's peace pact.'

'Hitler,' said Churchill, 'demanded a pound at the pistol's point. When it was given, he demanded £2, and then he consented to take £1. 17*s*. 6*d*.'

Lady Astor, whose Cliveden home had been a social centre for the pro-German appeasers, protested loudly when he said that Britain had suffered an unmitigated defeat and France had suffered even more. Churchill rounded on her and said, 'The noble lady must recently have been receiving a finishing course in manners!'

Thus the tragic year of 1938 drew to its end, with the London air dank from the miasma which arose in the late autumn and winter evenings from the waterlogged trenches and the neglected and bursting sandbags. There was a gallows jest to come. In a final act of political inanity and social deference, *The Times* invited the views of the Aga Khan on the European scene.

'Apparently hard up for a Chief Diplomatic Adviser,' said the *Mirror*, 'the eccentric *Times* newspaper has had to fall back upon that genial gentleman the Aga Khan for inspiration in this department of journalism.

'Well, what is his message?

'It is that we ought to trust Herr Hitler.'

Like the hallucinated German nation, the British people were now being invited to put their trust in a murderous and lying monomaniac. With eminent common-sense, the *Mirror* rejected the Aga Khan's views. It preferred those of Churchill, to whom Cecil King offered a platform in the *Mirror*. On January 1st, 1939, the *Sunday Pictorial* appeared with a prophetic leader entitled 'Be Ready by Spring.' The British public had time to contemplate in their beds the *Pictorial*'s warnings.

'For three weeks,' it said, 'a dread secret has passed from lip to lip among the politicians and diplomats.

'There has been no official announcement from London, Paris, or from Washington, and for some weeks there there will be no official admission of the facts which we disclose here today.

'But the *Sunday Pictorial* believes that the public should be acquainted with this grave diplomatic news without further secrecy or dangerous delay.

'Hitler has instructed his general staff to be ready in the early spring for another move that will plunge the world into a state of acute crisis.

'We think you should know the facts, for without armed strength there can be no such thing as a happy New Year.'

And the *Pictorial* repeated the familiar message:

'Armed might is our stoutest bulwark in 1939. Be ready by spring!'

Cecil King was determined that Churchill should be in the Cabinet, and on April 23rd, the *Pictorial*'s front page carried the question, 'Why isn't Winston Churchill in the Cabinet?'

'Churchill,' it said, 'more than any other politician foretold the crises that Germany's rearmament would inflame. His virility and vigilance have spurred on the Cabinet remorselessly—but they still will have nothing to do with Churchill himself.

'No one questions his integrity, his ability, his eagerness to serve.

'His fame is already too gloriously illumined for friend or foe to insinuate that he could be motivated by a zest for personal splendour or material gain.

'But while there gathers sullenly the hurricane that threatens to wreck our generation, this one man who could stem the dark forces, this one man whom Hitler fears, is thrust into the background and forced to endure a political impotence which is as shameful as it is premature.

'Why isn't Winston Churchill in the Cabinet?

'The answer is that the personal suspicions and fear and jealousies of others are crushing him out, and the desire of the nation is disregarded with contempt.

'The people now demand that this fantastic duel shall cease, and it is time that the truth about Churchill was told.'

Winston Churchill always had a respectful attitude towards Northcliffe (though Northcliffe suspected Churchill's attitude to censorship), and handled him with a combination of courtesy and forthrightness. Shortly before the First World War he had written to Northcliffe, thanking him somewhat sycophantically for his kindness in giving such wide coverage to his speeches. Northcliffe replied:

'I have not been in the least kind to you. I judge public men by their public form, and I believe that your enquiring, industrious mind is alive to our national interest.'

After the war, when Northcliffe in his eccentric decline started campaigning for the '*Daily Mail* hat,' a hat of novel shape invented for the paper, Winston Churchill was among the first to wear it. The idea failed to catch on. But the fact that Churchill, though no stranger to stunts himself, was willing to join in a stunt which, to Northcliffe's own staff, foreshadowed the onset of his final madness, illustrates Churchill's regard for Northcliffe as well as his own exhibitionism.

Between the *Mirror* and Churchill in 1939 there was then a traditional sympathy, qualified by a certain reserve about each other's judgments. But in this case the *Mirror* was solidly behind Churchill in his warnings, and on March 21st, 1939, it underlined his words in Parliament.

'We are told we must not divide Europe into two armed camps. Is there then to be only one armed camp? The Dictators' armed camp, and a rabble of outlying peoples wandering round the outskirts, wondering which of them is going to be taken first?

'Europe *is* divided into camps,' the *Mirror* warned.

While backing Churchill, the *Mirror* did not hesitate to take on the Establishment. The Archbishop of Canterbury had said earlier in the month that people should keep calm. The *Mirror* indignantly challenged his complacency.

'What about the Jews?' it asked. 'What is happening in the streets of Madrid? And ruined Czechoslovakia?'

A few weeks later Italy launched her attack on Albania. Again the *Mirror* warned under the heading, 'Another Scrap of Paper.'

'We said the other day that Hitler never rests and that he cannot stop. The Government's slow conversations with Poland have infuriated him, as the Nazi press ravings show. He answers by a rapid word of command to the lower end of the axis.

'Lieutenant Musso has been expecting that word for a long time—too long for his own prestige. He makes this move under orders from Berlin or Innsbruck. When, for Hitler's counter-move? Will it be east again, or at last a fierce move towards the west—another threat of general war? If that threat comes shall we meet it with resolution? or will another Minister oblige the whole British Commonwealth with a famous speech babbled in the easy atmosphere of a jolly dinner-party amongst pals?'

It was in this atmosphere that in July, 1939, Cecil King, then a director of the *Mirror*, together with Hugh Cudlipp, the editor of the *Sunday Pictorial*, visited Churchill at his home in Kent to discuss a series of articles to be written by him for the *Mirror*. Churchill's immediate interest was to use the power of the *Mirror* to awaken Britain to the Nazi menace. He was relying at that time for his income on his professional writing, and he could not have been indifferent to the substantial fee.

King and Cudlipp listened to Churchill for an hour as, in the manner of an elder statesman, he gave them a world tour of his views. As a result of this meeting, Churchill wrote a spectacular series of articles, with the final warning, 'At the 11th Hour' in August, 1939.

He began with an admonition to Germany.

'Let there be no delusions in the Nazi Party and among its grim chiefs that, for instance, Poland, the Baltic States, the Ukraine, Hungary and Rumania could be overrun, and that the aggressors could then turn round and make peace with the Western Powers.

'Napoleon, sword in hand, sought victorious peace in every capital in Europe.

'He sought it in Berlin, in Vienna, in Madrid, in Rome and finally in Moscow.

'All he found was St. Helena.'

Then he went on to pre-figure a famous phrase of his war-time speeches.

'There were years in that struggle when England stood quite alone, all the world against her.

'The unaccountable delay—whoever is to blame for it—in concluding an all-in alliance between Britain, France and Russia, aggravates the danger of a wrong decision by Herr Hitler.'

What sort of country was it that retained its composure, as Churchill pointed out, in the face of the Nazi threat? On August 22nd, 1939, the day on which the non-aggression pact between Germany and the Soviet Government was signed—a pact which the conscious dilatoriness of the Chamberlain Government had made possible, if not encouraged—Ivor Lambe, the gossip columnist of the *Mirror*, published this paragraph:

'Lord Stamp, chairman of the L.M.S. railway and the biggest railway noise in the country, is having his leg pulled about the way in which he spent part of his weekend.

'A crisis is blowing up in the railway world, for railwaymen are claiming a minimum wage of 50*s*. a week.

'Lord Stamp couldn't apparently get trains out of his mind; he was staying at Birchington-on-Sea and he took his three grandchildren, the little daughters of Mr. and Mrs. Wilfred Carlyle Stamp, for a ride on a model train that runs in the grounds of a local hotel. He even drove the engine himself.'

It was an ingenuous paragraph, written for a public which regarded human personality as being enhanced by a title. But it also recorded a period of social contrast when it was thought normal for a wage-demand of 50*s*. a week to be resisted within a setting of conspicuous affluence.

Unemployment in Britain, as in Germany in the early part of the decade, had begun to dwindle with rearmament. Paradoxically, the prospect of war lightened the burdens of the working classes. Wage claims and work problems were beginning to become secondary to questions of survival.

By March 16th, the *Mirror* was no longer talking hopefully about Britain seeking only to be left alone in order to enjoy the delights of Spring. Cassandra, who after visiting the Reich had reported with much sympathy such genuine grievances among the Germans as he could detect, now said in an article called 'The Dagger at Europe's Heart':

'The dagger at the heart of Europe may turn West.

'Pray God that our armour be strong and that the courage of unrivalled defensive might shall be ours.'

'W.M.' wrote on March 16th:

'Hitler is never satisfied with submission. His "dark Satanic mind" rejoices in humiliating the downfallen. He stamps on the faces of his victims. We know his methods and we have studied his programme. Nothing that he does surprises us. What does surprise us is the surprise of our rulers here.'

'They never seem to suspect their Hitler. When he lets them down, they just can't make out what's come over the Fuehrer. Why, he promised to be good!'

The following day the new Protectorate of Bohemia and Moravia was proclaimed by Hitler in Prague. He had, he said, forestalled a new threat to peace. In the name of peace he would shortly be turning, the *Mirror* prophesied, to Holland, Belgium and Alsace.

'What are we to do?' asked the *Mirror*. 'We ask most earnestly. Will *anything* persuade our Government, at once, with all the means in its power, to rally the non-aggressors together; at once to seek conference with Russia; with the U.S.A.; with the Scandinavian group; with all whom we have neglected or forgotten during the futile course of our vain attempt to disarm the dictators by being nice to them and believing their promises or their lies?'

'Words will not stop Hitler,' Cassandra wrote on March 21st. Urgently the *Mirror* warned in its leading article, 'Back to our Real Friends.'

'There are two ways of losing a war. One is to be defeated in the field. The other is to lose the war before it begins.

'We have indicated this peril for months past. It is now obvious. It is now admitted.

'Why is so plain a peril—plainly revealed in Hitler's book—why, we ask, is it only now recognized by our rulers?

'Simply because, even if they have read Hitler (which is still doubtful) they have not believed what he has said in *Mein Kampf*.

'Not believing him, not knowing the sort of lucid lunatic with whom they have had to deal, they have believed it possible to disarm him by smiles, handshakes, pacts and scraps of paper.'

Churchill's own warnings quickened. On July 27th, Parliament was going into a three-months recess. Churchill from his lonely position in the Tory Party protested. Hitler had done a deal with Mussolini over the future of the Tyrol. German forces had arrived at the Brenner Pass. All this was ominous for the future of peace.

A fortnight later in August, Churchill was offering a warning to Japan. But the warning, though stern, reads tragically in the light of subsequent events, with something of the irony of Chamberlain's later claim that the Germans had missed the bus in their Norwegian campaign.

'Singapore,' said Churchill, 'is as far from Japan as Southampton from New York.

'Strong reinforcements of troops have been sent from India to bring its garrison up to full war requirements.

'A great fortress like Singapore, armed with the heaviest cannon and defended by aircraft and submarines is in no danger from a purely naval attack.

'In order to capture Singapore the Japanese would have to send not only their main fleet, but an immense convoy of transports with an army of not less than fifty or sixty thousand men.

'They would have to disembark on the peninsula, and begin a regular siege amid its deadly marshes.'

Then Churchill went on to compare the operation of the siege of Port Arthur, the difference being that the Japanese would have to transport their troops and casualties over two thousand miles of British submarine infested waters. He concluded with:

'A stubborn defence should enable the fortress to hold out for at least nine months, or perhaps a year.'

It was a nice calculation which failed to take into account the possibility that Singapore might be attacked, as in fact happened, from the rear.

On August 23rd came news of Hitler's non-aggression pact with the Soviet Union. Now at last it was clear that the anti-Comintern pact was in fact what the *Mirror* called the anti-British pact. At last Rothermere's fond belief that Hitler stood between Britain and the Soviet Union was exploded. 'W.M.' wrote:

'Fools have for years supposed Hitler to be a "bulwark against Bolshevism"—he with his own "inverted Bolshevism" of the Third Reich! They believed, because he talked so loud about killing Communism in Spain.

'At the right strategical moment he becomes the benignant friend of the Soviet Government which he has treated so courteously of late. Just so—his racial-Aryan mania is compatible with his understanding with Japan.

'Power first and conquest! Convictions as a barrage of words to deceive fools.

'Now, at one stroke, two sets of delusionists are blown sky-high—(1) the-bulwark-against-Bolshevism sheep who thought that Hitler would never, never talk to those horrid "Reds"; (2) the Communist sheep who got all their ideas of an ancient political doctrine from Stalinism and believed that Stalin would never, never compound with what he has repeatedly called "German Fascism."'

Churchill himself summed up the world crisis on August 24th with his article, 'At the 11th Hour.'

'In view of the Soviet-German intrigue and all other information to hand,' he wrote, 'it is becoming increasingly difficult to see how war can be averted. It is certainly not right to give up hope. . . . There is no truth and no sense in the plea that Hitler has gone too far to stop. He could stop now.

'By a single impulse of will-power he could regain the solid foundations of health and sanity.

'He has but to send his reservists to their homes, and his example would be followed step by step in every country.

'He has but to restore to the Czech nation the freedom, the independence and the frontiers he solemnly promised at Munich to bring about an immediate revulsion of feeling in his favour throughout the world.

'There can be no question of buying peace.

'No further concessions can be made to threats of violence.

'We cannot pay Germany to leave off doing wrong.'

This was the ultimate affirmation of non-appeasement. War was now inevitable. On September 1st, the Government decided to evacuate children and 'priority classes' from London. The *Mirror* gave its full support and this sensible advice.

'Do all you can to help those who are trying to help you. Keep steady and cheerful. Be kind to one another. We who stay behind wish you a safe journey and a safe return.'

On the same day the call-up began and A.R.P. emergency control was put into effect. The next day, on September 2nd, the *Mirror* under the headline, 'No Choice Left,' soberly reported the words of Hitler in order to refute them.

' "In order to put an end to this lunacy I have no choice than to meet force with force from now on." '

'With these lying words Adolf Hitler prepares to plunge the world into the supreme lunacy of his war on two fronts. The sort of war he had denounced for years past!

' "In order to put an end to this lunacy." '

'That makes a good maxim and motive for ourselves. The time has indeed come for *us* to put an end to this lunacy.'

'The lunacy of a man and of the gang behind him.'

On September 3rd, 1939, war broke out. And the following day the early edition, with a roaring lion as its symbol, carried the headline splashed over the front page:

'Britain sets up War Cabinet: Churchill is new Navy Chief.'

On the inside page Cassandra had compiled a page headed 'Wanted! For Murder . . . for Kidnapping . . . for Theft and for Arson. This Reckless Criminal is Wanted—Dead or Alive!'

The back page gave the *Mirror*'s list of 'dont's.'

'Don't listen to rumours. Don't broadcast information. Don't lose your head. Don't listen to scaremongers. Don't cause crowds to assemble.'

By September 13th the paper had begun its campaign for efficiency in the conduct of the war.

'In 1939 we cannot endure fools in high places as we did after 1914. The self-revealed blunderers must go. We endured muddlers too long in the last bitter struggle.'

It wasn't only a warning for the obstructive. It was a specific warning to Chamberlain. The year of the Phoney War had begun.

CHAPTER V

The End of the Chamberlain Era

A WEEK BEFORE Christmas, 1939, with an apathetic Government and nation going through the motions of war rather than waging it, the *Mirror*'s rousing headline, 'The Canadians Are Here,' was followed by the report that the first Canadian combat troops had arrived on British soil. Under this despatch from 'A Western Port' was a protest that the War Office and the censor had held up the announcement so that Churchill could make it personally in a speech the night before.

'The nation should be told the news at once,' said the *Mirror* trenchantly. 'It should not be saved up to colour Mr. Churchill's speeches. . . . After all, we are fighting one form of dictatorship. We don't want to acquire another.'

It was an early shot in the running skirmishes between the *Mirror* and the War Office which were to last throughout the war.

The year was ending in discontent, only lightened by reports on the same day, December 19th, of twelve Nazi planes shot down, and a German cruiser sunk among mines.

In the country and the press generally, mistrust of Chamberlain, paralleled by Hitler's mounting confidence and braggadoccio, reinforced the public's anxiety to find a man who would grasp the situation, master it and thus lead the nation to victory. The *Mirror*, surveying the Cabinet through a Zec cartoon, saw nothing but a row of empty seats in an empty Cabinet Room. Among older men, a nostalgia was rising for 1916, when Lloyd George took over from a palsied Government and earned the title of 'The Man who won the war.' Among the younger men of the *Mirror*, there was a fierce concern to shrug off the past and get on with the war with new men and means.

In 1940, Lloyd George himself was living on his estate at Churt, a few miles from Farnham, where he had become a model scientific farmer. His political interventions were rare and Olympian. His battles with the Press Lords, chief of them Northcliffe whom he had accused in the House of Commons on April 16th, 1919, of 'a diseased vanity,' belonged to history. The founder of the *Mirror* had abused the politician, but, as Lloyd George said of himself, 'he hadn't bowed his head.'

Perhaps for that very reason, Northcliffe's nephew held him in a particular respect. Cecil King asked Hugh Cudlipp to visit the old statesman at Churt to discuss with him a proposed series of articles on the war.

On January 3rd, 1940, Cecil King recorded in his diary:

'Cudlipp had lunch with Lloyd George in the country and spent about four hours with him. Ll. G. was very active and communicative, though very pessimistic. He considered that we had been completely outwitted and out-manoeuvred in the last five years. The Russo-German pact had nullified our naval blockade, and though he did not actually say so, left Cudlipp with the impression that to seize a peace move by Hitler in 1942 or '43 would be the only alternative to military defeat.'

Cudlipp turned the conversation to Churchill, already the natural candidate for the nation's leadership.

'I told Churchill three weeks ago,' said Lloyd George, 'that he was unwise to take the job at the Admiralty. If he succeeds in sinking all the German U-boats, he'll be very popular. But what if they launch four hundred new ones? What if there are serious reverses? Winston will get it in the neck.'

Referring to the outbreak of the war, Lloyd George said, 'Churchill telephoned me three weeks before the war, and told me Hitler's latest terms for Danzig settlement. He said, "I think they are not unreasonable," and I agreed with him. We should have called a halt when Hitler interfered in Spain. The people who say Hitler is a fool are mad themselves. He is not an epileptic. He has a fine head.'

And then Lloyd George, his short legs dangling over his armchair, said.

'This is a damn crazy war. For years the menace of Germany has been rising—but what did Baldwin do? He was too lazy to make great decisions.'

Laziness in Lloyd George's view was the supreme demerit in a statesman. When Cudlipp referred to Hore-Belisha, Lloyd George dismissed him with the single word, 'Lazy!' But the old Welsh wizard refused to lend either his energies or his magic to articles on the war. What inhibited him wasn't the inertia of his own old age; it was a profound pessimism about Britain's chances of outright victory.

'People call me a defeatist,' he said, 'but tell me how we can win! Can we win in the air? Can we win at sea—when the effect of our naval blockade is wiped out by Germany's connections with Russia? How can we win on the land? The Germans cannot get through the Maginot Line; when do you think we can get through the Siegfried Line? Not until the trumpet blows, my friend. Even if Hitler marches into Holland and Belgium it will be to get nearer England—to build submarine bases and aerodromes; not, in my view, to invade France. In what field can action be decisive—for either side? In none. Hitler cannot win any more than we can—and he has the brains to see it. The war will drag wearily on. There will be no spectacular appeals to the emotions. The people will become bored and dreary, and in the end they won't stand for it. There is no excitement in a war like this. In the end they will demand peace.'

Two days later, the Secretary of State for War, Hore-Belisha, the man the generals disliked, the man who wanted to open up the war, was sacked by Chamberlain. On January 5th, Cecil King, hearing the news of Belisha's 'resignation', telephoned the *Mirror*'s editor, Cecil Thomas, and told him, as he recalls in his diary, 'to treat the news in a very anti-Chamberlain sense.' Belisha went, a pebble swept away by events. But his going started the avalanche that overwhelmed Chamberlain, falsified Lloyd George's pessimism and finally smothered what had seemed the indestructible monster.

Under a banner headline, 'Belisha Resigns,' the *Mirror* spoke of 'the sensational change in the Army Cabinet . . . the man responsible for purging the Army Council of its old men has resigned.' It called his resignation 'the biggest political sensation since hostilities began.' Hore-Belisha's political methods, said the *Mirror*, had aroused the opposition of the military caste—the old gang of the Army Command.

On January 6th Cecil King wrote in his diary:

'To the office at three o'clock, where I find Cudlipp has had breakfast with Belisha. Apparently Belisha had no suspicion whatever that any trouble was brewing, and was as surprised as anyone when he was asked to move from the War Office to the Board of Trade.'

King recorded Belisha's story as Cudlipp gave it to him.

'Chamberlain sent for me on December 24th,' said Hore-Belisha. 'He was highly congratulatory, and said he had complete confidence in me, and the highest admiration for my work. "It will live in the Ministry," he said, "and you will be remembered as the greatest War Minister." Chamberlain went on to discuss various aspects of my work and asked, "Have you got complete confidence in Gort?" "Yes," I replied. "Have you got complete confidence in Ironside?" Before I replied, he told me his opinion of Ironside. "I hear nothing but evil of him," he said. "He is an intriguer." I disagreed, and praised Ironside and did not want to change him.

'On January 4th, Chamberlain sent for me again,' said Hore-Belisha. 'He opened with more praise for me. Then he said there had been a lot of prejudice. "I am re-arranging the Cabinet, and it is in your interest that they should get you out," said Chamberlain. I was staggered. "If you go now history will do justice to you," he went on.'

The dialogue that followed was dramatic.

Belisha: This is completely amazing.

Chamberlain: I am offering you the Board of Trade and am sure you will accept it.

Belisha: I'd like to think it over.

Chamberlain: Think it over? Surely you're not hesitating?

Chamberlain pressed hard for an immediate acceptance.

Belisha: But what is the reason for the hurry, in any case?

Chamberlain: Well, there must obviously be no leakage.

Belisha: But how can there be a leakage? Who else knows about this?

Chamberlain: Oh, not a soul.

He went on to urge Belisha to take a post in the Cabinet. He couldn't refuse. The public would think there was a difference of opinion; it would be bad. 'Besides, what will you do?' said Chamberlain. 'You're an ambitious man.'

Belisha: Of course I'm ambitious. You are yourself. Is there any M.P. who doesn't want to be Prime Minister? But I have lived for the War Office. I regard it as my great job in life.

An hour after the interview, Chamberlain wrote Belisha a personal letter. It was four pages long, amazingly friendly and almost sentimental. In it Neville Chamberlain described a personal experience. In the First World War he had interviewed a soldier about to be

Daily Mirror

THUR JULY 5 1945

FORWARD WITH THE PEOPLE

No. 12,960 ONE PENNY

Registered at G.P.O. as a Newspaper.

DON'T LOSE IT AGAIN

Vote for them

WE reproduce on this page Zec's famous VE-Day cartoon. We do so because it expresses more poignantly than words could do the issues which face the people of this country today.

As you, the electors, with whom the destiny of the nation rests, go to the poll, there will be a gap in your ranks. The men who fought and died that their homeland and yours might live will not be there. You must vote for THEM. Others, happily spared, are unable for various reasons to have their rightful say in this election. You must represent them.

Vote on behalf of the men who won the victory for you. You failed to do so in 1918. The result is known to all. The land "fit for heroes" did not come into existence. The dole did. Short-lived prosperity gave way to long, tragic years of poverty and unemployment. Make sure that history does not repeat itself. Your vote gives you the power. Use it. Let no one turn your gaze to the past. March forward to new and happier times. The call of the men who have gone comes to you. Pay heed to it. Vote for THEM.

Remember the issues. They are national not personal. Your own interest, the future of your children, the welfare of the whole country demand that today you do your duty and

VOTE

"Here you are—don't lose it again!"

(Reproduced from our VE-Day issue without apology.)

ZEC'S CARTOON ON ELECTION DAY, 1945, REPRODUCED FROM THE MIRROR'S VE-DAY ISSUE

Daily Mirror

THURS OCT. 25 1951

1½d

FORWARD WITH THE PEOPLE

No. 14,915

Registered at G.P.O. as a Newspaper.

WHOSE FINGER?

BIG ISSUES OF 1951

Today YOUR finger is on the trigger

SEE YOU DEFEND

PEACE with SECURITY and PROGRESS with FAIR SHARES

VOTE FOR THE PARTY YOU CAN REALLY TRUST

The 'Daily Mirror' believes that Party is Labour

WHOSE FINGER ON THE TRIGGER? THE MIRROR'S FRONT PAGE ON ELECTION DAY, 1951

executed. To console him Chamberlain said, 'You are making a great sacrifice!' Hore-Belisha found the parable unconvincing.

The two men met again, and their conversation sealed their divorce.

Chamberlain: Is your decision irrevocable?

Belisha: Yes.

Chamberlain: Well, how can we tell the public?

Belisha: I suppose I'll have to write a letter.

Chamberlain: Not a nasty letter, of course. The public mustn't think there are any differences in the Cabinet.

Chamberlain urged Belisha to insert a sentence, 'I am glad to think there is no difference of policy between us.'

Belisha: You are going to give no reasons, Prime Minister?

Chamberlain: It's all prejudice—prejudice and criticism.

Belisha: What prejudice?

Chamberlain would go no further.

Belisha: But it's staggering, the whole thing. Only a fortnight ago you sent for me to praise me. I take it that this prejudice was in existence then? What you are doing is to deliver me up to my enemies. How can I take another post now? You will let me down again. I'm absolutely staggered and perplexed. I can't go to Clarkson's and put a wig on and turn up as somebody else next week.

The interview finished with Chamberlain making further vague references to prejudice. He thanked Belisha for his work at the War Office and again expressed his personal liking and admiration.

Belisha said to Cudlipp that there had been no controversy between him and the generals, though a small clique didn't like his reforms. There had, however, been one *démarche* by the generals about the new officers' courses. They were critical of promotion from the ranks and wanted the old Sandhurst methods.

Belisha: Of course, the Palace was in it.

Cudlipp: How?

Belisha: Well, they worked through those quarters (the generals).

Cudlipp: Was that the pressure Chamberlain referred to?

Belisha: I can only tell you, old man, what I know. The Duke of Gloucester is in the Army, remember, and they worked through him. 'Too much democracy in the ranks!'—and that sort of rubbish.

What was the prejudice? It was the kind of prejudice that no one wanted to make explicit. It was, in fact, the prejudice of the established social and military order against a Jew of middle-class and foreign descent, who sought publicity for his work, rejected the caste attitudes of his day and who, for short, was referred to by his critics as a 'cad.' The *Mirror* did not need any personal sympathy with Belisha to defend his cause. His superficial demeanour—brash, arrogant, and thrusting—alienated many. But his democratisation of the Army was the essential preliminary to a total democratic counter-attack against Hitler's total onslaught.

On January 6th, 1940, the *Mirror*'s leader, inspired by King, was headed 'Bombshell!'

'What is behind the sudden and surprising departure of Mr. Hore-Belisha from the Cabinet of Antiques in Downing Street?' it asked.

'He is (for a Minister) young. He has proved himself a man of ideas and energy.'

'So far as we know, much of the recent modernization and reform of Army methods, much of the Army's recent mechanization, together with a part at least of such remarkable achievements as the passage of a big expeditionary force to France, may be set to his credit. At any rate, his name is known to the men at the front, to the men in training at home, and to the civilian public.'

The attack on the Government became even sharper at the end of the column.

'We fear that the Museum Ministry may well collapse earlier than the enemy. And today we begin to ask whether the other and larger Ministry—whether the Government as we now have it—may not collapse also before the end of the war.'

After considering the matter over the weekend, the *Mirror* returned to the subject with a savage editorial called 'Questions.'

'Apart from Mr. Chamberlain, that (War) Ministry possessed two men whose names are not merely names to the people: Churchill and Hore-Belisha.

'One of them has gone. Mr. Churchill remains as the lone possessor of an imagination and therefore of a popular appeal.'

Then it went on to ask some questions.

'Can it be that Mr. Hore-Belisha was too democratic? Had he made enemies amongst true "gentlemen"? And have those gentlemen, in typical gentlemanly fashion, retaliated upon Mr. Hore-Belisha? Suppose that Mr. Hore-Belisha didn't believe that to lose as a gent is better than to win as a "bit of a bounder"? What if the old gang have surrounded Mr. Hore-Belisha?

'Are these foolish or subversive questions?

'Then answer them! Refute them. Give us some explanation, if not in public, at least in secret session to M.P.s.

'Failing an explanation, we repeat, the Government has dealt itself a staggering blow.

'It has relapsed with a thud lower into the morass of its own mediocrity.'

Almost a week passed in which public discussion of the changes remained lively. Belisha's reforms had been popular, and the *Mirror* had no intention of abandoning the theme of a need for the right kind of change, or of altering its view that a shifting of the furniture in what it called the Museum Ministry of Chamberlain wasn't the proper way to get it. On the Thursday following its leader 'Questions', Cudlipp, at King's suggestion, met Belisha to talk to him about the speech he was due to make in the House the following week.

King wrote in his diary of January 13th, 1940:

'On further reflection Belisha feels sure Churchill must have known about his impending dismissal, and he is also fairly sure that he intends to become Defence Minister. The reason is presumably that things may go wrong in the Navy, and as Defence Minister his risks would be spread. Belisha said he learnt that Churchill had dinner several times with Ironside in the last month or so, and he is convinced that Ironside is in the plot. When asked why Churchill didn't use the opportunity to resign and force Chamberlain out, Belisha said that clearly Churchill assumed that he (Belisha) would take the Board of Trade; secondly, that he was out of the country and could not quickly take advantage of the situation when Belisha refused the Board of Trade; and thirdly, that in any case Churchill was a bad political tactician and probably did not see his chance.' In fact, Hore-Belisha underestimated Churchill's political skill and overestimated the esteem in which Churchill held him. Churchill wasn't prepared to sacrifice his own chances of power in favour of a man who often couldn't be found when his officials wanted him—a supplementary criticism often made about Belisha by his colleagues.

When Belisha made his resignation speech, it fell far short of the challenging, dramatic tone which the *Mirror* had hoped for. Belisha, despite his blandness in face of anti-semitism, was acutely sensitive to the danger that his Jewish origin might embarrass the Government. Supremely confident of his ability to lead, he nevertheless didn't want to add to Chamberlain's trouble at a critical time.

Cecil King was deeply disappointed. He wrote on January 17th:

'The Hore-Belisha episode has ended in a complete fizzle. Belisha made an innocuous speech in the debate. Up to Saturday night he was determined to fight; on Monday night he rang up Cudlipp and was less sure about the wisdom of fighting, and when the moment came he climbed meekly down. Chamberlain denied in the debate that Belisha had had any disagreement with anyone, but declined to give any reasons for the dismissal. An interesting feature was the statement by Attlee that the Socialists were not going to swing in behind a newspaper campaign. Apart from the tactical absurdity of the remark, it was significant as it brought the House down, and was thus interesting proof of the intensely hostile attitude of the House of Commons to the Press.'

If with the departure of Hore-Belisha there had been some improvement on the various fronts, the generals and Chamberlain might have been vindicated, and the *Mirror* confounded. But the military position crumbled. The Russian attack on Finland was a cruel and treacherous addition to Britain's difficulties as well as being a catastrophe for the Finns. By March 14th, 1940, Finland had capitulated, and the *Mirror* with great prescience said of the Scandinavian countries which had refused to intervene:

'It is evident that the fears of Norway and Sweden, their desperate shrinking from the risk of intervention, have contributed to the catastrophe. . . . The Scandinavian countries have made their choice. We must leave the consequences to them.

'For ourselves—why deny it?—the "hard peace" thrust upon Finland by her brutal neighbour is indirectly another defeat.

'It will set Stalin free to help Hitler. It will help Hitler to plot further aggression with Stalin. It will open supplies to Germany from Russia. And it will once more give all our wishful thinkers and hopeful babblers an opportunity of explaining that it doesn't matter, because, one day, after they've got all they want, Hitler and Stalin will fall out and begin scrapping over their immense booty.'

Zec marked the occasion with a powerful cartoon showing the figure of a Finnish soldier crucified on a huge hammer and sickle. The caption read, 'Russia Declares Peace on Finland!' With an unintended irony, Miss Patience Strong contributed in her Quiet Corner, just below the cartoon, a rhyme entitled 'Jog Along.'

'Laurels may be yours one day,
Who knows what fate may bring?

You may be called upon to do
Some big and splendid thing . . .
But for the moment take your place
—Just one among the throng—
You may get your chance—but in the meantime,
Jog along.'

This was exactly the opposite of what the *Mirror* was recommending to the Government. The *Mirror* wanted a new and dynamic approach to the war. It had no confidence in Chamberlain, and wanted Churchill to take over the Premiership and lead the nation to victory.

Early in February Winston Churchill invited Cecil King to lunch at Admiralty House, with Mrs. Churchill, Miss Mary Churchill and an American woman who, as King says in his diary, 'talked too much.'

'Mrs. Winston,' King wrote, '(is) a very good-looking woman, with good eyes and good features, but rather thin, dried-up and nervy. The daughter, aged seventeen to eighteen, is a real winner; huge eyes, big mouth, wide across the eyes and a full figure. Winston wore black boots with zip fasteners, the first I have seen. At lunch the conversation was general for a bit, that is to say, largely a monologue by the American, when suddenly Winston said, "How do you think the war is going?"

'I said that was a big question; he said, "You shouldn't be afraid to answer big questions." I said, "Well, put like that—not very well." From then on we talked mainly politics and the war—say for an hour or so in all—the latter half of the time alone with him after the ladies had withdrawn.

'When I saw him in May or June, he had spoken of Belisha without affection, but said he was one of the best men Chamberlain had. But on this occasion his whole attitude was quite different. Churchill said that he had formed a very poor opinion of Belisha's conduct of public business since the beginning of the war; that though he had to give him credit for the introduction of conscription, he thought the work of the War Office would go forward more smoothly and expeditiously under Oliver Stanley; that the War Office ("and not particularly the Brass Hats", meaning the civil servants there), were delighted to see the last of him; that for Belisha's sake (this more in sorrow—the old humbug! than in anger) he was sorry he did not take the Board of Trade when it was offered to him, but that now he thought it was as well Belisha had not.

'Mrs. Churchill then chipped in and said Belisha even had to have his papers read out to him, and the American lady said he never got out of bed till 11.00 (this is very widely stated and may be true). I said I thought that judged by the very low standard of the present Government Belisha was quite good. Mary Churchill clapped her hands at my mention of the poor quality of the present Government and thanked me for saying it! By their reference to the excellence of Stanley's speech at Newcastle this week, I got the impression that Churchill is very pro-Stanley—probably mainly on social grounds—which confirms my guess on Churchill's part in the downfall of Belisha and the promotion of Stanley.

'On Chamberlain, Churchill said he had formed a better opinion of him since he had worked with him; that he was very tough; and that he was 100 per cent for the vigorous prosecution of the war. I said he was too old, dreary, with a sorry record of appeasement, and that his speeches lacked substance. In fact that he lacked all the qualities of leadership in anxious times; that the country regarded Churchill as leader, and yet he had not the authority of a Prime Minister.

'Churchill said, "The Premiership isn't much of a catch these days; I would only take it if offered to me by common consent." He would not take the job as a prize in a fight, as then he would have two fights on his hands—with his opponents in the party and with the Germans. Churchill's attitude was that Chamberlain had the entire support of the Conservative Party, therefore he was quite safe—and public opinion?—to hell with public opinion. And Churchill actually said that anyway in time of war the machinery of Government is so strong it can largely afford to ignore popular feeling. *He also said he would rather have Chamberlain than Eden as Prime Minister by eight to one.*

'From the course of our conversation I gathered that Churchill was not planning anything so definite as becoming Defence Minister, though I hear on all sides he is playing a stronger hand over the whole field of government.

'Churchill attached importance to the fact that the Germans were putting out peace feelers in all sorts of hole and corner ways. He thought this showed the Germans to be uneasy and afraid of the war's outcome.'

King's own comment was that if the Germans would get Britain to sign an armistice now, 'they would have us where they want us. We should not make another great war effort on any account for several years, and in those years the Germans could take anything that struck their fancy—in fact, peace would be a victory for Germany, leading in about eighteen months' time to our complete downfall.'

King saw clearly that an armistice on German terms could only be a halfway house to a defeat as inexorable as Czechoslovakia's after Munich. But the conduct of the war created in him a pessimism which he didn't seek to hide. Unlike Lloyd George's, it was a pessimism which sprang from Britain's immediate circumstances, not from her potentialities. Churchill understood his point of view, and despite King's 'very plain speaking' was friendly, saw him into the lift at Admiralty House, and urged him to come again.

'He looks puffy and old,' was King's verdict. 'He drank port and beer alternately at lunch—ending with beer.'

King's personal view of Churchill was always one of esteem tempered by scepticism. At this luncheon the Churchill myth had not yet flowered to the fullness it was to achieve at the end of the war. The great speeches had not yet been spoken. The stern face and the parted fingers had not yet been national symbols of determination. Churchill was still a political figure, a Conservative with a past. At home, the word 'Tonypandy', where he sent troops to restrain rioters dogged him in Labour circles and labelled him a reactionary. As a strategist, 'Gallipoli' was his political epitaph.

Nor, in family tradition, did Churchill occupy a place of unqualified confidence in his attitude towards Press censorship.

In a First War letter to Lord Murray, the former Liberal Chief Whip, Northcliffe wrote about censorship and the First Lord of the Admiralty:

'What the newspapers feel very strongly is that against their will, they are made to feel part and parcel of a foolish conspiracy to hide bad news. English people do not mind bad news.

'Every newspaper man that I know regards Churchill as responsible for many of the wicked evils of the Press Bureau. . . . I have always liked Winston personally, and he knows that.'

Over twenty years later, King was to re-echo his uncle's doubts about Churchill and the Press. And, Churchill, in turn, was to be at least as hostile to the *Mirror*'s criticisms as he had been to those in Northcliffe's *Daily Mail.*

In the meantime, the search for a national leader went on. From France came reports of disintegrating morale, of defeatism and betrayal. The oppressive feeling continued at Geraldine House that when the moment of supreme crisis came for Britain, Chamberlain, through indecision and lack of imagination, would make British arms as ineffective as they had been during the Phoney War.

On March 20th, King went to see Anthony Eden at the Dominions Office, 'a gloomy place,' as he put it, 'great high ceilings, enormous empty passages, tiled floors and drab walls—the whole effect incredibly gloomy and depressing. Eden sat at a large desk at the far end of a large gloomy room, a sort of dining table in the middle with several chairs around, and three oil paintings on the wall. We started the discussion,' says King, 'by referring to the attack on Sylt last night, which seems to have cheered the Government (and everyone else) no end. Then we went on to refer to the French political troubles. In the debate in the Commons yesterday, Chamberlain got an ovation; in the debate in the Chamber of Deputies last night—the subject Finland, the progress of the war being the same—Daladier got a vote of confidence carried by 240 to one with 311 abstentions! And so he has resigned. Eden seemed to have no inside knowledge of the French political situation, but, I gather, was voicing the views of his colleagues when he said he very much hoped Daladier would form a new government—anyway, that they wouldn't have Flandin. I gathered, though, that they are all a bit nervous about the maintenance of French morale.

'Arising out of the debate in the House, I said that after all it was only Chamberlain as usual explaining why he had done nothing. Eden said, 'No, I think it's more than that. It was a wonderful performance!' We then began to talk about Finland. He said that Mannerheim in the early stages did not want men, as he doubted their value in deep snow unless they could ski; that at one stage some time in the middle of February an observer returned from Finland with a highly optimistic account. But before he had been in London twenty-four hours, reports began to come in that the position was very bad indeed. Eden said that the Government thought that to keep the Finn war going would weaken Russia and diminish her power to help Germany, but that they were well aware at the time that if they offered help and the Finns cracked on us, we should get the worst of both worlds—as has proved to be the case.

'I said I thought on our side the whole Finnish campaign was to be an excuse to bag the Gallivare iron mines in Sweden. He said that was being very crude, wasn't it?—though doubtless that was what the Swedes feared. He repeated that we mainly wanted to keep the war going so as to weaken Russia and reduce her power to help Germany. He said he had had lunch with Churchill alone that day; and expressed the warmest admiration for him—Churchill full of ideas —not all good—but how could they be with a man who had so many?

'In the course of further conversation I expressed the view that we were heading for defeat, that the war could certainly not be won by anyone of Chamberlain's age or by anyone with the very limited capacity of many of his colleagues.

'I mentioned the hostile attitude of the newspapers to the Government and told him (he was quite unaware of the fact) that in the last war the papers were absolutely uncritical until the shell scandal broke out and that they would prefer not to criticize now. Under these circumstances, was it not a point requiring more attention that the Press, even to the sycophantic *Daily Telegraph*, was all so critical or hostile?'

Eden shrugged his doubts away, and King noted in summary:

'My impression was that Eden was most charming, most intelligent, but as a future leader quite pathetic. He has no independent point of view, has clearly no intention of upsetting the political status quo—is in fact a very small straw on the current of events—with no ambition to be anything else. Really, as I walked down Whitehall after leaving him, I was nearly in tears.'

And so there remained Churchill. After the false hopes aroused when, as the *Mirror* put it, 'the British Navy steamed into Narvik and did some real bull-dog breed work,' and the news that 'speedy and effective aid' had reached Norway, came the Nazi occupation and the British withdrawal. Quisling and Hitler had jointly triumphed. The Nazis hadn't, after all, missed the bus. It was the Allies who once again had tripped and fallen.

In the desperate days that followed, the *Mirror* was in the dilemma which must always come upon a national newspaper in a time of national crisis. Should it minimize the danger in order to avoid a fall in public morale? Or should it tell the harsh truth and risk panic among the fainthearts in order to rally the brave? It was the strength of the *Mirror* when Norway fell and Holland and Belgium were overrun on May 10th, that it trusted the people, and believed that the shock of truth would stimulate and not paralyse it.

There are times in a country's history when even without elections the voices can be gathered. The *Mirror* sensed the dissatisfaction with the inert Chamberlain Government. Another few months, and all might have been lost. With Holland and Belgium crumbling, Britain needed a new Government with a new spirit. In this recognition, which the *Mirror* had done so much to make possible, the debate on Norway, essentially a debate on confidence in the conduct of the war, ended with Chamberlain begging his personal friends for support in the Lobbies, with Leo Amery exhorting him in God's name to go, with Arthur Greenwood speaking for Britain, with Lloyd George urging Chamberlain to set an example of sacrifice by sacrificing the seals of office, and with a Division in which Chamberlain was deserted by some of the best and most patriotic members of his own party.

Chamberlain had to resign. On May 11th, the *Mirror* wrote under the headline, 'Silence':

'Mr. Neville Chamberlain is no longer Prime Minister. We feel sure that his resignation has been prompted by a high sense of public duty. His broadcast message to the nation last night was admirable in its self-effacement. He has honestly tried to serve our cause—whatever his mistakes in dealing with the ruffians to whom honesty is a foreign word. Therefore, in the moment of his withdrawal, we salute him in silence and say not one word about or against his record as the nation's leader during the gravest crisis in our history.'

The second leader, entitled, 'And Now—Forward!' offered Churchill, Chamberlain's successor, an explicit programme.

'He has the task,' it said, 'of retrieving a position by no means desperate, but difficult. And he has this enormous advantage—he realizes what he has to face and what, under his leadership, we all have to face.

'Proof of that is provided by the words that ended his speech in the House of Commons on Wednesday night: words already quoted in this column—

"At no time in the last war were we in greater peril than we are now."

Then the *Mirror* went on:

'The man who spoke those words is under no delusions. That is good. We feel henceforward we shall not be deceived.

'And we feel no discouragement. We are in great peril. But we have known perils nearly as great. In the sentence of the Homeric hero—"Stand fast, my heart, for thou hast endured worse evils than this."

'Not worse, perhaps! But dangers nearly as dark and as pressing. We have fought with our backs to the wall and we have won. We shall win again, if we have faith, endurance and patience.

'We feel that our new Prime Minister has great gifts.

'We believe that he will place our cause before personal and political loyalties.

'That may be the heaviest part of his burden—to sacrifice those whom he believes to be unfitted for the supreme struggle, whatever their private virtues, whatever their merits as men.'

Those words were a warning as well as a programme. Churchill, whose opinions and claims the *Mirror* had steadfastly supported, wasn't to be given a blank cheque in his leadership. Among other things, Churchill was to be, so to speak, Belisha without Belisha. He would be expected to maintain and extend the democratic nature of the new Army and to blow away antique cobwebs with the breath of reform. But he would have to be Churchill too—a man ready to carry the war on to enemy soil.

If there was any doubt, it was about his post-war intentions, and about these the *Mirror* was deeply concerned.

But for the present, the war had to be won. On May 11th, on the page headed, 'This Page is dedicated to Victory!', the *Mirror* said:

'There will be no mercy this time. The new world in which you find yourself this morning is a world of glorious opportunity!'

The statement was a just one. The hour had found the man. The Churchillian era had begun; and the *Mirror* could speak with a prophetic confidence of a New World which had been ushered in, paradoxically, by the dismissal of Belisha, one of its harbingers.

CHAPTER VI

The 'Mirror' Wars with Churchill

CHURCHILL, THE COALITION Government, and a new Cabinet weren't enough to satisfy the *Mirror*'s demand for an end of what it called the 'Munich Muddlers.' The Phoney War enveloped Britain in listlessness, and laid its mould on administration and public alike. No one expected anything to happen. The forces at their action stations were apathetic. Among the civil population the fatalistic belief had grown up that the stalemate would last until the war itself died of boredom.

Even when Hitler struck in the West and Belgium capitulated on May 27th, 1940, thus exposing the French flank, the public as a whole failed to realize the meaning of the *Blitzkrieg*. The *Mirror* was prompt to understand the catastrophe and to attack the trade union of kings and generals which tried to explain away the defection of Leopold III. It described him as a 'skunk . . . the most distinguished and accomplished of all Generals of the Fifth Column in any European country to date.' For Admiral of the Fleet Sir Roger Keyes, a friend of Leopold, who had asked that judgment be suspended on 'a very gallant soldier,' the *Mirror* had nothing but lacerating scorn.

'And what were you up to in Brussels where you've been special liaison officer since Belgium was invaded?' it asked. 'Did you sniff the Rat King? Smell any stench of treachery? Lost your nose and your guts, man? Don't know a damned deserter when you see one? Surely *you* were not bootscraping and bowing on Brussels carpet in a Rat King's palace?

'For the Lord's sake, as for your own, don't come gabbling here about gallant soldiers and suspended judgment. You must have been misreported surely. You ought to deny the report.

'Until you do we must revise our own views of gallantry. Until you take back your words we must suspend judgment.'

But the Men of Munich and the Men of Brussels suddenly seemed an irrelevance compared with the Men of Dunkirk. On

June 1st, when the long-drawn-out evacuation was almost complete, the *Mirror* appeared with a headline, 'Bloody Marvellous!' and a cartoon by Zec entitled 'This way, Chum!' showing a wounded but smiling soldier being carried ashore on the back of a sailor. For the next few days while the Army was passing through its agony and the nation was absorbing the shock, the *Mirror* gave all its energies to rallying Britain. 'Never Lose Heart,' it urged on June 3rd. 'We Will Repay,' said a gaunt and defiant soldier from the shattered memorial at Vimy Ridge in the Zec cartoon.

The evacuation had succeeded. At last the *laissez-faire* of the Phoney War was ended as the heroic men of the R.A.F. prepared, in Churchill's words, to 'claw the Nazis from the skies.' But in the rising elation of a people facing a life-and-death challenge, the *Mirror* still warned.

'Mr. Churchill certainly will not suggest that a retreat, however brilliantly executed, is a victory. What we need is a victory, and Lord Gort has gallantly assured us that "next time victory will be with us."

'To that end—however distant—every man and woman in this country can set hand and brain to work. And with these—heart.

'To keep up heart, as our men did out there in their peril. Never to lose heart! That is the prelude to victory.'

The *Mirror* rallied to Churchill. 'We Never Surrender', it said in its biggest and blackest type on June 5th, 1940. And there followed an extract from his speech to the Commons, a speech which was to become historic but which as it was heard and read for the first time was as fresh and new to his audience and readers as Lincoln's speech when he delivered it at Gettysburg.

'Even if large tracts of Europe fall into the grip of the Gestapo and all the odious apparatus of Nazi rule, we shall not flag or fail. We shall go on to the end, and shall fight in France, on the oceans and in the air. We shall defend our island, whatever the cost, and shall fight on the beaches and landing grounds in the fields and streets. We shall never surrender.

'Even if—which I do not for a moment believe—this island or a large part of it were subjugated, our Empire abroad, armed and guarded by the British Fleet, would carry on the struggle until, in God's good time, the New World, with all its force and men, set forth to the liberation and rescue of the Old World.'

The *Mirror* passionately endorsed his words.

'It is,' it said, 'above all a time to swear, in the Prime Minister's words, that we shall not flag or fail. We shall not, because failure means our extinction. And because, to flag would be to prove ourselves pitiably unworthy of those brave men who lie dead along the shores of France.'

By June 18th, France had fallen, and with its fall came the recognition that the Continental policy of Britain had failed. The Nazis stood on the Channel. Invasion was now a probability. Soon the sirens were to sound not for single reconnaissance planes but for massed attacks which were to kill thousands and maim tens of thousands. A *Mirror* editorial summed up the nation's reaction in a single proud word, 'Alone!'

'The collapse of French resistance,' it said, 'leaves us in our island —hardly an island any longer—alone as the last fortress and hope of civilization in Europe.'

But the *Mirror* showed a profound political understanding and foresight.

'No blame for the true France! The next phase concerns ourselves alone—with America, friendly but largely impotent, in the background.

'For ourselves—Mr. Churchill expresses the soul of Britain: "What has happened in France makes no difference to our actions and purpose. . . . We shall fight on unconquerably until the curse of Hitler is lifted from the brows of mankind!" '

Yet the *Mirror* returned to its theme, attacking the relics of the Chamberlain Government and the Chamberlain mentality in a comprehensive self-reproach to the nation.

'For ourselves, have we at last given up our dream mentality, our mentality of inveterate muddle, our tragic lack of foresight, our perilous patience with fools?'

Churchill spoke to the Commons on June 19th.

'The battle of France is over,' he said. 'I expect that the battle of Britain is about to begin.'

To this the *Mirror*, as in a dialogue, replied:

'You need not worry about the men and women of Britain, Mr. Churchill. The common people of this land have the courage. Give them arms and give them leadership, and they will not fail as they have been failed. But above all, give them—(and splashed across the bottom of the page was the word)—Leadership.'

When the *Mirror* spoke of the common people, it had the undertones of Walter de Reynel, who first said, '*Vox Populi*, *Vox Dei*.' The source of the aphorism may have been forgotten, but its meaning bore a truth which in the centuries between had often been blanketed by rulers. The turning point of the popular revolution which took place during that war and culminated in the Election of 1945 was the recognition in 1940 that the old, closed establishment had failed the nation. The *Mirror* made the feeling articulate. It found words for the malaise, and helped to formulate the slogans of change. Above all, it gave 'the common people', now conscripted for total war, the recognition that they themselves were the makers of the new world. 'The civilian is in this war,' it said. 'He knows it at last.'

'Urgency' was the watchword which the *Mirror* pressed on the Government. 'Make this country a fortress!' it demanded. It called for a *levée en masse* of local Defenders. It published news stories to expose bureaucracy, such as the one about Corporal Jack White, V.C., who had to leave the Local Defence Volunteers because his father, a refugee from Tsarist Russia sixty years earlier, had never been naturalized. It welcomed a French General called de Gaulle, 'thin-lipped, super-efficient, once head of France's tank school,' who, 'spoke to the real France with the message, "Fight on".'

Bartholomew's great discovery was the use of the imperative mood for the *Mirror*'s readers. 'Do this' and 'Do that' was the injunction which a public, eager to be led and already conditioned by the disciplines of war-time Britain, welcomed. It was all the more welcome since it was accompanied by the assurance that the *Mirror* was in fact speaking for the people when it called for 'this' or 'that' to be done. Bartholomew was essentially a visual journalist. He liked the curt order in black headlines.

This imperative mood wasn't displeasing to Churchill, provided that it supported his policies. When it contradicted them, he reacted sharply. At the beginning of 1941, Churchill's friendly disposition towards the *Mirror* was beginning to alter in face of the daily criticisms, which threaded its exhortations. Churchill had no doubt about the *Mirror*'s vast influence among the forces. He recognized that nothing could more effectively reduce his and his Government's prestige than the *Mirror*'s derision.

Thus, when Cassandra wrote a paragraph, drawn from the magazine *Life*, in which Churchill was alleged to have returned a long-winded memorandum to Anthony Eden with the note, 'As far as I can see, you have used every cliché except "God is Love" and "Please adjust your dress before leaving",'—Churchill took the unusual step of writing to Cecil King to say that 'this offensive story is wholly devoid of foundation.' He added that another story by Cassandra forecasting changes among a 'gang' of Ministers—'ex-this and ex-that but never ex-a-job'—was untrue, and that the writer was dominated by malevolence.

'Talk about musical chairs,' Cassandra had written. 'The trouble is that this particular game (of shuffling Ministers) is being played to a funeral march. Ours!'

King replied to the Prime Minister in friendly terms.

'Dear Prime Minister,

'Thank you for your letter of yesterday's date. The story printed in our issue of January 1st, was taken from the very well-known American paper *Life* and was described by Cassandra as 'apocryphal.' The story of impending ministerial changes was originally hinted at fairly circumstantially on the front page of the *Daily Sketch*. It then appeared in the *Evening Standard* in its more detailed form, and most of the newspapers reprinted the story, supposing from its appearance in the *Standard* that it was semi-official. I have brought both these cuttings to Cassandra's notice and he is sorry, as we all are, to have given publicity to reports of a change in the Presidency of the Board of Education which prove to be without foundation.

'Cassandra is a hard-hitting journalist with a vitriolic style, but I can assure you his attitude neither to you personally nor to Mr. Eden is in any way "malevolent." Quite the contrary. Though we continue to take an unflattering view of some of your colleagues, our criticisms are only directed to the fact that the nation's war effort is less intense than it might be—less intense than it would be if more young men were employed in positions of real authority.'

This amiable, though independent, letter failed to pacify Churchill. He may well have had the mistaken thought that some of those in authority at the *Mirror* were sympathetic to the idea of a negotiated peace. Nor did he hesitate to express his thought in blunt and aggressive language, mitigated only at the end by a politician's pat on the back.

'Dear Mr. King, (he wrote on January 25th, 1941),

'I don't think the mere adding of the word "apocryphal" is any justification for foisting upon the British public an absolutely untruthful story, which is of course extremely offensive both to me and Mr. Eden. Nothing that appears in the *Evening Standard* or any other paper is "semi-official." Any news about appointments will be given to all newspapers equally from Downing Street. I thank you, however, for your expressions of regret.

'These give me the opportunity of saying one or two things which have struck me very forcibly on reading the *Daily Mirror* and the *Sunday Pictorial*.

'First, there is a spirit of hatred and malice against the Government, which after all is not a Party Government but a National Government almost unanimously chosen, which spirit surpasses anything I have ever seen in English journalism. One would have thought in these hard times that some hatred might be kept for the enemy.

'The second point is more general. Much the most effective way in which to conduct a Fifth Column movement at the present time would be the method followed by the *Daily Mirror* and the *Sunday Pictorial*. Lip service would no doubt be paid to the Prime Minister, whose position at the moment may be difficult to undermine. A perfervid zeal for intensification of the war effort would be used as a cloak behind which to insult and discredit one Minister after another. Every grievance would be exploited to the full, especially those grievances which lead to class dissension. The Army system and discipline would be attacked. The unity between the Conservative and Labour Parties would be gnawed at. The attempt would be made persistently to represent the Government as feeble, unworthy and incompetent, and to spread a general sense of distrust in the whole system. Thus, large numbers of readers would be brought into a state of despondency and resentment, of bitterness and scorn, which at the proper moment, when perhaps some disaster had occurred or prolonged tribulations had wearied the national spirit, could be suddenly switched over into naked defeatism, and a demand for a negotiated peace.

'I daresay you will be surprised when I tell you that as a regular reader, I feel that this description very accurately fits the attitude of your two newspapers. I am sure this is not your intention, nor the intention of the able writers you employ. It is, none the less, in my judgment, the result. It amounts to the same thing, even though the intention may be the opposite. It has given me much pain to see that newspapers with whom I have had such friendly relations, and from which I have received in the past valuable support, should pursue such a line. It is because of our past relations that I write thus plainly.

Yours sincerely,
Winston S. Churchill.'

To this letter, King replied that the *Mirror* was dedicated to victory and supported the Prime Minister personally; that it would conform to his wishes in so far as it conscientiously could; and he ended by asking for an interview.

On January 30th, 1941, King arrived at Downing Street at 2.55. An air-raid was going on—the fourth that day—and the slamming of gunfire was the accompaniment of his interview with the Prime Minister. An usher led King into a small library ante-room, and from there into the Cabinet room, where Churchill was already standing with his back to the fire behind his usual chair at the long table. He sat King down on his right hand, and promptly launched into a tirade. The *Mirror*, he said, was engaging in a clever form of treachery—praising the Prime Minister and vilifying his Ministers. It was rocking the boat. What was King going to do about it?

During his prolonged reprimand—the interview, King noted in his diary, lasted an hour and ten minutes by the clock—Churchill kept getting up, striding about and sitting down, sometimes leaning on the fireguard, at other times re-lighting his cigar. His words were often tangential to his main theme. 'Our conversation followed no logical path at all,' King said later. The key-note word was 'malignancy'—one of Churchill's favourite ways of describing hostile criticism, and which he was to use indiscriminately about Hitler, the *Mirror* and, after the war, about the Labour Party.

King said to Churchill that the *Mirror* backed him and various of his Ministers. Did that mean it had to support, say, Attlee and Arthur Greenwood?

Churchill didn't disagree with the inference; but then he turned to the question of who owned the *Mirror*. Some of his colleagues, he implied, felt that there were various sinister figures behind it all.

'Not a bit,' said King. 'There are five executive directors. I am one of them. I'm more interested in politics than the others, so they leave politics largely to me.'

Churchill returned from the window, and eyed King up and down for a few moments. Then he said:

'Well, you look innocent enough!'

King wrote in his diary after the interview:

'Churchill *is* wartime England.'

He had no doubt about the Prime Minister's will, his capacity or his consistency as an anti-appeaser. All that he suspected was his judgment of men. For Churchill, his censure of the *Mirror* was a necessary act in securing a free hand, even if it meant repressing criticism; his personal relations with King remained excellent. At the end of their interview, the air-raid was still on. Churchill insisted on sending King back to his office in his own official car.

A few days later, King enlarged to Churchill on some of the subjects which they had touched on during their meeting. In this letter, which remains a central statement of the *Mirror*'s purposes, King emphasized a theme which was the essence of the *Mirror*'s success both in the war and in the years immediately following the peace. He said:

'Any support we gave you and your policy before the war was not just a newspaper stunt to sell papers. It never did—in fact our readers (and some of my colleagues) wanted to hear that it would be roses, roses all the way. When I wrote to you on the outbreak of war to congratulate you (or rather the nation) on your going to the Admiralty, I said I hoped that when the inevitable demand came for a more vigorous prosecution of the war that you would step up to a still more exalted office, and when later, in October '39, we 'splashed' a prophecy that you would be the next Prime Minister, this was not idle flattery. It was the realization by me slightly sooner than by others that you were our inevitable wartime leader—not because of your particular experience or capacity or for any other reason but because you *are* wartime England. When you make speeches, yours is the voice of England with all its traditions, its courage, its strength and its limitations. You epitomise our past; you are our present. There can be no question of your replacement during this war. This is not said just on a shrewd view of the political probabilities, but because you and England could not be separated now without both disintegrating.

'But loyalty to England means not only loyalty to the past and the present, but to the future. This war is to you the crowning of a lifetime of public service; to us, who are much younger, it is the first step towards a new and better England in which we shall pay our way and not live—as we did in the years 1919–1939—on the accumulated wealth and prestige of our forefathers. This does not mean that I have some future leader up my sleeve or under the bed; I haven't. I have no idea whom he may eventually prove to be, but I think we shall not find him in any of the existing parties (in which I would include Mosleyites and Communists) and I think he is now much younger than I am (nearly 40).

'Loyalty to the future involves not only scanning the horizon for the new ideas and ideals which may shape the world, but also the discrediting of the men who made the period 1919–39 such an ignoble page in English history. This is not done to humiliate them, but to impress on the young people growing up (who read our papers) that that is an era which must not recur.

'Perhaps this would be clearer if I gave you an actual example of how it works. We advocate a statement by the Government of the country's war aims. Clearly to do so in any but vague and platitudinous terms would cause dissension among your ministers and between this country and its allies. Therefore you must think that to press such a demand is essentially mischievous. But look at it from a young man's point of view. The Middle East was conquered by the Mahommedans holding a sword in one hand and the Koran in the other—and who will deny that the Koran was the more potent weapon? At this moment we want our Koran and feel its possession would be the decisive factor of the whole war. Perhaps if you have read as far as this, you will see that there is no clear answer to this dilemma. One's loyalty is just divided.

'The staff here do not always see clearly what I am driving at. Mistakes occur; but behind everything printed in these two papers is the conviction I have just described expressed in terms of the tabloid newspaper—itself a raw, crude medium but very typical of its day.'

Churchill was obdurate in his reply. He wrote to King:

'Thank you very much for your letter and I was glad we had a talk. All this fine thought about the rising generation ought not to lead you into using your able writers to try to discredit and hamper the Government in a period of extreme danger and difficulty. Nor ought it to lead you to try to set class against class and generally "rock the boat" at such a time. Finally, I think it no defence for such activities to say that your papers specialize in "vitriolic" writing. Indeed throwing vitriol is thought to be one of the worst of crimes. No man who is affected with "vitriolism" is worthy to shape the future, or likely to have much chance of doing so in our decent country.

'There is no reason why you should not advocate a statement of war aims. I wonder that you do not draw one up in detail and see what it looks like. I see that Mr. Mander has tabled his war aims, which seem to me to bear out what I ventured to say in the House, namely that "most right-minded people are well aware of what we are fighting for." Such a task would be well-suited to the present lull.

Yours sincerely,
Winston S. Churchill.'

To a great extent, Churchill's phrase 'All this fine thought about the rising generation,' with its mocking undertones, expresses the reason for his failure with the electorate of 1945.

The correspondence ended in a slightly barbed truce. But neither the *Mirror* nor Churchill could change their nature. Bartholomew, like King, wanted to keep the *Mirror* as a paper with the aggressive theme of victory, challenging anyone, high or low, who failed to play their part or who tried to do well out of the war for themselves.

In the meantime, however, the military situation continued to deteriorate. The position in Singapore became desperate and the city, once described by Churchill as 'impregnable,' fell into Japanese hands on February 15th, 1942. The *Mirror* put the point.

'It is time that M.P.s asked themselves—"Are we doing our duty if we allow votes of confidence to be extorted from us on the personal appeal of the Prime Minister? Is it any longer true to say that we trust the Prime Minister, though we do not trust his Government?"'

This was followed up on the day that Singapore fell by G. M. Garro-Jones, a Labour M.P. who had been commissioned by King to write an article for the *Sunday Pictorial* called 'Who is to Blame?' It urged strongly that 'those responsible for the latest humiliation should pack up and get out.'

Garro-Jones followed up this attack with what seemed to Churchill an act of *lèse-majesté*. All over the country posters were being displayed showing a portrait of Churchill with the caption, 'Deserve Victory.' Garro-Jones claimed that the posters would be better placed in the offices of Ministers and in the War Cabinet room itself. Then he went on to the most sensitive question of all.

'Have we the wrong Prime Minister?' he asked. 'Last week I would have hesitated a little and said "no." Today I say that unless the Prime Minister acts, the answer will soon be "yes."'

His article ended, 'The people send back to their Prime Minister the noble message which their Prime Minister has sent to them, "Deserve Victory."'

At a time in the war when Churchill had established an unchallengeable psychological ascendancy, this was a bold defiance. Churchill himself was infuriated that the *Mirror* and the *Sunday*

Pictorial should have expressed criticism which in their original and milder form he had already resented and rebuked. To many in the office, it seemed that Churchill's later attempt to extinguish the *Mirror* sprang from his indignation at Garro-Jones' attack, which he called 'a stab in the back.'

In the meantime, however, the *Mirror* continued to increase its popularity among the forces and the war workers. Bartholomew turned out front pages that were like pictograms in their impact. The black headlines and the white spaces were calls to action.

To supplement the print, Bartholomew had found in Philip Zec a cartoonist with a strong line who could express in picture form—black with a lot of white space—the *Mirror*'s shorthand views on how to win the war.

Bartholomew, it will be recalled, had himself been a war photographer during the First World War. Impatient of abstruse argument, he wanted the *Mirror*'s message to come over in simple visual terms, whether in words or pictures.

The ancient wall-drawing found a modern form in the strip cartoon. During the war years, Bartholomew had been quick to see that a large proportion of the nation saw their fantasies and reveries in images. Tired men don't think in syllogisms. They think in pictures of love, power and liberty. For those who wanted to escape, the *Mirror* offered Jane; for those who wanted potency, Garth; for those who wanted liberty, Popeye.

Shortly after the outbreak of war, Cassandra had introduced to Bartholomew a cartoonist Philip Zec, then aged thirty, who at the time was the proprietor of Zec, Ltd., a commercial art studio specializing in photography, layout and industrial design. Zec had trained as an artist at the St. Martin's School of Art, and later worked for an advertising agency, together with William Connor, who was already established as an outstanding copywriter. After drawing a few experimental cartoons, he found that his bold black, unfussy line, his use of space and the visual message of his work exactly complemented the *Mirror*'s verbal message. Bartholomew told Zec to 'do a cartoon every day until the Service chiefs decide they can't win the war without you.'

The cartoons were popular. Zec was given a deferment from call-up, and for the next few years no one doubted the value of his work or the sincerity of his views. By March, 1942, accounts of Hitler's barbarities against the Jews in Occupied Europe were beginning to reach

Britain. Zec, himself a radical Jew on the Nazi Black List, had no doubt at all of what would happen to him in the event of a German victory.

On March 5th Zec, who was accustomed to draft the daily cartoon at his home, cycled to the *Mirror* office carrying in his saddle-bag a drawing showing a torpedoed sailor with an oil-smeared face lying on a raft in a sinister, empty sea. The cartoon conveyed all the desolation, the heroism and the horror of the Battle of the Atlantic. It spoke more in its stark lines than a whole Hansard of debates on the conduct of the war and the conduct of those at home. Zec had chosen as his theme, during a lull on the war-fronts, the need for a clamp-down on the black marketeers at home who were profiteering from the hardship and sacrifice of the fighting men.

The Government had just authorized an increase of a penny in the price of petrol. Zec in his cartoon wanted to emphasize that the cost of petrol was in human life as well as in cash, and that the public should know that casualties as well as prices were rising. His main object was to urge on the public that precious petrol shouldn't be wasted. That there were undertones of bitterness in the cartoon against those who exploited shortages for private gain is certain. But these were secondary to Zec's dominant theme, which was simply, 'Don't waste petrol. It costs lives.'

Zec gave his cartoon the caption, 'Petrol is dearer now.' When Cassandra, who shared an office with Zec, saw the cartoon, he said, 'You're a genius. But it needs a stronger caption. Bring in the penny rise. It'll dramatize the whole thing.'

Zec, an easy-going, cheerful, unargumentative man, agreed. He had worked hard at the cartoon. He respected Cassandra's judgment. The caption was changed, and became 'The price of petrol has been raised by a penny (official).'

The next morning at breakfast several million readers looked with awe and many with guilt at the tragic, exhausted figure on the raft who symbolized the struggle of British sailors to bring them petrol through the dangerous Atlantic seas. At the *Mirror* Cecil Thomas, the editor, Zec and Cassandra were elated with the cartoon. It had shocked the nation as it had intended to shock. The *Mirror* had given a magisterial rebuke to those who were letting the forces down. From all over the country requests came from shops, from petrol stations and church halls for copies of this moving and inspiring cartoon. Its traumatic effect had been salutary. The nation responded.

But Churchill studied the cartoon with profound resentment.

The *Mirror*, which had done so much to bring him to power, had become increasingly sharp in its criticisms, despite his earlier rebuke. This cartoon, he felt, could only depress the morale both of the merchant sailor and the honest public at large by suggesting that the sailor's life had been put at stake to enhance the profits of the petrol companies. Herbert Morrison, Ernest Bevin and the Lord Chancellor, Sir John Simon, all agreed that the drawing would have that effect. Like Churchill, the War Office, long the butt of *Mirror* cartoons and editorials, became interested in the *Mirror*'s ownership. What fingers pulled the strings and articulated the mouths of the puppets? Churchill himself ordered that the *Mirror*'s ownership should be investigated, together with the background of Zec himself, the somewhat Dostoyevskyan innocent with uncomplicated Left-Wing views, who now found himself at the centre of a great counter-operation designed to uncover subversion in the *Mirror* offices.

'I spent the next few weeks in a kind of trance,' Zec said. 'It was hard to believe it was happening.' After it was all over, a detective told him in a Fetter Lane bar that he had been 'investigated'. 'He knew all about me,' said Zec. 'He seemed surprised I had led such a blameless life.'

So it was to prove, too, with the investigation into the *Mirror*'s ownership. The most frequent suggestions during the war were that the majority of the *Mirror*'s shares were owned by William Randolph Hearst, the American isolationist, by Israel Sieff, director of Marks and Spencer and a Jew, and by Sir John Ellerman, publicity-shunning and reputedly one of the world's richest men. These charges were designed in the case of Hearst to suggest that the *Mirror* was controlled by an anti-British influence; in the case of Sieff by a Jew who had special reasons for opposing Hitler; and in the case of Ellerman by a capitalist who made money from the sale of Left-Wing opinions. Of these three, only Sir John Ellerman at the end of the war had a holding in the *Mirror*. Out of a total of 5,600,000 shares, he and his associates held just over 150,000.

As far as Hearst was concerned, the *Mirror* disposed of the charge made in the House that he was an owner of the paper with the editorial words.

'At no time in our history has this evil man Hearst had any financial or other interest in our newspaper.'

The *Mirror* couldn't have said plainer than that.

CHAPTER VII

Critics and Censors

AT THE END of Questions on Thursday, March 19th, 1942, Mr. William Patrick Spens, the Conservative Member for Ashford, rose to ask a question of which, in the traditional phrase, he had 'given Private Notice.' The Prime Minister, who had just made a statement about the appointment of Mr. William Casey, then Australian Minister in Washington, as Minister of State in the Middle East, remained in his place, to listen; and his presence gave pause to other M.P.s who might have drifted from their leather benches in the Chamber of the House of Lords, where the Commons were sitting after the destruction of their own Chamber.

Spens, a King's Counsel with an earnest manner, asked the Home Secretary, Mr. Herbert Morrison (who had inspired the question) whether he had seen a cartoon recently published in the *Daily Mirror* of a distressed seaman on a raft over the words, 'The price of petrol has been raised by a penny'; and as this suggested that seamen were risking their lives in order that bigger profits might be made, and 'was calculated to discourage seamen and readers of all classes from serving the country in its time of need, and was conducive to defeatism, whether action could not be taken to prevent a newspaper from publishing irresponsible matter likely to influence public opinion in a manner prejudicial to the efficient prosecution of the war.'

Herbert Morrison rose at the Despatch Box in an attentive House, where the uniforms of men in the Services alternated with the dark suits of older Members, and began to read a prepared statement in a voice as aggressive as his terms were harsh.

'The cartoon in question,' he said, 'is only one example, but a particularly evil example, of the policy and methods of a newspaper which, intent on exploiting an appetite for sensation and with a reckless indifference to the national interest and to the prejudicial effect on the war effort, had repeatedly published scurrilous misrepresentations, distorted and exaggerated statements and irresponsible generalizations. In the same issue,' he went on, 'the leading article stated:

' "... the accepted tip for Army leadership would, in plain truth, be this: All who aspire to mislead others in war should be brass-buttoned boneheads, socially prejudiced, arrogant and fussy. A tendency to heart disease, apoplexy, diabetes and high blood pressure is desirable in the highest posts...."

'Reasonable criticism on specific points and persons,' said Morrison, 'is one thing; general, violent denunciation, manifestly tending to undermine the Army and depress the whole population, is quite another. Such insidious attacks are not to be excused by calls in other parts of the paper for more vigorous action. The Press in general recognizes that the principle of freedom for the expression of opinion which Parliament and the Government are determined to maintain imposes on newspaper proprietors, editors and journalists an obligation to exercise that freedom with a proper sense of responsibility, and that if a particular paper so abuses that freedom that the war effort is hindered, that abuse is as injurious to the interests of the Press itself as to the national interest.'

The Government, Morrison went on, had decided that the right method of dealing with a newspaper which persistently disregarded its public responsibility and the national interest was to make use of the powers contained in Defence Regulation 2D, which authorized the suppression of a paper that systematically published matter calculated to foment opposition to the successful prosecution of the war.

'The issue,' he said, 'raised in such a case is—Will the continued publication of such a paper prejudice the successful prosecution of the war? On such a question it is incumbent on the Government to form a judgment, subject always to their responsibility to Parliament.'

Heard at first in silence, Morrison was at this point encouraged by cheers on all sides of the House, except from below the gangway where some of the Government's sharper critics like Emmanuel Shinwell, Richard Stokes and Seymour Cocks sat.

'The provisions of Defence Regulation 2D,' Herbert Morrison went on, 'cover not only overt or disguised incitements to refrain from helping the war effort on the ground, for example, that the war is waged for unworthy ends, but also the publication of matter which foments opposition to the prosecution of the war by depressing public support for the war effort, by poisoning the springs of national loyalty, and by creating a spirit of despair and defeatism.'

He had caught the mood of the House. No one could approve of words and actions which led to the 'poisoning of the springs of national loyalty' or the creation of 'a spirit of despair and defeatism.' The rest of the statement was accompanied by rumbles of 'Hear! Hear!' and muttered approval.

'I have seen those responsible for the *Daily Mirror*,' Morrison ended, 'and I have made clear to them the considerations which I have outlined to the House. A watch will be kept on this paper and the course which the Government may ultimately decide to take will depend on whether those concerned recognize their public responsibility and take care to refrain from further publication of matter calculated to foment opposition to the successful prosecution of the war.'

Morrison sat down to loud Government cheers. He had warned the Mirror, satisfied the Government and antagonized, as he felt, no one but the inveterate back-bench grumblers. But he hadn't reckoned with Emmanuel Shinwell, the conqueror of Ramsay MacDonald at Seaham in 1935, who rose and in his high-pitched voice protested that the statement with 'all its possible ramifications' was a very serious one. It endangered the right of public expression of opinion. It filled critics of the Government with alarm and despondency. Would there be the opportunity for a debate?

'Yes,' Morrison replied. The matter was serious, and he hoped that the proprietors and the editor of the *Daily Mirror* would realize it. Shinwell was supported in various degrees by Seymour Cocks, ('Will the Home Secretary arrange,' he asked ironically, 'that in future newspapers should be edited by Ministers' Parliamentary Private Secretaries?'), James Maxton, the I.L.P. leader, and Hore-Belisha.

'Who are the proprietors now?' an M.P. called out.

Morrison was waiting for that question. At Churchill's special request, he had investigated the *Mirror*'s ownership.

'This is a newspaper which has not got a wealthy single owner as its proprietor. It is a mixed proprietorship. (Hon. Members: 'Who are they?'). I do not know that the information would be illuminating. It is one of those mixed financial controls in which you cannot trace a single directing financial influence, so far as I can see at present.'

At this point Commander Locker-Lampson shouted:

'Hearst is part-owner.'

This repetition of an untrue statement added to the miasma of suspicion with which the *Daily Mirror*'s critics were trying to surround it. Morrison made no comment on the charge. If the House wanted a debate, the House could have one on a Motion—and a Division. He wanted a chance to demonstrate that despite the *Mirror*'s vast circulation in the country the Government had the backing of the House.

*

The Home Secretary's statement hadn't come as a surprise to Bartholomew or Cecil King, despite the fact that Churchill had told King in a letter dated February 13th, 1941, that he would be 'very glad to see (him) at any time,' and invited him not to hesitate 'to propose a visit.' Churchill, it was known from his private statements, had been smouldering with anger throughout a year made tense by air-raids and the developing Battle of the Atlantic, at what he called 'the airy and jaunty detachment' of the criticisms in the *Mirror* and the *Pictorial* of his conduct of the war. During the First World War at the Admiralty, he had clashed with Northcliffe over the elbow-jogging of the Press, and had indeed urged in Cabinet that *The Times* should be suppressed and some form of *British Gazette* (a project which he was to realize during the General Strike) should be substituted.

Those were the days when a despatch from *The Times* correspondent Arthur Moore dealing with the Battle of Amiens, though 'improved' by the chief censor, F. E. Smith, had sounded an alarm to a complacent public. Later, Northcliffe's *Daily Mail* had criticized Kitchener over the shell shortage on the Western Front—a bitter and unpopular attack which made the paper lose 238,000 copies in circulation within a month. *Punch*, indeed, had carried a cartoon of John Bull trampling the *Daily Mail* underfoot while he patted Kitchener's shoulder, saying, 'If you need assurance, Sir, you may like to know that you have the support of all decent people.'

Now, once again, Churchill felt that the war effort was being jeopardized by a dissenting press, and he urged Morrison to invoke Regulation 2D. It was the instrument by which he could realize a long-held ambition to restrain the *Mirror*. Herbert Morrison, backed by Lord Beaverbrook and the Minister of Information,

Brendan Bracken, favoured the milder course of warning the *Mirror* that 2D would be invoked unless it stopped, as he put it, 'fomenting opposition to the successful prosecution of the war.' Grudgingly, Churchill agreed 'to give the paper a last chance and a last warning.'

The warning was to be a grave one. On the night of March 18th, 1942, John Cowley and the editor, Cecil Thomas, were summoned by telephone to attend at the Home Office the following morning. Morrison at that time was fifty-four, approaching the height of his authority. He had been briefly Minister of Supply in the Coalition Government, but it was as Home Secretary that he really found scope for the special brand of pragmatic and selective tolerance which he had inherited from his father, a London policeman. The truncheon in the hall at home remained his mace. He was a disciplinarian, an organization man, and within the Labour Party one of his tasks for many years was to make its members toe the line, a duty which was to bring him into many a clash with Aneurin Bevan. Towards the *Mirror*, though, he was in an ambiguous position since he had to rap over the knuckles the very paper to which he himself had been a frequent contributor.

In many other respects, the *Mirror* had deserved well of Herbert Morrison. Indeed, on May 24th, 1940, when Morrison was Minister of Supply, the *Mirror* had published an editorial insert under the heading, 'Thanks a Lot.'

'When a politician lives up to his policy and his promises,' it said, 'he always deserves a word of thanks. Before Mr. Herbert Morrison became Minister of Supply he told us what should be done. Now he is doing it.

'The weakness of our supply system became all too apparent in the first few months of war. When Mr. Morrison says "twenty-four hours a day, seven days a week, on arms," he has the country behind him. The muddlers have gone and the new Minister shows us in a few days what whole-hearted efficiency can do.'

Now, Morrison had to justify these words of praise in an unwelcome context.

Instead of Cowley, Bartholomew himself arrived with Cecil Thomas at the Home Office, and was ushered into an impressive room overlooking St. James's Park. It was a cold day. A fire burned in the large, old-fashioned grate. And standing underneath a Kneller portrait with John Jagger, his gaunt Parliamentary Secretary, and

Sir Alexander Maxwell, the Permanent Under-Secretary of State, at his side, the Home Secretary began:

'What I've got to say is going to be rather unpleasant. What I've got to tell you is the unanimous decision of the Cabinet.'

For half an hour, Morrison gave Bartholomew and Thomas a dressing-down, his quiff bobbing with indignation as he said of Zec's cartoon that it was 'worthy of Goebbels at his best.' His cyclopean eye—he had lost the other as an infant—transfixed Thomas as he added, 'Only a very unpatriotic editor could pass that for publication.' Then he turned to Bartholomew and said, 'Only a fool or someone with a diseased mind could be responsible for *Daily Mirror* policy.'

This was strong stuff, even from an old and praised contributor, but Bartholomew and his editor had agreed that whatever the provocation they wouldn't reply except to say that the charges were misconceived.

Morrison ended with the taunt:

'Now you can go away and start lobbying your M.P.s. Nothing I've said is secret. I'm going to answer a question about it in the House today.'

The session ended with pleasantries on the Home Secretary's part. Morrison sent his regards to John Cowley, the *Mirror*'s seventy-two-year-old chairman, and as Bartholomew and Thomas left, Morrison hummed a little tune to himself.

*

After the Home Secretary made his statement to the House later in the day, a small group of the *Mirror*'s defenders demanded a Debate. The Leader of the House agreed, and fixed Thursday, March 26th, for a Debate on the Adjournment with the short title, 'Freedom of the Press.' And so, for a few hours on the day before the Easter recess, Parliament turned from its preoccupation with waging war to the consideration of one of the war's major aims—the preservation of the rights of a free press and of free speech.

Wilfrid Roberts, a Liberal M.P. for North Cumberland and Parliamentary Private Secretary to Sir Archibald Sinclair, Secretary of State for Air, opened.

There had, he began, been an increasing encroachment by the Government on the liberty of the press.

'The Home Secretary's statement,' he said, 'was a warning to the

Press as a whole, as well as to one particular paper. Most of the London dailies, and the provincial papers, commented on that statement in leading articles, and with one or two exceptions the Press has reacted with disapproval of the Home Secretary's actions, or if not with disapproval, with alarm. As I see it, a free Press is a vital part of a free Parliament. The Press moreover is a vital part of this House, and a threat to the freedom of the Press is a threat also to the freedom of Members of Parliament. Neither the Press nor this House has ever liked Regulation 2D, the one which the Government threatens to use again on this occasion. Regulation 2D was an unfortunate afterthought of the previous Home Secretary. It was justified to this House as an extreme weapon, to be used only at moments of crisis, such as invasion. Even so, as the last weapon in the armoury of the Government, it was only approved in this House in July, 1940, at that critical and dangerous time by a very small majority of 38.'

He went on to say.

'There is no opposition in this House or in the Press or in the country that I can see to vigorous and energetic action by the Government when it is necessary. The crime that the *Daily Mirror* is accused of is that it criticized the Government irresponsibly, sensationally—to quote words that have been used—and "with a reckless indifference to the national interest." The crime of the *Daily Mirror* is to criticize the Government, and all I ask on this point is that, if the crime is against the Government, the Government should not judge that crime, but that the normal processes of law should be invoked. Having said that, it will be clear that I do not think a Member of Parliament in this House is the right person to advance the case of the *Daily Mirror*, but yet, as we are living under the threat of the possible immediate suppression of a very large newspaper, possibly even during the Easter Recess when the House is not sitting, it seems to me absolutely necessary to say something about the *Daily Mirror*.'

Wilfrid Roberts was an uninspiring speaker who could not normally attract a large 'House'; but on this occasion, the benches began to fill rapidly. The word had got around that the Government had decided to have a showdown with the *Mirror*, and there was speculation as to who would be bold enough to challenge the Home Secretary, or through him, Winston Churchill. Brendan Bracken, the red-haired Minister of Information and never a man to refrain from pouring oil on the flames, was on the Front Bench next to Morrison. At one stage, he interrupted Roberts, who was complaining that the Minister of Information had given currency in a telegram to Buenos Aires to a rumour that the anti-British Hearst was connected with the *Mirror*.

'You're giving information to Goebbels,' said Bracken.

Shinwell protested on a Point of Order. The Speaker rose, frowned and said there must be freedom of debate.

Roberts went on:

'. . . this paper, the *Daily Mirror*, has followed quite a consistent policy for many years now. I think that the Foreign Secretary will perhaps remember that one time before the war it supported him. I would like to make one quotation from the issue of September 27th, 1938. I do not think there is much difference in this from what the *Daily Mirror* is saying at the present time:

' "Make Britain strong. Britain stands for peace. But she must be strong for war. It is your duty to give her strength. By joining your Defence units. By growing all the food you can. By avoiding waste. By making aircraft, ammunition, ships. By keeping calm, cheerful, determined. To make the nation so strong that none may dare challenge the peace of the world."

'There was a time before the war when the Prime Minister himself was a contributor, a very notable contributor, to the *Daily Mirror*. I believe that the writer of the editorial now under consideration prizes letters he has, both from the Prime Minister and Lord Beaverbrook, congratulating him on his work. But at that time, before the war, there was a similar rumour to the present one. Then it was stated that a prominent Jew influenced the *Daily Mirror*, because the *Daily Mirror* was anti-Nazi perhaps a little before some of our papers and some other gentlemen. Then it was supposed that it was the Jews who were influencing the policy of this paper; now it is the hidden hand of the isolationists of America.'

Then he turned to the question of the *Mirror*'s ownership.

'I shall risk making a statement about the ownership of the *Daily Mirror* which the Home Secretary, with his superior power of knowledge, ought to be able, with his powers, to get. If he has not the powers, he ought to get them. The *Daily Mirror* belonged originally to Lord Rothermere. About ten years ago, Lord Rothermere sold his shares, gradually, on the Stock Exchange. They were bought up in small blocks. There is no big, or controlling, group of shares now held by any one person. The shares held by nominees represent only between five and ten per cent of the whole shareholding of the paper. In other words, this paper, unlike many others, is run by a board of directors and a chairman. I am not sure that that is not a very much better way than for great organs of opinion to be at the mercy of the whim of one owner, who may change his policy overnight. I say that the policy of the *Daily Mirror* has not changed in the last five or six years. Its staff has not changed, since the time when the Prime Minister wrote for it and when I remember the Leader of the Opposition quoting it with such effect from the Box after the occupation of Austria.'

As Roberts went on, the recriminations faded. His listeners laughed when he said, 'I want to end with this. I was in the Army, and I read the *Daily Mirror* like many other officers.'

'Jane!' shouted an irreverent Member.

'Yes,' said Roberts. 'Jane *is* popular in the Army. Strips *are* popular.'

No one could doubt it. Nor the telling quotation from Brendan Bracken with which Roberts ended his speech.

' "A blindfolded democracy is more likely to fall than to fight." '

He was immediately supported by a Tory, Sir Irving Albery, whose point of view in turn was castigated by the Durham miner Jack Lawson, later Lord Lawson, who argued, amid many interruptions, that as some miners had had their liberties restricted in being compelled into the pits when they would have preferred to work in factories, so too should the Press agree to be restricted. Miss Ellen Wilkinson, Joint Parliamentary Secretary to the Ministry of Home Security and a dedicated supporter of Morrison, urged Lawson on, goading the *Mirror*'s defenders with her shrill interjections.

'The hon. Lady on the Front Bench opposite should really restrain herself,' said the Member who followed her. He was Aneurin Bevan, ex-miner and Left-Wing critic of Churchill who, with his skilled dialectic, never failed to stir his friends and infuriate his opponents. Brushing Ellen Wilkinson's objections aside, he went on to tackle Morrison himself, an old adversary in the Labour Party, and as he spoke, the Benches filled as Members returned from the Smoking Room and the Tea Room.

'I should be the last person,' he said, 'to suggest that there ought not to be such restrictions upon personal liberty as are necessary to win the war. I am not one who argues that there ought never to be restrictions upon liberty in any circumstance . . . the amount of liberty afforded to the people must be governed by the necessities of war. . . . Therefore, there is no argument here for liberty in the abstract. What we are discussing is whether the definite proposals to restrict liberty here and now, are necessary for the effective conduct of the war, and whether they promote the war morale of the country or undermine it. I do not like the *Daily Mirror*, and I have never liked it. I do not see it very often. I do not like that form of journalism. I do not like the strip-tease artists. If the *Daily Mirror* depended upon my purchasing it, it would never be sold. But the *Daily Mirror* has not been warned because people do not like that kind of journalism. It is not because the Home Secretary is aesthetically repelled by it that he warns it. I have heard a number of hon. Members say that it is a hateful paper, a tabloid paper, a hysterical paper, a sensational paper, and that they do not like it. I am sure the Home Secretary does not take that view. He likes the paper. He is taking its money.'

Amid cheers from his friends, he waved in the air a handful of cuttings of Morrison's articles in the *Mirror*.

Stung by Bevan's taunt, Morrison rose to say:

'If the hon. Gentleman wants to be personal, so is someone closely connected with him.'

*

Jennie Lee, Aneurin Bevan's wife, had in fact left the Ministry of Aircraft Production in 1941 to become the political correspondent of the *Mirror*, at Bartholomew's invitation.

'It was a crazy world we were living in and this was a crazy little tabloid,' she has said in her autobiography. Bartholomew's great theme was that 'we were fighting a People's War, and he intended to slant the news from the People's point of view.'

When Bartholomew engaged her, he said that he had no intention of making the *Mirror* 'a frowsy political news sheet that no one would want to read.' What he intended was a simple, warm-hearted championship of the rights of ordinary men and women. Jennie Lee recalls that she listened, much impressed.

*

Bevan brushed aside Morrison's reference to Jennie Lee, and went on:

'Be as personal as you like. As far as I am concerned, I do not mind how direct the right hon. Gentleman is, because in this matter the harder the hitting the better I like it. But the right hon. Gentleman will not be able to hit back as hard as I can hit him. He does not dislike the *Daily Mirror* because of its bad journalism, because of its sensationalism, or because of its strip-tease artists. He took the *Daily Mirror* money, so he does not dislike it. I have here a copy of the *Daily Mirror* in which there is an article headed "My Report on What the People Want. By Herbert Morrison." This is on 1st February, 1940, when the country was at war. He says:

' "They want the war to be fought with energy. They want to see every factory and every man at work. They want less muddled advice from the top."

'As a matter of fact, the headline at the start of this series of articles is:

' "Morrison's important page. Regularly you can read these articles in the *Daily Mirror*. The Right Hon. Herbert Morrison, P.C., M.P., writes a hard-hitting page which is winning an extraordinary reputation among the people."

'Of course the right hon. Gentleman was not in the Government then.' (There were shouts of 'The country was at war.') 'Yes, but what sort of war? The same sort of war as that which is happening now—no air raids and no attacks on the enemy. What was the right hon. Gentleman doing there—undermining the morale of the country and the confidence of the country in the leaders of the nation and the Army? He made an attack (in the *Mirror*) when the right hon. Gentleman for Devonport, Mr. Hore-Belisha, resigned from the office of Secretary of State for War.'

'Read it!' shouted Members. It was the encouragement that Bevan wanted.

'He suggested,' Bevan went on, 'that the right hon. Gentleman was removed by the brass hats because he was in favour of democratizing the Army. Could there be anything more calculated to undermine the morale of the Army than to suggest that the generals shifted a Secretary of State for War because he wanted to democratize the Army?'

Morrison rose to intervene, and Bevan gave way.

'I have no notice of this,' Morrison said. 'It would have been helpful. I am only asking my hon. Friend, in order to help everybody, including myself, to quote what I wrote.'

'Certainly,' Bevan replied. 'I have not given the right hon. Gentleman notice, but *he* gave me no notice of his warning of the *Daily*

Mirror. I am pointing out that at the time when he wrote these articles, the British Army was in France facing the enemy—not in Britain and not in camps, but right opposite the enemy—and suggesting that he was writing articles in the *Daily Mirror* as much calculated to undermine the confidence in the higher-ups as anything which the *Daily Mirror* has written since. I will quote something else from the *Daily Mirror*.'

'Will the right hon. Gentleman quote what I wrote about the brass hats? That is what I want,' said Morrison.

'I assure my right hon. Friend that he must not play with me the Parliamentary game of asking me to read,' Bevan replied, amid interruptions. 'I do not want to read these articles because they are rather dull. This is another article headed, "Sensational attack on Belisha," He writes:

'The more the House of Commons can be told about the episode, the better it will be for the public interest. . . . All sorts of explanations of this business have been canvassed. The most prominent one is that the ex-War Secretary is a victim of the brass hats of the Higher Command of the Army.'

'I want to know what I said about it,' Morrison insisted.

'I am reading what you said,' Bevan retorted. He quoted:

"And if that should stand revealed as the real issue in this episode, it would be the duty of the Labour party to fight it out with all the vigour at its command."

'This is Britain, not Japan,' he ended.

'I only wanted my hon. Friend to quote that,' Morrison replied, 'because, having started with the statement that I said that the brass hats removed my right hon. Friend, it is now perfectly clear that somebody else said it.'

'I leave it at that,' Bevan said. 'But it makes it worse. The right hon. Gentleman was the purveyor to 1,800,000 people of a story he could not verify. I am anxious not to delay the House. I ask the House to consider this: Why does the House always look upon the soldiers in the Army as children? Why do you not treat them as adults? Which will do more harm to the Army—for the Army to be told, as it has been told, that this paper is being warned and may be in danger of suppression, or for the Army to be allowed to read what the paper says morning by morning? This paper is, in a special sense, the paper of the Armed Forces.'

'They like it, that is why,' said Edgar Granville, the Member for Eye.

'Certainly they like it,' said Bevan, stuttering a little. 'I am asking the House this serious question, because if what the *Daily Mirror* says about the administration of the Army is not confirmed in the daily experience of the soldiers, they will not take any notice of it. The British Army consists of adult men as good as we are. So if these men, when they read these criticisms, know from their own experience that the criticisms are exaggerated, that they are not correct, then those generalizations will fall upon barren ground. But if in their experience the criticisms are confirmed by what they know, you will not stop the demoralization by preventing them from being told, because they know it, and unfortunately most of the criticisms made by the *Daily Mirror* about the leadership of the British Army have been confirmed by many military events. The Prime Minister said that. What is the use of pretending that you can restore the morale of the British Army by preventing the Army reading what a paper like this says?'

Seconds later, Black Rod interrupted the proceedings to summon the House to the Lords for the Royal Assent to the Landlord and Tenants (Requisitioned Land) Act, 1942. His intervention reduced the temperature of debate, and ended the immediate duel between Bevan and Morrison. When Bevan resumed his speech, the passion of its opening had fallen, but the seriousness of its tone had deepened.

'The right hon. Gentleman,' he said, 'has been connected with the Labour party for many years. He is the wrong man to be Home Secretary. He has been for many years the witch-finder of the Labour party. He has been the smeller-out of evil spirits in the Labour party for years. He built up his reputation by selecting people in the Labour party for expulsion and suppression. Indeed, the House of Commons ought to be warned by the career of the right hon. Gentleman. He is not a man to be entrusted with these powers because, however suave his utterance, his spirit is really intolerant. The House of Commons ought to consider what has happened. The right hon. Gentleman exorcized with bell, book and candle from the Labour party a gentleman who has now been taken into the War Cabinet and appointed Leader of the House. In fact, the right hon. Gentleman is the worst possible counsellor on issues of this kind. His own political records denies what he is doing now. I say with all seriousness and earnestness that I am deeply ashamed that a member of the Labour party should be the instrument of this sort of thing. It has been my experience in the House, which now goes over a number of years, a sad thing that the two Home Secretaries whom this party has provided have been among the most reactionary Home Secretaries in half a century. It is a shameful record.'

The Parliamentary Labour Party was, in those days, highly tolerant of its most pungent critic.

'The right hon. Gentleman is doing great damage to the Labour party and great damage to the country as a whole. I ask the House seriously to take into account what would be the consequence of the policy suggested by the right hon. Gentleman. We shall go through very difficult times in the next few months. We shall have to call upon our people to make supreme spiritual exertions. We shall have to address meetings in an unprecedented way in the next few months if we are to face the crisis which lies ahead. Why do the Government take our arguments away from us even before we begin to speak? Why do they make nonsense of our pleas before we make them? How can we call on the people of this country and speak about liberty if the Government are doing all they can to undermine it? The right hon. Gentleman wrote an article in the *Daily Mirror* on 23rd November, 1939, which puts my thoughts more succinctly. He said:

"Democracy is not without its faults. I know. I have to lead a democracy and it is my business to know. But a Government of parliamentary democracy fighting a war know whether or not its people are with it. A free press and a free Parliament can successfully fight for the elimination of the incompetent. Ability generally becomes known in due course, as does corruption and inefficiency. Praise and blame are freely handed out by a public opinion that can express itself, even though it is not always just. But in some way or another the accused can usually defend themselves and demand justice. Public criticism is one of the essentials of good government. Under dictatorship public criticism—even private criticism—is a crime. . . . Beware of the foes of democracy using the excuse of war for its suppression!"

Bevan quoted the Home Secretary's words, more familiar in Morrison's cockney voice than in his own cadenced Welsh accent; but the words came equally well from Bevan's mouth.

'I ask the right hon. Gentleman,' he said, 'could the argument be put better than that? Is he not today using the war emergency as an excuse for invading the rights of the Press and of free public criticism in Great Britain? I can understand now why the right hon.

Gentleman does not take the *Daily Mirror* to the courts. His case is too bad. He has to appeal to a packed House of Commons—packed by over 200 Members immediately attached to the Government. He dare not put his case to the courts because the *Daily Mirror* would then have the right to defend itself by putting the Home Secretary in the box as one of its principal witnesses. That is the reason he does not go to the courts.'

Bevan sat down amid muttered cheers from many parts of the House. The debate wore on, till eventually Morrison decided that he should intervene.

His speech began with a jangle of objections from Members whom he accused, in effect, of being willing to wound but afraid to strike in case their ineffectiveness would be exposed. He teased Bevan ('who poses as a great Parliamentary strategist'), with not putting down a Motion which could be tested in a Division, and added:

'My right hon. Friend, the Member for Ebbw Vale, was up to his usual hearty and thoroughly irresponsible, enjoyable and hectic standard. My hon. Friend is never happier than when he is having a shot at his own political friends, and he has never been happier than he was today.'

Bevan answered with the fraternal observation:

'And the right hon. Gentleman is never happier than when he is attacking his own political principles.'

Using a technique of accusation by juxtaposition and rhetorical question, Morrison went on to talk of the *Daily Mirror* and Fascism.

'Supposing a secret Fascist organization wished to conduct propaganda for the purpose of undermining morale. If it had sense, it would not go about it by openly opposing the war. Not at all. It would set about vigorously supporting the war and then it would paint the picture that the House of Commons is rotten or corrupt or incompetent or something like that, that the Government is the same, that the chiefs of the Armed Forces are the same, in that way effecting a steady undermining of public confidence and a spread of the belief that defeat is inevitable and why should the needless spilling of blood and suffering continue. That would be a perfectly understandable Fascist technique.'

Dr. Haden Guest, the Labour Member for Islington North, asked:

'Is the right hon. Gentleman aware that this paper—I have a copy of it in my hand—advocated precisely the same line of general policy as long ago as May, 1939, and does he consider that in May, 1939, this Fascist conspiracy which he is hinting at, this Fascist intent, had then taken shape in the mind of the newspaper's proprietors?'

Jack Lawson asked another question.

'Can he tell us how it is, if they pursued this course previous to the war, that they are now deliberately doing their best to lose the war?'

There was a shout of 'Nonsense!' and Morrison said:

'I noticed what both hon. Members said, and there is point in both their observations. The basis upon which judgment must be delivered is: Is this calculated to have the very effect that the Fascist enemies in the war would wish?'

He ended by saying:

'Let me say that we have no wish or intention improperly to interfere with the proper freedom of the Press, which we are upholding and we will uphold. I myself would be no party to any such policy. If there was any danger I certainly should not be a party to it. There is no danger of it with this Government. There is no such intention; but we say boldly and clearly to the House that this is the kind of thing we will not tolerate; that this newspaper has been told that the evidence against it exists; that the systematic publication of which we have evidence entitles me, in our opinion, legally to suppress that newspaper tomorrow—or last week—and that is our view. I told the newspaper that in future there will be no question of building up another such systematic case. We are not waiting six months to build up another systematic case. If that newspaper goes on with the pernicious line it has conducted. I tell the House—because I will not be a party to deceiving the House—that if that happens, that newspaper will be suppressed, and having done it, we will submit ourselves to the judgment of the House. I can only hope that that will not be necessary. The newspaper has, I think, been much less objectionable since the statement I made in the House on Thursday of last week. I hope that it will learn from the warning and the experience that it has had, and will conduct itself in a proper and responsible spirit. If it does, it has nothing to fear from His Majesty's Government, but if not, then I tell the House openly and frankly that we shall not be afraid to act.'

He sat down to loud Government cheers, but the debate wasn't over. First, Hore-Belisha called for vigilance in the cause of freedom of the press. 'The descent is easy. You start on a firm principle. The ground gradually gives way, and your foothold becomes less secure and in the end you cannot even hold on to the cause for which you started this war.'

After him, Wing-Commander James, the Member for Wellingborough, said, 'No one can contend that the *Daily Mirror* is a serious political paper. . . . Its circulation has been very largely built up on the publication of deliberately salacious muck to tickle the palates of its public.'

But the debate showed that the House as a whole saw the *Mirror* as a political force acting powerfully for good or ill on the Services and the civilian population alike. It ended without a Division. Enough had been heard to make it clear that the *Mirror*, even if it were thought at fault through the ardour of its expression was nevertheless, dedicated to helping the war effort; that the Zec cartoon, though ambiguous, was well-intentioned; that the Government was in earnest in its intention to ban newspapers if it thought it necessary for the war effort; and that the *Mirror* was fully aware of that intention.

The *Mirror* commented in its editorial the next day, under the heading, *Personal Explanation.*

'So much attention has been concentrated in Parliament and in the Press upon a leading article printed in this column on March 6th that the author of it may be permitted to explain his meaning and his intentions in writing it.

'In substance the article was not more than a plea for the appointment of younger, perfectly fit and able men to "positions of authority and responsibility" in the Army.

'Had *one* sentence in the now notorious, irresponsible, despairing, and defeatist article been more tactfully phrased, it would seem that we should not have been accused of "trying to weaken the confidence of the country and the Armed Forces in the quality and character of our devoted corps of officers," as the Prime Minister put it yesterday.

'Nothing could have been further from our intention. Our praise of General Wavell, as of other Army leaders, will be remembered by our readers. Our encouragement of younger men has received a response in grateful letters from them.

'But, with all that, it is plain that caricatures (i.e. of Colonel Blimp) are bitterly resented at a time when the sense of humour (ours included) wears thin.

'Had we realized that one of ours might produce an effect, now denounced as deplorable, we should have been glad to withdraw it at once.

'That is now done.'

Churchill himself, despite his earlier wish to ban the *Mirror*, was well-satisfied with Morrison's strong language. But despite the debates in Parliament—the Lord Chancellor, Viscount Simon, introduced a similar debate in the Lords the same day—Churchill allowed himself a final growl. On March 27th, 1942, he spoke to an enthusiastic rally of the Central Council of the Conservative Party at their annual meeting at Caxton Hall. His account of the past year involved a long tale of 'an almost unbroken series of military misfortunes.' The British had been driven out of Cyrenaica, and were now only partly re-established there.

'We have been attacked,' he said, 'by a new and most formidable antagonist in the Far East.'

Hong Kong, the Malay Peninsula and the Dutch East Indies had been overrun. Singapore had been the scene of the greatest disaster to British arms yet recorded. The Allied squadrons in the Netherlands East Indies had been virtually destroyed in the action off Java. Burma was invaded; Rangoon had fallen; and to cap it all,

'The Battle of the Atlantic,' he said, 'is now for the time being . . . worsened again.'

Churchill hadn't come to jolly the delegates along. He wasn't there 'to speak smooth words or make cheering promises.' But on the other hand, he reassured them, 'in 1942 we need not expect to have reverses unrelieved by successes.'

As the meeting laughed and cheered, Churchill went on to refer to the *Mirror*.

'We have succeeded,' he said, 'in preserving our traditional free institutions, free speech, full and active parliamentary government, and a free press. We have done that under conditions which at times were more strained and convulsive than have ever beset a civilized State. But there is one limit which I must ask shall be respected. I cannot allow . . . a certain propaganda to disturb the Army—'. At this point his sentence was interrupted and ended by cheers, and that was virtually the last word in a bitter and prolonged argument.

Or almost the last word. As in a fairy-tale, Bart and Morrison became firm personal friends, and the *Mirror* lived happily with the National Government till the end of the war and the General Election of 1945, when it played a major part in kicking it out.

CHAPTER VIII

The Landslide: Beveridge to the Welfare State

On June 10th, 1941, Arthur Greenwood, the Minister of Reconstruction, announced to an indifferent House of Commons the appointment of a Committee with the drab title, 'The Inter-Departmental Committee on Social Insurance and Allied Services.' The chairman was to be Sir William Beveridge, a public servant with a distinguished record, first in the Ministry of Munitions in the First World War and later as chairman of the Unemployment Insurance Statutory Committee. He was a Liberal in politics, an administrator who had shown his sympathy both in his writings and in his practical work with the unemployed and poverty stricken in the 1920s and 1930s.

Among the Conservatives in the Coalition Government the Committee, which was ultimately to produce the Beveridge Report, was regarded as a tolerable sop to the Left, since the Royal Commission on Workmen's Compensation set up in 1939 had resigned its charge on the ground that it couldn't sit under war conditions. The T.U.C. had protested, but in the hustle of more important things, had acquiesced. Among the general public, the appointment of the Beveridge Committee struck few sparks at first. The war was in an active phase.

Churchill's first and justified priority was to fight the war and win it. Yet the war itself was the lancing of a chronic carbuncle of social pain, injustice and human indignity whose chief symptoms, the unemployment of the post Great War world, marked millions in the Western world with a sense of personal shame. In Germany, Hitler treated the disease with the homeopathy of total degradation; he gave work to the Germans in building the war-machine that destroyed them. He also gave them social incantations like 'Strength through Joy' which cheered them to their suicide.

In Britain, the British Communists had been discredited by the

Russo-German Pact of August, 1939, and their ideologists had exhausted themselves in dialectical acrobatics intended to make their contortions seem like the posture of upright men. Victor Gollancz's Left-Wing Book Club no longer offered the same inspiration to Socialists as in 1938. The war had moved on, and new forces were stirring among those who wanted to end the evils which in their different ways Jarrow and Hitler symbolized. Progress was no longer the property of the self-styled 'progressives'.

Belisha, politically extinguished, had nevertheless made a vital contribution to the idea of a New Britain, a phrase which was coming into fashion in 1941. Conscription and democratization of the army had introduced the classes to each other. Although the social divisions of wealth and privileged education had not been removed, men of different origins met in the Services in a way which hitherto had been a curiosity, as in the Duke of York's camps for public school men and working class lads. During the war's latent periods, the Army Bureau of Current Affairs gave opportunities for discussion to the formerly inarticulate. The huddling together in air-raid shelters of factory workers, shopkeepers, teachers, business-men and a hundred others—a comradeship through *force majeure*—loosened the nation's tongue. Except in country strongholds, untouched by war and where the enemy seemed not Hitler but the evacuees, the British had become less insular and reserved. Ernest Bevin, Minister of Labour, imported Indians to enlarge the labour force, and everyone thought them quaint and engaging in their turbans and saris. Everywhere at their vigils, men and women talked together about their post-war plans.

'After the war,' was the heart-cry of every soldier. From Clacton to Cairo, they spoke with hope and concern about their own post-war world.

Yet this talk might have dribbled away like spilled water into the sands where they stood guard if it hadn't found a container of post-war planning. Churchill himself was impatient of the planners. His dreams, like his actions, were concerned with high military strategy, the machines and the modes of war. He accepted that the Labour Party was the 'social' party, nor did he use the term in a friendly sense. He regarded it as a weakness, though a convenience, that the Labour leaders left the job of waging war to him while they concerned themselves with social and economic affairs.

The aim of the National Government was to stay national. Therefore, it had to avoid internal arguments. As Churchill wrote to King, the unity of the Conservative and Labour Parties should not be 'gnawed at.' The Government had to avoid language that would lead to controversy. The keyword of 1941 was 'reconstruction'—'a mild, vague word which frightened nobody,' said the *Mirror*. Not even Lord Croft, the former Sir Henry Page-Croft, the extreme Right-Wing Tory M.P. for Bournemouth, where it was said that at the General Election two humble women had been heard to say, 'Where do servants vote?' But behind the 'mild, vague word' was a revolutionary doctrine. It was essentially the doctrine of the Welfare State which in 1945, with the *Mirror* as its popular voice, was to sweep the Labour Party to power.

There is no reason to think of the Beveridge Committee as a device foisted on the National Government by its Labour supporters in order that Labour should win the post-war election. The affirmation of the rights of human personality was a weapon in the war against Hitler, who had denied them to the darkened European continent. The pressure on the Government to set up the Beveridge Committee was the pressure of history rather than of ideologists. The generation of the 1920s and 1930s wanted something better for the 1940s than a return to their old condition. Arthur Greenwood, Minister of Reconstruction, was the spokesman for the new Britain, not its inventor.

At the beginning of 1941, Bill Greig, the *Mirror*'s lobby correspondent, anxious to bring his paper into close touch with these trends, had invited Bartholomew to meet Arthur Greenwood at lunch. The meeting at L'Apéritif was a failure, a dialogue of the deaf, because while Bart on the one hand had little interest in abstractions, Greenwood with his high principles had little in common with the monosyllabic pragmatist. Yet Bart was preoccupied with the links between the home front and the Forces. Bart had appointed Greig to write a regular column dealing with soldiers' grievances. The idea had immediately caught on. Thousands of letters flooded into the office, not only with servicemen's grumbles but their wives' as well. These were down to earth complaints about delays in sending wives their allowances, about red tape in telling families of casualties, about unfairness in rationing and a hundred other things.

Greig himself, early in the war, had been summoned to the War Office and told by someone with red tabs that 'this must stop.' It was, he claimed, demoralizing the army. He cited an article by a soldier's widow complaining about a delay in paying her pension.

'She needs the money,' said Greig.

'Why,' asked red-tabs, 'doesn't she draw on her bank account meanwhile?'

When Greig reported the rebuke, Bart said, 'We go on printing.' A few weeks later, Greig was summoned to General Paget, C.-in-C. Home Command, and congratulated on a column which he described as an 'excellent safety valve.'

But already the *Mirror* was emerging not as a safety valve but as a moulding force for Britain's future. Greig introduced Bart to Emmanuel Shinwell, and the three men had a friendly luncheon at Ciro's. Bart liked Shinwell's bluntness. He was surprised to discover in him not just a doctrinaire Socialist but one who was also a constructive critic of the part that the trade unions were playing in the Labour Movement.((The need to reform the trade unions remains one of the *Mirror*'s themes.) Indeed, through Shinwell's influence, the *Mirror* was to appoint Sidney Elliot, a dedicated Left-Wing Socialist, as a political adviser.

At first the work of the Beveridge Committee seemed unexciting, and the public as a whole was unexcited. But there were many men with a strong social conscience like J. B. Priestley, Edward Hulton and King who recognized that winning the war was only worthwhile if it meant a worthwhile life to live. Priestley in his 9 o'clock wartime broadcasts was listened to with a tense hope, not because he was privy to the secrets of the war, but because he spoke as an ordinary man to ordinary men and women about why it was worth fighting the war at all. He spoke about simple virtues and simple fulfilments—jobs, homes and security. If Churchill in a rancorous mood was later to refer to him dismissively as 'a man called Priestley' who talked while others fought, he was merely underlining his own failure to see that Priestley's vision of the post-war world sustained millions. So it was that journals like *Picture Post* and the *Mirror* cheered the public not with pep-stories but with a down-to-earth, realistic appraisal of what could be done in the New Britain. The public answered with a curiosity about the Beveridge Committee which was to show itself dramatically.

Beveridge, recognizing the urgency of his task, plunged himself into the writing of the Report and, as information gradually leaked out about its progress, Beveridge's five giants—sickness, want, squalor, ignorance and idleness through unemployment—became like characters in a morality play. When, at last, the Report was ready, the *Mirror* formed the opinion, later to prove well-founded, that inside the Government there were doubts and divisions about the advisability of publishing it.

Sir Stafford Cripps, the Lord Privy Seal and Leader of the House, asked Cecil King to come and see him at his flat in Whitehall Court on 'a matter of great importance.' When King arrived, he found Cripps in an unusual anxious state. The reason for Cripps' tension wasn't simply the prospect of meeting a fellow Wykehamist. He was deeply worried that some of his Cabinet Colleagues wanted to temporize with the publication of the Beveridge Report. Did they want to kill it? Not exactly. The principle was, 'Thou shalt not kill, but need'st not strive, Officiously to keep alive.' Hearing the general contents of the Report, King reacted quickly. His attitude had always been, 'Let the public know the truth, good or bad.' Here was good truth, an inspiring truth, which stirred his radical spirit while appealing to his judgment of what should be a realistic administrative scheme. He returned to the *Mirror* offices through the mist and black-out of an early November nightfall, walking through the emptied streets with a sense of exhilaration. He had decided that the *Mirror* would throw its full weight behind the Beveridge Report.

On November 21st, 1942, the *Mirror* printed an editorial challenging the Government to issue the Report so that it could be publicly discussed.

'If, as Mr. Arthur Greenwood has suggested,' it said, 'Party truces and coalitions mean no Parliamentary controversy, and therefore no debate on matters that matter, it would seem to follow that the Beveridge Report cannot be discussed at all! It looks as though it might be hush-hushed after publication. It has at any rate been sniped at before we know anything about it.'

'Reformers must console themselves by the reflection that the Report must be publicly discussed some day. It cannot be indefinitely pigeon-holed on the excuse that it might disturb the national unity—or equanimity—of those who see Moscow in any proposal for social reform.'

Just over a week later, on December 1st, the Report was in the Vote Office of the House of Commons, and within a few hours a queue a mile long formed in Kingsway to get copies from the Government Stationery Office. The Beveridge Idea had worked in silence in the British mind. The Report was called simply, 'Proposals to the Government.'

The public welcome to the proposals was overwhelming. *The Times* spoke of the Report as 'a momentous document which should and must exercise a profound and immediate influence on the direction of social change in Britain.' The *Daily Telegraph* called it 'the consummation of the revolution begun by Mr. Lloyd George in 1911.' So Beveridge himself had acknowledged. The *Manchester Guardian* called it 'a big and fine thing,' and the *Daily Worker* 'a courageous attempt . . . to alleviate some of the worst evils of present day society.'

Lloyd George himself left Churt to lunch with Beveridge and to congratulate him on his achievement. But it was the *Mirror* which, more than any other newspaper, realized what hope the Report would bring to the men and women who were thinking of the post-war world. In a banner headline, 'Banish Want', it described the Report as a Cradle to Grave Plan', and it summed up the principles as 'All pay—all benefit.'

With simple diagrams, the *Mirror* set out, step by step, 'How to be born, bred and buried by Beveridge.' This was an over-simplification of the Beveridge Plan, and may well have led at a later stage to some of the difficulties of the Welfare State. But the *Mirror* recognized that the Beveridge Report contained the essence of a new society worth fighting for. And its faith in the Plan was confirmed by the public response.

At first the Government, and in particular Winston Churchill, were reluctant to give the Report publicity. They feared it might prove a distraction from the war effort itself. But shortly before it appeared Brendan Bracken, the Minister of Information, had decided that the Report would prove a valuable weapon in fighting against Nazism, since it presented a picture of a social state worth fighting for. Sir James Grigg, the Secretary of State for War, took a different view. The Army Bureau of Current Affairs, known as ABCA, had asked Beveridge to prepare a summary of his Report. Two weeks later, the War Office ordered the summary, which had been circulated for discussion, to be withdrawn. Immediately questions were raised in Parliament by Major John Dugdale and Tom Driberg, who quoted an official description of the withdrawal as 'an inconceivably stupid action.' Sir James Grigg's reply was:

'Whatever the hon. Member for West Bromwich (Mr. Dugdale) may think about it, there does exist—and I find evidence of it in my post-bag and in what Members say to me in the Lobbies—a suspicion, or at any rate a fear, that this scheme can be used to propagate one particular set of views, and this, besides being contrary to the spirit on which the present Government is founded, is definitely not in the interests of the Army educational scheme, which will then become the football of those holding extreme Party views. The reason I deplore the fuss which has been made about this is that more has been done by the creators of the fuss to make the ABCA scheme the football of extremists on either side than I could ever have believed possible.'

In one way, Sir James Grigg was right. The scheme did propagate a particular set of views—those which were to lead to the foundation of the Welfare State and its general acceptance by Tories as well as by Socialists. What is remarkable, though, is the political myopia which prevented Grigg from recognizing the public longing for ideas and measures which would end the abuses of the pre-war years. To equate Beveridge's social plans with extremism was to ignore the fundamental longing for change and reform which, as events were to prove, the majority of the British people felt.

Beveridge himself, though deeply hurt, preserved a dignified reticence. Winston Churchill made no attempt to receive him or to engage even by correspondence in a discussion of the Report with its author. In Parliament, on the other hand, there was a continuing curiosity. Question followed question, till at last the Government had to put down a Motion welcoming the Report, while damning it with the limited description of it as 'a comprehensive review of the present provisions in this sphere and a valuable aid in determining the lines on which developments and legislation should be pursued as part of the Government's policy of post-war reconstruction.'

The Motion had all the signs of a formula designed to paper over the division between contradictory views. The Labour Party, represented by Arthur Greenwood, called on the Government 'to begin implementing, without a day's unnecessary delay, the Social Security Scheme.' But Sir John Anderson, Lord President of the Council, and Kingsley Wood, the Chancellor of the Exchequer, went out of their way to say that 'there can be no binding commitment.' Kingsley Wood said the Scheme was costly, while Sir John Anderson emphasized its weaknesses.

In the meantime, the *Mirror* made its position clear. On January 20th, 1943, it said:

'We believe that the Beveridge Report is one of the most able documents on any subject ever presented to any Government by anybody. We think it should be accepted, and the machinery for putting it immediately into operation at the war's end should be set up.'

A curious exception among forward-looking people to the general enthusiasm for the Report was the Minister of Labour, Ernest Bevin. 'Man cannot live by Beveridge alone,' was one of his early comments. To the Scottish T.U.C., he called it 'a coordination of the nation's ambulance service on a proper footing.'

Bevin disliked the enthusiasm that the Report had aroused in the Labour Party, and in a small act of spite blamed Beveridge at a party in Claridges for not having given credit to his Civil Service colleagues of the Inter-Departmental Committee in the presentation of his Report. This was the only time when Bevin spoke to Beveridge after the Report had been published. When Beveridge pointed out in a letter to Bevin that the Report itself contained these acknowledgements, Bevin didn't reply.

The outcome of the debates in the Commons and the Lords was that the Plan was referred to a committee of civil servants so that they could draft plans for legislation. But the committee of civil servants took longer to comment on the Report than Beveridge had taken to produce it. The year previously, the *Mirror* had published a Zec cartoon entitled 'A Slight Technical Hitch', showing a body of striped-trousered diehards obstructing the laying of a foundation stone. It bore the inscription, 'The New World. This foundation stone is being laid by the sacrifices of the armed forces of the united nations.' It was not, however, till September 26th, 1944, that the Government published two White Papers on the social services. They were in substance a rewritten Beveridge Plan. The *Mirror* at once gave the White Paper its full support.

'The *Daily Mirror* welcomes the Government's proposals for social security. Whether the proposals are bigger and better than those of the famous Beveridge Report, or whether, in some respects, they fall short of the original hope, makes no matter. We have at last arrived at a national scheme of insurance, and that in itself marks a big step forward in the social reconstruction of the country. But while the step is a big one, it is only the first one, and, in our view, represents not an end but a beginning.'

An editorial summarized the White Paper.

'The full and efficient functioning of the scheme depends on full employment, which, of course, is a Government responsibility.

'A rising birth-rate is essential to the success of the scheme. Otherwise it becomes top-heavy owing to the increasing proportion of old people.

'Details of the medical scheme are vague. It is doubtful whether the scheme can work in the absence of a State medical service. The Government's proposals in this respect will be awaited with interest.

'The decision to use neither the trade unions nor the approved societies as agents is wise. The scheme must not become tainted with "vested interest" from the start.

'The scheme depends on practical efficiency and therefore the Minister appointed to work it must be not only a good administrator but a strong man; a man who commands the country's respect.'

This summary is as valid today of the Welfare State in being as it was of the White Paper.

Beveridge himself at his rooms in University College, Oxford, saw the White Paper on the Beveridge Scheme for the first time when a *Mirror* reporter handed him a copy. When Churchill was asked on March 18th, 1943, whether he had consulted Beveridge on the setting up of machinery to implement his Plan, and whether he proposed to do so, the Prime Minister said, 'No.' When Beveridge asked for an interview with him, the reply was that Churchill was too busy. This was less a failure of courtesy than a failure to recognize that Beveridge had become the symbol of a new age. It was a failure which was to prove politically expensive. Not only had the debates in Parliament made it clear that the Government was dragging its feet about the Beveridge Report, but the *Mirror* had indelibly impressed on the minds of millions of servicemen the need for 'Beveridge.' It was their hope for the future. Those who obstructed the Report were also obstructing the fulfilment of their hopes.

Herbert Morrison himself, who took part in the debate on the Beveridge Report in February, 1943, was friendly to it; but because he had to speak to a Government brief, he appeared lukewarm. His defeat by Arthur Greenwood for the treasurership of the Labour Party later in the year was partly due to the unpopularity he had to endure for that reason. Churchill's coolness to the Report was also a decisive factor in his defeat in 1945. The Welfare State was on its way, and the Coalition Prime Minister hadn't noticed it.

*

After the flurry of blows between the *Mirror* and Churchill there came a lull, and the war leader and the forces' journal settled down to fighting the enemy in their own separate ways. Jennings ('W.M.') fell ill, (he died in 1953) and ceased to take an active part in the paper. He had performed a vital part in expressing the *Mirror*'s policy against appeasement. While others had dithered, Jennings had been firm. As a commentator, he had achieved a national stature between 1939 and 1940. With his vivid sense of language—'the pale spy Ribbentrop, so recently the darling of the treacherous upper-crust riff-raff in this country'—he had reintroduced to Britain a vehemence which had not been known in political controversy since the age of the pamphleteers. As with the eighteenth-century satirists, his passion went with an acute mind and a courageous character. The *Mirror* itself wrote of him in his lifetime words which might well serve as his obituary.

'He was,' said the *Mirror*, 'a man who made all England sit up, the one voice that has unswervingly warned our people of what would happen next, who has revealed the ultimate aims of the dictators, who has hammered home the lesson that Britain must be strong.'

Jennings' successor as chief leader writer was Bernard Buckham, who wrote under the initials 'B.B.B.' Writing in a similar capsule style to Jennings, his editorials were blunt rather than bitter, and expressed the general tone of frank but prudent criticism of the Government which the *Mirror* was to maintain till the end of the war, parallel with its rumbustious attacks on the enemy.

At this stage, the *Mirror*'s style became less strident and more analytical. 'B.B.B.'s manner was to begin his leader with a principle which he then analysed and developed in informed detail. On November 3rd, 1943, his theme was 'United at Last.'

'The Moscow Conference,' he wrote, 'marks the real turning point in the war, for it means that Hitler's last throw, which was the attempt to sow internal dissension among the united nations, has failed.'

At the beginning of 1944, the *Mirror* set out a series of good resolutions which were fundamentally a statement of its policy. The *Mirror* urged that everyone should stop talking of the certainty of victory and get on with the job of securing it. Reports, blueprints and optimistic oratory should be translated into action. The Labour Party should in its own interest admit young people to its ranks and get rid of the old men. Then came the repetition of the *Mirror*'s constant theme, which at the time had the merit of novelty—politicians should combine to lay the foundations of social security and full employment.

Though tied to no Party, the *Mirror* urged the Government to nationalize the mines and coordinate and control basic services such as transport, light and power. Anticipating the formation of the United Nations Organization, it urged the U.S.A., Russia, China and Great Britain to consolidate their alliance by making themselves the nucleus of a new and better League of Nations. To fight the war, it called for a fairer distribution of food, better meals for miners and more milk for the aged. Rent sharks and house profiteers should be sternly dealt with, and the Black Market finally wiped out.

This was a powerful prescription—the very formula of the British Left—and it undoubtedly found acceptance among the forces. The *Mirror* was proud to regard itself as the forces' newspaper. It encouraged correspondence from serving men about their grievances, not just to grumble about them but to seek redress. The *Sunday Pictorial* engaged Captain Fred Bellenger, M.P., who had been evacuated from Dunkirk, to act as a Serving Man's Friend, and his articles obtained a wide popularity with titles like 'Back to Spit and Polish,' 'More Concerts Please,' 'Glass House Scandal', 'Release These Men Now!' and 'When an Airman's Wife is Untrue.'

The choice of a Labour Member of Parliament who had the glamour of the evacuation from Dunkirk to aid him in pressing for a fair deal for the forces was not accidental. For the whole of the 1930s, the Labour Party had been associated with pacifism. The Captains and the Colonels almost all belonged to the Tory Party. But now in the ranks and among the commissioned officers who had been able to rise from the ranks with the new opportunities in the democratic army available to those who were not 'hereditary gentlemen,' there were hundreds and thousands—perhaps millions—of new Labour supporters. Captain Bellenger could champion the men in the services more successfully because his military rank blurred the division between 'Them' and 'Us', and gave notice that Labour too was fit to command as well as to represent. (Bellenger in Attlee's first Labour Government was to become Secretary of State for War.)

The *Mirror* was a paper of the rank-and-file, easy to read, uncomplicated in its politics. It was on the side of the under-dog, and that meant, psychologically, almost everyone who had to take orders in war-time. 'What the *Mirror* Says' had a steadily increasing influence in forming opinion not only among the forces but also in the factories and among the families at home. A. J. P. Taylor, in his *English History 1914–1945*, has written:

'There was (during the War) no cheap organ of hate on the (Horatio Bottomley) *John Bull* model. The war had one important outcome in the newspaper world. For the first time the masses—other ranks in the forces and factory workers—read a daily newspaper, and this carried the *Daily Mirror* to the top of the circulation list. The *Mirror* was popular in a special sense. Previous popular newspapers, the *Daily Mail* and the *Daily Express*, were created by their proprietors, Northcliffe and Beaverbrook—men not at all ordinary. The *Mirror* had no proprietor. It was created by the ordinary people on its staff. . . . The *Mirror* was, in its favourite word, brash, but it was also a serious organ of democratic opinion and owed its success to its sophisticated columnist Cassandra as to Jane, its strip-tease strip-cartoon. The *Daily Mirror* gave an indication as never before of what ordinary people in the most ordinary sense were thinking. The English people at last found their voice, and the historian is the more grateful for this voice since the Second World War, unlike the First, produced no distinctive literature.'

Despite the *Mirror*'s popularity, or rather because of it, the politicians persisted in *Mirror*-baiting. Cudlipp, who perhaps more than anyone had given the *Mirror* its distinctive voice, had joined the forces in 1940 after a Parliamentary episode which already reflected the sensitivity of the Government's supporters to his pre-war goading. On 4th December, 1940, Quintin Hogg, then M.P. for Oxford, asked in the House:

'Why Mr. Hugh Cudlipp, aged about twenty-seven years and editor of the *Sunday Pictorial*, had not been called up for military service; and whether steps would be taken to see that any advantage granted to him was removed in order to secure the equal operation of the Military Service Acts.'

Ernest Bevin, the massive Minister of Labour and Trade Unionist, who was gradually to emerge as one of the *Mirror*'s heroes, replied:

'The calling-up of Mr. Cudlipp was deferred on the application of his employers supported by the Ministry of Information. I understand that this deferment was against the strong desire of Mr. Cudlipp himself, and that as a result his employers later withdrew the request for deferment. Arrangements are accordingly being made to post Mr. Cudlipp to the Armed Forces.'

In fact, long before that date, Cudlipp had written to J. H. Brebner, then Director of the News Division at the Ministry of Information, asking to be taken off the reserved list. Brebner had replied:

'I have received your letter and have already taken the matter up with our people to get you off the reserved list.

'May I be allowed to express my own personal admiration of your action, as it comes like a breath of fresh air after the many applications I receive from people to go on the reserve list. Good luck and good wishes to you.'

Cudlipp joined the army, and in 1942 was followed by Cassandra, who on March 27th, 1942, wrote this elegiac note on his *Mirror* opinions and attitudes.

'By 1938 I had graduated from pickle kings to Neville Chamberlain. I fought hard against him and I fought fiercely against Munich. I had been in Germany nearly every year from 1929 to 1938 and it seemed incredible to me then, as it does now, that anybody could possibly mistake Hitler's preparations as being designed for anything but gigantic war.

'I campaigned for Churchill, and my support was early and violent. But since he came to power I have distrusted many of his lieutenants—and I have said so with scant respect either for their position or their feelings.

'Churchill told a former colleague of his that "there are paths of service open in wartime which are not open in the days of peace, and some of these paths may be paths to honour." '

'I, who have not transgressed, am shortly following the Prime Minister's advice. I am still a comparatively young man and I propose to see whether the rifle is a better weapon than the printed word.

'Mr. Morrison can have my pen—but not my conscience.' Or, as a French satirical paper said to Clemenceau in the First World War when he threatened to ban it, 'You can have my feathers but you can't have my carcass.'

With the war-time passing from the *Pictorial-Mirror* scene of Cudlipp and Cassandra, its controversial temperature fell somewhat, and its energies turned towards the post-war problems already exercising the men and women overseas as well as the factory workers at home.

The *Mirror*, under its editor Cecil Thomas, was interested in radical change, and had many points of sympathy with Aneurin Bevan. Indeed, at one stage in the war when the *Mirror*'s correspondents reported a sagging in morale, Bevan wrote three unsigned articles designed to raise the forces' drooping spirits. But Bartholomew himself had fundamentally more in common with Herbert Morrison than with Bevan. Bart and Morrison were Organization Men, technicians in their trade and highly sensitive to the mood of the British public. Their empirical approach differed from the idealism of Bevan. Both men of great energy, they believed in the long haul rather than in the tempestuous onslaught which marked Bevan's political approach.

Bevan might call Morrison a 'Tammany Hall politician.' But to Bartholomew, a master of the craft of journalism, Morrison was a master of the craft of politics who had the quality he admired above all—a lack of social stuffiness and an irreverence in face of the pretentious, whether of the *Mirror* or of the ideological Left. Between Cudlipp and Bartholomew there had been 'the affinity of two porcupines', as Cudlipp himself put it. Between Cecil King and Bartholomew, there was respect without affection. But as the war went on, they became allies in the steadfast purpose of the paper—the determination that a better Britain should come out of World War II. Bartholomew had his own hobbies in fighting the war, such as his newspaper for submarine crews called, *Good Morning*, and his activities as a volunteer fireman. But his real contribution on the paper was to support those, like Herbert Morrison, who wanted democratic change. And despite personal antipathies, he and Cecil King worked closely together in order to achieve it.

D-Day came, and the *Mirror* published a stirring leader entitled Destiny's Hour.'

'We can,' it said 'with reason select a sacred invocation for the battle-cry, and say, with Montgomery: "Let God arise, and let His enemies be scattered." '

This was not pietism. It expressed the solemn mood in which the people of Britain faced Hitler as a personification of evil. The passage of time has not erased this valid belief.

A week after D-Day, when the battle of Normandy was at its height, the *Mirror* returned to its theme that politics mattered. It reminded the forces that one of their weapons was the vote.

'The soldier,' it said, 'has a tough job on hand, but he is wrong to think that despised "politics" should be brushed aside as a matter of no moment. On the contrary, every effort should be made to instruct him in the importance of having a vote in his own future. Votes are weapons fit for heroes. Our soldiers should make sure that they have got them.'

And then the *Mirror*, with its usual realism, ended,

'How to stake your claim—see opposite page.'

Another week passed, and the *Mirror* had to decide what to do about the V.Is, which had made their sinister appearance over England.

'We have the measure of the thing now,' said the *Mirror*, hopefully, 'and our answer to the buzz-bomb is Buzz Off!'

But even while the flying bomb raids were at their height, the *Mirror* still concentrated on the need to plan for the future, and in the leader 'Work and Play' B.B.B. set out some of its ideas on full employment and trade union responsibility.

'The T.U.C. demands a five day week,' it said, 'and the *Daily Mirror* supports the plea. Prosperity depends on production, and production depends on efficiency. The idea should be to make as much as possible with the least expenditure of human labour, in which case every worker would need to pull his weight while he is at work. We hope the T.U.C. accepts this obligation. Increased privileges entail increased responsibility. The trade unions will have to consider whether they can extend their discipline to factory and workshop in a manner which will prevent the honest worker having to make up for the deficiences of the amiable lounger and the deliberate shirker.'

As 1944 came to an end, Lloyd George, who had failed so completely to grasp the issues of the Second World War, despite his incomparable leadership in the First, announced his retirement from political life. The *Mirror* noted his passing with a sermon entitled 'Political Veterans.'

'Mr. Lloyd George's retirement from political life will be much regretted from the personal point of view, but if his decision to stand down at the next election acts as an example to others, great advantage may accrue. . . . There is nothing to prevent constituencies taking the matter into their own hands. They should refuse to support candidates in their dotage.'

The *Mirror* was repeatedly to return to this theme in the next ten years.

And so on to April 13th, when on the front page the *Mirror* headlined the news 'Roosevelt Dies on Eve of Allied Triumphs.' The same day the Commons adjourned in tribute .The end of the war in Europe was approaching.

'Wait for it,' said the *Mirror* on April 30th. 'We shall wait for it—the official announcement that peace has returned to Europe. We shall not receive it in the spirit of irresponsible pleasure-seekers, but in a mood of thankfulness, of sympathy with those who have suffered bereavement and loss, of remembrance of those who carry on the battle of the Far East.

'For us the end will be a solemn and uplifting occasion, and a time of dedication. Dedication to the task of restoring love and mercy and justice among men. Dedication to the hope that these human qualities will never more perish from the earth.'

On May 2nd Hitler died. On May 8th the *Mirror* proclaimed 'V.E. Day!' in its heaviest type across the front page. It marked the end of the war with an obituary on Hitler which was a call to a new age in international relations.

'Never must the slothful years return,' it said. 'Who shall say that there are not in the world other Hitlers waiting to rise up if the time comes ripe? The end of German power is the end, or ought to be, of that evil thing "the balance of power." We can make it the beginning of a collective system, thus to fashion a world in which no man anywhere can have the chance to debase the human race.'

At the same time, the *Mirror* coined a new slogan, 'Forward with the People.'

'Happy indeed shall we be if we can feel that our system is fair to all; that a real attempt is being made to bridge the gap between rich and poor. To weld the nation into a contented, busy, prosperous whole is a noble cause. And so we say, Forward with the People.'

In the meantime, as early as 31st October, 1944, Churchill had declared that it would be wrong to continue with the existing House of Commons after the Germans had been defeated. Yet after V.E. Day the Japanese war remained still to be won, and Churchill was anxious to carry out the Government's own proposals for reconstruction, anaemic though they seemed to the Labour Party. On 18th May, he proposed to the Labour and Liberal Parties that the Coalition should be continued. Attlee dithered, and at the Blackpool Conference he could be seen wandering in zig-zags through the main lounge of the hotel absorbed like some political Hamlet in his uncertainties. Ernest Bevin was more definite; he believed that the convulsion of a General Election would be bad for the nation. Aneurin Bevan, by contrast, was raring to go. The whole tone of the Labour Party Conference was one of youth, eagerness and will for change. Under the chairmanship of Ellen Wilkinson, and with the guiding hand of her colleague and friend Herbert Morrison, the speakers at the Conference were carefully stage-managed in order to reflect the backing which the Labour Party had in the forces, and the new-type of Parliamentary candidate. Major John Freeman, later to become a Minister in Attlee's Government, evoked tremendous applause when he was announced as 'a Desert Rat.' Major Denis Healey, destined to be Minister of Defence in the 1964 Government, aroused raptures of enthusiasm by his denunciation of corrupt and reactionary monarchies in the Balkans. 'The people are on the march,' he cried, and the audience applauded the partisans of Yugoslavia and Greece.

Many Tories for their part were as eager to get to grips with the Labour Party in an electoral contest as the enthusiastic young men of Blackpool. Attlee wanted the election to take place in October. Now that the Coalition was to be broken, Churchill, under the pressure of his supporters, who wanted to exploit his prestige as a war-time leader, was anxious to have the election forthwith. On the 23rd May, Churchill resigned and the War Cabinet was dissolved.

*

When the Election campaign began, nobody could successfully have forecast the Labour landslide in which it would end. Petty war-time grumbles didn't add up to a pattern of discontent on party lines. Restrictions of every kind made the nation as a whole long to be free, but no one could say that this desire would not express itself in a great vote of confidence for Churchill as a war leader who promised to bring Britain to the fair uplands of victory, liberty and plenty. Nor could anyone be sure how the forces, still scattered and still at war, would vote.

Contrary, however, to its situation in previous elections, Labour was not overwhelmingly outweighed in the National Press by the Tories. The *Daily Herald*, *News Chronicle* and *Mirror* were selling approximately 6,000,000 copies daily. The most potent factor in redressing the old imbalance between press support in favour of the

Socialists and Tories was of course the *Daily Mirror*, whose circulation at the time was approximately 2,400,000. On the Conservative side the sales were about 6,800,000.

Low summed up the dominant mood of the electorate in a *Manchester Guardian* cartoon. Entitled 'On a Higher Level,' his cartoon showed a massive figure like Rodin's *Penseur* sitting on a plinth in an attitude of profound thought, holding in its hand a large document with the words, 'Haphazard Enterprise for Private Profit, or Planned Development for the Common Good,' followed by a question mark. Below, in swirling clouds, the cartoonist had expressed some of the stunts and diversions of the campaign with the caption, 'Politics for the Child Minds'—a Colonel Blimp entitled, 'My Nest-Egg Right or Wrong,' two urchin Blimps saying, 'Is Churchill Prettier than Attlee?', and Churchill himself in napkins with a placard 'Totalitarian Tosh.' Above the clouds floats Lord Beaverbrook, a witch on a broomstick, while below a Diogenes Low in a barrel waves a lamp, looking for truth.

In the battle fought during the month's campaign, the *Daily Herald* was most blatant in its imitation of the traditional electoral virulence of the Tory Press Lords. Its headline of 26th June said, 'Frauds, Cheats, Wrigglers Seek Power;' on the 18th June it claimed 'A Vote for Churchill is a Vote for Franco.' The Tory press, on the other hand, concentrated most of their energies on elevating the image of Churchill as first in war and first in peace, and the climax of this projection was the report of his thousand-mile Election tour.

The violence of the *Daily Herald* found no counterpart in the way in which Attlee conducted his campaign. Churchill in his first broadcast had told the nation that 'Socialism is inseparably interwoven with totalitarianism,' and that it could not be established without political police—a Gestapo. He had over-inflated his attack, so that it was not taken seriously, and Attlee's mild but sensible reply on the BBC the following night, in which he said, 'The voice we heard last night was that of Mr. Churchill, but the mind was that of Lord Beaverbrook,' not only diminished Churchill's authority as a responsible person but Lord Beaverbrook's as well. As Attlee later put it in a speech at Camberwell on July 3rd, 'Mr. Churchill has rather old-fashioned views about fighting an Election.'

The Labour Party had been prepared for press scares, and during the Election engaged for much of the time in a prophylactic campaign, warning the public that sooner or later the opposition press would try some sort of stunt. Churchill's attack on Harold Laski, the Labour Party Chairman, for having claimed that Attlee would go to the Potsdam Conference as an observer responsible to the National Executive of the Labour Party rather than as a political leader in his own right, failed to whip up the public and constitutional anxiety that he had hoped for. The country was not interested in abstractions, nor indeed in the passions of ideological slogans. It was tired of the stale faces in the National Government. It wanted simple domestic things—homes, security and settled jobs. The soldiers wanted to come home and raise families. Their wives wanted the stability of a domestic relationship after separation.

Of all the newspapers engaged in the campaign, the *Mirror* had its ear most closely attuned to the mood of the electorate, which was admitted by all who took part in the campaign to be one of sober and thoughtful consideration, completely unlike the mood of hysteria which was successfully whipped up after the First World War, when Press Lords and politicians stampeded a semi-literate working-class by scare headlines.

As Election Day approached, the *Mirror*, in contrast to the *Daily Express*, which was beginning to treat the Election as 'the greatest circus of all time,' became more and more sober in its appraisal of the issues. Not that it didn't occasionally lash out at individuals. On June 30th, it attacked Mr. A. T. Lennox-Boyd, Tory candidate for Mid-Bedford, who had sneered at Bevan's plan for building a million houses as 'a military operation.' It accused him as a Junior Minister in 1938 of giving great comfort to the Nazis by announcing that he 'could imagine nothing more ridiculous than for Great Britain to guarantee Czechoslovakia's frontiers against Hitler's threats of aggression.'

At the same time, in a leading article 'Your Sacred Trust,' it demanded that the voice of the fighting man should be heard on polling day. It ended with the slogan that was to become classic for millions of working-class women, 'The women will vote for *him*.'

Three days before the Election, in large type it instructed the women how to 'Vote for Them.' The theme had been initiated by a Mrs. C. Gardiner of Ilford, Essex, who had written a letter to the *Mirror* which ended, 'I shall vote for him,' referring, as Morrison mentions in his memoirs, to her hopes of a better Britain for her soldier husband. Morrison had been consulted by the *Mirror*, and gave his warm support to the idea of using 'Vote for him!' as a slogan.

'How does a woman vote for a serving man who has no vote? How does she make sure that his fighting views get into the ballot box? the *Mirror* asked.

'The answer is easy. *She* puts them there herself *using her own vote to do it*.'

On the same day it congratulated Churchill for having 'escaped from the influence of his confidant and henchman Lord Beaverbrook, who sought from the beginning to conduct the campaign at the lowest level.'

On July 3rd it hammered home the theme that the Election was to be a fight for *him*.

'Let the votes of the people decide,' the *Mirror* said. 'Let *his* vote decide. To the electors we would say: You know what the fighting man wants. You know which party is likely to give him what he wants. You know the only way to make his future safe. Go then and do your duty. Vote for *him*.'

Within the *Mirror* at the time a small group of journalists, chief among them Ted Castle, the picture editor, was giving considerable aid and comfort to the Labour Party by assisting Herbert Morrison, Labour's campaign manager, with technical advice on propaganda. Zec, whose innocent cartoon had made the *Mirror* clash with Churchill, was now drawing cartoons for the Labour Party at Morrison's personal invitation.

In previous elections, Labour manifestos and broad-sheets had suffered grievously from old-fashioned, chunky presentation. Socialist earnestness kept breaking through. However worthy the subject and argument may have been, only the most masochistic or dedicated could persist in reading it. But Castle and his team helped Morrison to give something of the same new look to Labour Party literature as they had for several years been giving to the *Mirror*. Though not wholly successful in transforming the old-fashioned hostility of the Labour Party towards bright presentation, they eventually succeeded in substantially improving a great deal of Labour's campaign literature, and their influence has persisted to the present day, when it is no longer thought indecorous for Party literature to be cheerful. The nature of the election manifesto, 'Let's Face the Future!' reflected itself in their new presentation.

On the eve of the Election on July 4th, the *Mirror*'s full page, signed 'The Editor', read:

'A Message to the Voters of Britain!

'Vote for Them!

'The man who would fill that chair in your home. The mate you miss at work. The pal you liked to meet in the pub. The boy friend.

'These men are still fighting all over the world. Thousands of them are denied the chance to vote. You can restore what, for party purposes, has been filched from them.

'You can Vote for Them.

'The woman in home and factory has a special responsibility. Her public duty and personal interest is to put the fighting man first.

'Fighting men would vote for courage, for the homes they hope to build, for the social security which fosters happiness in the home.

'Vote for Them!

'Vote for Them,' it shouted on July 5th, with a reproduction of Zec's magnificent cartoon of a wounded soldier holding out a laurel with the label 'Victory and Peace in Europe,' and the caption, 'Here you are—don't lose it again!'

'Vote on behalf of the men who won the victory for you,' said the Mirror. 'You failed to do so in 1918. The result is known to all. The "land fit for heroes" did not come into existence. The dole did. Short-lived prosperity gave way to long, tragic years of poverty and unemployment. Make sure that history does not repeat itself. Your vote gives you the power. Use it. Let no one turn your gaze to the past. March forward to new and happier times. The call of the men who have gone comes to you. Pay heed to it. Vote for *them*!'

'The slogan,' Morrison wrote in his autobiography, 'was simple, brilliant and undoubtedly influenced large numbers of women, who had hitherto imagined that politics were of no importance to them.'

Its brilliance was that at no time did the *Mirror* specifically urge the voters to vote Labour. Yet by its constant references to the need not to repeat the political errors which followed the First World War, and by its specific disparagement of Churchill's electoral methods and of the pre-war Tory party, the *Mirror* made its message unmistakeably clear. Free from party attachments, despite its close sympathies with Herbert Morrison, the paper under King's political inspiration had a team of radical young men (among them the future M.P. for Gravesend in 1945, Garry Allighan, head of the paper's information service for the forces under the slogan, 'Write to the *Mirror* about it!'), who daily encouraged the electorate to vote for a genuine new order. The Welfare State was an embryo. But its nucleus had been the subject of argument and approval not only among the radical Left but also in the forces and by millions who, without seeing the issue in ideological terms, believed in the principle of a Welfare State to end the abuses of the past.

The injunction 'Vote for him' was more than a general exhortation. It was a specific act of guidance for women voters to use the proxy votes of their husbands and sons serving overseas to vote Labour. Of 2,867,836 registered service voters, 1,873,510 had nominated proxies. In Australia and New Zealand and other difficult areas, either inaccessible to the postal vote in time or where men on the move couldn't be reached, thousands were disfranchised. The *Mirror*'s slogan, 'Vote for him!' was thus an especial instruction for women with proxy votes to use them for Labour, and for women whose husbands lacked a vote, to defend their interests by voting 'for him.' The Service vote proved, in effect, to be something like 90 per cent in favour of Labour.

It would be inaccurate to claim that the *Mirror* was responsible for Labour's victory in 1945, since the whole tide of history was flowing in Labour's favour. Yet it is certain that never before had a newspaper of the Left exercised such decisive influence in forming opinion at the time of an election or in guiding the electorate towards its decision.

For a decade the *Mirror* had resolutely marched with the Left, sometimes out of step and sometimes ahead of the column, but always carrying a guiding light.

THE CARTOON THAT CAUSED THE TROUBLE

(*top left*)
H. G. BARTHOLOMEW ('BART')

(*top right*)
WILLIAM CONNOR ('CASSANDRA')

(*bottom*)
PHILIP ZEC, WARTIME CARTOONIST AT THE MIRROR

CHAPTER IX

The King Era

WHILE THE *Mirror* was fighting its two-front war against Hitler and the Tories, an internal revolt had broken out, directed against Bartholomew's dogmatism, which had increased as his touch became less sure. Despite his own radical objections towards establishments of any kind, he himself, now chairman of the *Mirror* Group, dominated its affairs with an increasing arrogance. Especially resentful of the up-and-coming men on his staff, chief among them Hugh Cudlipp, who had returned from the services, he grasped at the opportunity of sacking him at Christmas, 1948, for having failed to publish a news cable about a strike and a riot involving the death of a number of Africans at the Enugo coalfield. The story had, in fact, been personally despatched by Cecil King from Africa, and Bartholomew, whose relations with King had become progressively more strained, felt this was a heaven-sent opportunity to break up the King-Cudlipp alliance. Cudlipp left the *Pictorial*, to the regret of his friends and the pleasure of Lord Beaverbrook, who promptly gave him a job on the *Sunday Express*.

But Bartholomew's joy didn't last. There had been growing dissatisfaction on the *Mirror* board with his hectoring manner and a developing misanthrophy which drink didn't relieve.

King decided in 1951 that the time was ripe for a Palace revolution. He telephoned Zec, now a member of the board, to tell him that he and three other members had decided to ask for Bartholomew's resignation. Zec's support was essential because, of the seven directors one, Cook, was in Australia, and Bart thought he could rely on the support of at least one of those who remained. Zec was astonished at King's proposal; so might one of the German generals have felt when invited to join the bomb plot against Hitler. But Zec reacted in a traditional manner, and asked King to lunch.

There King told him that, together with Sylvester Bolam, the editor and a close friend and dependant of Bartholomew, he had come to the conclusion that Bartholomew, now nearly seventy, was in his dotage and had to be disposed of. Zec himself had suggested to Bartholomew six months previously that he ought to resign since, as a colleague put it, 'the old man was drinking too much and had become incoherent and unreliable.' And so, after lunch, Zec saw Bartholomew and advised him that the best thing he could do would be to resign. Bartholomew refused. He couldn't believe that he didn't have a majority, since his friend Bolam had the casting vote. Zec then had to tell him that Bolam had in fact given the casting vote against him. Bartholomew's comment was a short one. 'Judas!' he said. After that he broke down and wept for twenty minutes, interrupting himself only to finish a bottle of whisky.

For the next four days, Zec had the unhappy task of persuading Bartholomew to write the four necessary letters of resignation. It was rather like persuading a man under sentence of death to write his will when he couldn't believe that the sentence had been pronounced. Bartholomew wept intermittently, saying, 'How could Bolam do this to me?' One of his difficulties was that although he had joined the *Mirror* at the age of fourteen and had played a major part in building it up, he had no shares in the firm. In the event, however, King arranged for Bartholomew to have a pension of £6,000 a year, together with a golden handshake from the various companies totalling £20,000. Over the years Bartholomew had, in fact, received capital sums from the *Mirror* totalling £80,000.

At this time, Cudlipp himself was working for the *Sunday Express* as deputy to John Gordon. It was an uneasy relationship, since Cudlipp's arrival had given Gordon a new lease of life. On the other hand, Cecil King, despite the fact that Hugh Cudlipp had 'spiked' his message from Enugo, held him in the greatest affection and esteem and wanted him back on the *Mirror*.

The King revolution, dramatic and irreversible, marked the movement of the *Mirror* Group into a new and successful phase which King was to control and dominate. He celebrated his accession to the chairmanship by inviting Cudlipp to return to the Group, first as editor of the *Sunday Pictorial* and later as editorial director of both newspapers.

Whereas Bartholomew had developed the *Daily Mirror* and *Sunday Pictorial* companies in a series of commercial impulses, some of which, like the purchase of *Public Opinion*, brought disappointment and failure, King, a new type of business-man intellectual, planned his newspaper expansion by entering profitable fields hitherto unploughed by his organization. He bought the Amalgamated Press, later renamed Fleetway Publications in 1959, and Odhams Press two years later. The resulting alliance of companies, now called the International Publishing Corporation Ltd., eventually contained two hundred periodicals and twenty-one newspapers, twelve of them overseas.

The first ten years of King's dispensation was a period in which he was more concerned in setting a stamp on his reign than in expanding his empire. Sylvester Bolam, the editor he inherited from Bartholomew, was a Durham University graduate who joined the *Mirror* in 1936 as a sub-editor. In the Crippsian atmosphere of austerity that followed the war, he was an appropriate choice as editor. A radical with his roots in Newcastle, he was an enthusiastic supporter of Christian Action, and dedicated to the idea of building the Welfare State and in telling the people how it should be done. But his chief fault—an unpardonable one in a *Mirror* editor—was dullness. His interpretations of Cripps' White Papers by means of graphs was to King and some of his colleagues like the scraping of a knife on a rusty saucepan. The *Mirror*'s function was to interpret, not to bore.

Bolam's editorship was a sad one. He served three months in Brixton Prison for contempt of court in the Haigh murder case, and the *Mirror* was fined £10,000 plus costs. At last, in 1953, he resigned because of what was formally described as 'a disagreement with the management.' The Crippsian radical whom his best friend called Judas, the supporter of Christian Action who was gaoled for contempt of court, the deferential editor sacked for disagreeing with his superiors—all went to make an unhappy paradox.

Bolam's successor, Jack Nener, who joined the *Mirror* as a sub-editor in 1943, was a forthright Welshman but sentimental, warm, offering the right blend of bounce and emotion for the *Mirror* readership. He remained editor till 1961, contributing in his own person a cartoon of what a tabloid editor should look like, a down-to-earth image of the *Mirror* itself.

The interplay of King, Cudlipp and Nener was an ideal mechanism for the *Mirror*'s expansion. The political emphasis tended to change from programmes to causes, and the decade of 1951 to 1961 marked the height of the *Mirror*'s campaigns. While King was acquiring newspapers like the *Daily Times* of Nigeria, he was also supporting the causes for which the men under his command were fighting.

In a later television interview, King was asked, 'Why are you in journalism at all? What are you using your newspaper for?' He replied, 'I think I have tried to serve the interests of my readers, who are virtually the country—43 per cent of all adults over the age of sixteen read the *Mirror* every day.'

The interviewer continued, 'Are you trying to lead them?'

King said, 'It isn't the business of a newspaper to lead; it's the business of a politician to lead and a newspaper to comment.' Pressed further on this point, he added, 'I think leadership should be supplied to the country by the Prime Minister, and the newspapers should comment.'

'But what about causes?' he was asked.

'I'm interested deep down in the underdog,' King answered.

As the interview went on, King said in reply to a question as to whether his attitude necessarily led him to the Left,

'It certainly did when I became very politically conscious. That was between the wars when we had masses of unemployed and an utterly inept government doing nothing at all.'

King was never a member of the Labour Party, but always described himself as 'very sympathetic.' (In the 1964 General Election he put a red flag on his Rolls Royce with the slogan, 'Vote Labour.') Despite many a disappointment with the Labour Party, not least a lack of grace on Attlee's part in acknowledging the *Mirror*'s part in victory, he never gave up his sympathy for the Labour cause. His policies were as intuitive as they were intellectual.

How much power has a newspaper? What is the value of a newspaper campaign? Lord Beaverbrook once said that he owned newspapers in order to exercise power; then spoke with a sense of failure of his campaign for Empire Free Trade. To Beaverbrook, the reason for this particular lack of success always remained a mystery. Yet to a less dogmatic mind, it would have been apparent. A newspaper campaign can only succeed if it strikes a right balance in its pressure on public opinion and on government.

It can stimulate governments to act on public opinion; and it can excite public opinion to act on governments. It must explain as well as exhort, though in exhorting it mustn't bully. And above all, it must give the public the feeling that it is being championed in its own cause. If the Empire Free Trade campaign failed, it was first because the public couldn't understand it, irrespective of its merits and demerits; and secondly, because it was excessively personalized as Beaverbrook's own crusade. No one likes to be tugged by the lapel.

Again, with the rise in literacy and secondary education in the 1930s, the printed word lost some of its unchallenged sanctity. Beaverbrook's private battles, elevated into public causes, like his attacks on the British Council, could attract interest but not passion. At the turn of the second half of the twentieth century, young readers were looking for causes where their energy and idealism could express themselves. But they refused to involve themselves in the out-of-date, egotistical wrangles of old men.

The *Mirror* was the paper read by the young. During and after the war, a complex of ideas had crystallized around it so that eventually the *Mirror* became a character in its own right, an entity, a personality. When its editors in the post-war years had to make a policy decision, the question they asked themselves was, 'What would the *Mirror* say about it?'

There was nothing mystical about this; nor, on the other hand, was it an impersonal computerization of opinions and attitudes. The *Mirror*'s personality had developed spontaneously through the fortuitous combination and interrelationship of radical, challenging men. It had become a newspaper of the Left. Yet it might have fallen into the dreariness then characteristic of most Left-Wing newspapers, if after the war it hadn't reinforced its social attitudes with a first-class system of political information strikingly presented.

In 1954 Sidney Jacobson joined the *Mirror* as political editor, appointed by Hugh Cudlipp with whom he had already worked on the *Pictorial* after Cudlipp's return. Jacobson already had an extensive journalistic experience. After working on the *Statesman* of India he had later joined the liberal *Picture Post*, served in the army where he won the M.C., and later edited the *Leader*. He was to stay with the *Mirror* till he became editor of the *Daily Herald* at his own request in 1962.

He was followed by John Beavan, who had previously been editor of the *Daily Herald* for eighteen months, and London editor of the *Guardian* for nine years, having earlier in his career worked as news editor of the *Observer* and as an assistant director of the Nuffield Foundation.

The significance of these appointments was that the *Mirror* now had a network of political intelligence which could convert hunches into effective policies. The task of both men was as much to inform their own colleagues as the *Mirror*'s readers. Reinforcing the close contacts of both King and Cudlipp with the policy-makers in Westminster and the City, they helped to make the *Mirror* as well informed as the best informed newspapers in the country—and often better.

The *Mirror*'s first major test of its strengthened political information, was at the time of Suez. The seizure by Nasser of the Canal had the same effect on the *Mirror* as it had on Gaitskell with whom, at the time, Cudlipp and King and Jacobson had close contacts. Gaitskell denounced Nasser in the House for his Hitlerian behaviour. The *Mirror* emphasized his rebuke in a front page story, 'Dictator Nasser,' on July 30th, 1956.

'A warning about a sticky end,' it wrote. 'Colonel Nasser is the boss of Egypt. He wants every Egyptian to realize this. He also wants to make it perfectly clear to the outside world.

'But he has chosen a crude and dangerous method to demonstrate that he is a Big Shot.

'He may believe that by grabbing the Suez Canal and tearing up a solemn international agreement he inflates his own personal power. In fact, he merely brands Egypt as a liar, a cheat and a menace.'

Within a fortnight both Gaitskell and the *Mirror* had shifted the weight of their attack. The *Mirror* sent a front page message to Eden in its biggest and blackest type: 'No War Over Egypt.'

'Today,' Cudlipp wrote, 'the *Mirror* earnestly warns Sir Anthony Eden to rid his mind of the dangerous delusions from which he is suffering about the state of British public opinion in this challenging but changing situation.'

Then the editorial took on *The Times*, the *Daily Mail* and the *Daily Express* in a slashing attack.

'Who are the sabre-rattlers? Which are the most belligerent right-wing newspapers still urging the Prime Minister to violent action?

'The answer is: *The Times*, the *Daily Mail*, the *Daily Express*.

'These are the three newspapers which—openly or by inference—advocated appeasement towards Hitler's Nazi Germany.

'*The Times* suppressed the warnings of its own correspondents about Hitler's plot to seize Europe. *The Times* was eating out of Neville Chamberlain's hand: it out-appeased the Arch Appeaser.

'The *Daily Mail* deceived its readers into believing that Hitler's unholy clique were a team of energetic patriots who would honour a deal with Britain.

'The *Daily Express* lulled millions of people into apathy by declaring again and again that there would be no war.'

In 1939, it reminded its readers, Britain fought a war over Jenkins' Ear. It was incredible that in 1956 Britain should go to war to save Eden's face.

Through the anxious August, the *Mirror* kept reminding its readers of the danger of a war with the Arab states and a prolonged occupation of Egypt. 'A Middle East adventure on this scale,' it said, 'could only be undertaken by a British Government fully backed by British public opinion. To pretend that such a backing exists for Eden's administration would be a woeful caricature of the truth.'

Was that indeed so? In the event, the Mirror's opposition to the Suez enterprise, cost it a 70,000 drop in circulation. Once the war had begun and British troops were involved, there was a keen public desire, not shared by the idealists nor the more far-sighted politicians and press men, that Nasser's forces should be crushed and the Egyptian power broken.

The *Mirror*'s theme at this stage of the Suez dispute was that 'Britain must not go it alone'. It favoured what Gaitskell favoured—that the crisis should be dealt with through collective international action. On the other hand, it also stated on August 15th that if Nasser closed the Canal to Britain's shipping, 'it would be Britain's duty to answer aggression by force.'

King, meanwhile, had got wind that the Government intended a landing at Suez. He told Gaitskell, who was at first incredulous. But King's urgency convinced him. Cudlipp himself hurried off to the T.U.C. Conference at Brighton, where he told Geddes, the vice-chairman, of the critical situation. As a result Gaitskell, speaking at Leeds, gave a new warning. He called on the Government to denounce 'reports from Whitehall' that force might be used to find a Suez solution. The T.U.C. followed with an emergency resolution:

'Congress hopes that the proposals of the eighteen Governments now being submitted by the committee of five to the Egyptian Government will lead to a speedy and satisfactory settlement. Should the talks break down, force should not be used until the question has been referred to the United Nations and with its consent.'

The *Mirror*'s streamer headline said:

'The time has come for Eden to tell the nation. Is he planning a war with Egypt? If so, under what conditions would he use military power?'

By September 7th, in mounting national anxiety, Eden agreed to recall Parliament. The decision had been taken, and by September 10th, on the eve of Parliament's recall, the *Mirror* wagged a finger at Nasser, saying that if he were 'insane enough to discriminate against Britain or British people with a violence that would amount to a declaration of war by Egypt,' a different situation would arise. Nasser should not forget that in these circumstances the militant resentment of the Labour Party and the T.U.C. might well be aroused.

The following day the *Mirror*'s headline was in Latin—the first headline ever to appear in the *Mirror* in Latin and, the *Mirror* hoped, the last. '*Si Sit Prudentia*' was its message to Eden. It was the motto of his coat of arms, and had the monitory meaning, 'If there be but prudence.' On Wednesday, September 12th, when Parliament reassembled, Richard Crossman put the Labour view in simple terms. He said:

'Labour has made it clear that the only kind of military action it could support would be United Nations sanctions against Egypt.'

As Parliament reassembled, the *Mirror* made a test of public opinion. The issue, it said, was one of negotiations or war. It quoted the Gallup Poll conclusion that four out of every five voters in Britain believed that the Suez dispute should be referred to the United Nations. Then it summed up its own attitude. Had it ever approved of Nasser's behaviour in the crisis? The answer was No. Had it ever approved of Nasser's grab of the Suez Canal? The answer was No. Did the *Mirror* express a view on the use of force when the crisis first blew up? The answer was Yes. But when it came to the question of whether the *Mirror* had directly criticized Eden's handling of the crisis, the answer was 'Yes, most certainly.' It called for his resignation as Prime Minister.

And so it returned to its original advice to Eden to be prudent and not to be hustled by the gun-boat diplomats. For once, the *Mirror* called for American intervention. 'Get moving, Mr. Dulles,' it exhorted the American Secretary of State, calling on him to meet Colonel Nasser.

'This newspaper,' it said, 'has attacked Mr. Dulles' self-proclaimed policy of taking the conduct of foreign affairs to the brink of war.' But now it was Eden and not Dulles who was bringing the crisis to the brink. 'The man to start the talks—the man who can prevent war—is John Foster Dulles,' it said.

Meanwhile, King and Cudlipp had been in close contact with Gaitskell, and on September 16th the *Mirror* gave him the front page with a massive headline, 'Gaitskell Tells the Nation. What Would Labour Do About Suez?' The essence of Gaitskell's statement was that despite the fact that nobody condoned Nasser's arbitrary behaviour or his inflammatory speeches, the dispute should be settled by the United Nations.

Following its policy of presenting a balanced view, the *Mirror* a week later published an interview with Selwyn Lloyd on BBC's 'Panorama', where the questions were put to him by Hugh Cudlipp, the *Mirror*'s editorial director. The key answer by Lloyd was that Britain would go to the Security Council in good faith.

By November 2nd, the battle was on not only in Egypt but also in Parliament, where Eden, daily more ill, exhausted and nervous, was being harassed by the Opposition. Despite Aneurin Bevan's attempt to present a philosophic and political indictment of Eden, passions in the House were so roused that there were times when the speakers on both sides were inaudible.

The House met again on November 3rd from 12 till 3 p.m., in an atmosphere of passion which reduced the proceedings to a bear-garden. The developing Hungarian Revolution with its threat of Russian intervention added to the hysteria.

Gaitskell condemned what he called 'Eden's war' as an act of 'suicidal folly, whose consequences we shall regret for years.' But even at this stage, no one could be sure how far Eden intended to carry the war on. Even his own supporters were beginning to lose faith. *The Times*, all for intervention earlier in the Suez crisis, admitted 'Doubts remain whether the right course has been taken now.' The *Mirror* was unyielding, and warned Eden again:

'Whatever fleeting military successes may be achieved, the truth is this: There is *no* treaty, *no* international authority, no moral sanction for Eden's war.'

On November 4th, while Britain was bombing Egypt, Russia, as the *Mirror* put it, 'seized her chance to murder freedom in Budapest.'

The leaders of the Hungarian Revolution, who had been negotiating in Moscow, were treacherously seized and imprisoned, and Soviet troops savagely crushed the rebellion.

'The twin tragedies of Suez and Budapest mark a turning point in history, said the *Mirror*.

'Perhaps Russia would have crushed the Hungarian fight for freedom in any event. But it was touch and go.

'There was always the chance she might have been daunted by pressure from the West. There was always the chance that the moral force of the United Nations might hold her back.

'But this much is certain. Once British bombs fell on Egypt the fate of Hungary was sealed. The last chance of exerting moral pressure on Russia was lost when Eden defied the United Nations over Suez.

'Air raid warnings over Cairo gave the all clear for Russia to march on Budapest.

'How can Eden condemn Russia for defying UNO when he has already set the example?'

The troops had gone in, and the *Mirror* echoed Hugh Gaitskell's words about Eden—'he is utterly, utterly discredited in the world.' But within a few days, the decisions had been taken out of Eden's hands. By November 7th, under American and Russian pressure, the shooting had had to stop.

'Back to sanity,' said the *Mirror*. 'Thank God the shooting has stopped in Suez.

'This is a last-minute victory for the forces of decency.

'Whom shall we thank for this?

'Thank the United Nations.

'Thank the Labour Party which challenged Eden at every move.

'Thank America. President Eisenhower's warnings to Eden played a big part in bringing him to his senses.

'Thank public opinion in this country—and in the free world.

'Eden's War, which was launched to depose Nasser and seize control of the Suez Canal for Britain and France shocked world opinion.

'Only four days ago, Eden was still laying down conditions and proclaiming that his attack on Egypt would continue until he had his way.

'Last night he went back to the path of negotiation. What a calamity that he ever left it!

'This country will never forget that in this day and age Eden started a war in defiance of the United Nations, in defiance of treaty obligations, and without any moral sanction.

'But today the first thought must be this:

'Thank God there will be no more killing.'

The Anglo-French intervention had achieved neither of its main objects, which were to overthrow Nasser and to establish Anglo-French control of the Suez Canal. On the 12th November the *Mirror* called again for Eden's resignation. He had, it said:

'Divided the country more sharply than at any other time in this century.

'Split the Commonwealth. Dismayed Canada. Brought India, Pakistan and Ceylon to the verge of walking out.

'Dealt a terrible blow at the Anglo-American alliance at the very moment when unity was imperative to meet the Russian menace to Hungary.

'Angered President Eisenhower. Sent a wave of anti-British feeling throughout the United States.

'Flouted the United Nations. Put Britain in the shameful position, of the first time, of having to use the veto to block a U.N. decision.

'But above all,' it claimed, 'Eden's War has destroyed Britain's moral leadership.'

The Suez campaign ended in national humiliation. Yet when the whole thing was over, the *Mirror* didn't forget its part as a champion of the British soldier.

'Heads High,' it said on December 18th. 'The man who can hold his head high today is the British soldier—Tommy Atkins, representing the do-your-job department.

'The British Army could have wiped out the Egyptians within forty-eight hours. Everybody knows this, including Colonel Nasser and all the other Egyptians.'

It was an editorial which skilfully reflected the changing mood of the British public, which after its early moral spasm had begun to feel resentment at the apparent humiliation of British arms.

'Who feels anything but admiration for the British forces who have done their best in impossible circumstances?' asked the *Mirror*.

It was important to distinguish between governments and those whom the *Mirror* championed. The *Mirror* had fought its own Suez campaign not just on the basis of policy, but also as a cause. How was the strategy of its campaigns arrived at?

*

During the hearings by the Royal Commission on the Press on June 26th, 1961, Cecil King was asked by the chairman, Lord Shawcross, how the *Mirror* decided its policies, quoting a memorandum of evidence which referred to committees of the newspapers, periodicals, trade and technical publications.

'You say there is a committee to discuss strategy?' asked the chairman.

Cecil King replied in magisterial tones, 'There is no committee; there are only two of us—Cudlipp and myself.'

The chairman continued, 'What I really want to ask is whether on broad matters of policy you meet your editors and reach a decision on what your line is going to be?'

"Very, very occasionally," replied King.

The chairman insisted. 'You say—'Editorial policy in the case of daily and Sunday newspapers is controlled as follows. Editors carry out tactically what has been discussed and agreed by them strategically with Mr. Cecil King?'

King replied, 'I would say that on editorial policy Hugh Cudlipp and I, who have been directors together for very many years, work closely and are in general agreement on what sort of line we are going to take. I suppose I see him very nearly every day, and if anything fresh crops up we decide what we are going to do, but I very rarely see the editors. He sees the editors and the editors are responsible to him.'

At that point Cudlipp expanded King's explanation.

'It does work precisely like that,' he said. 'Mr. King and I meet frequently; we know each other's minds and the policies of our papers have been settled for very many years; we're not suddenly going to be Right Wing instead of Left Wing, or unilateralists instead of multilateralists.

'If King is away, which he is frequently because it is a large company, I have the last word. If he is there and I am doubtful, I consult him, and if we differ, and I cannot remember any occasion on which we did, he would have the last word, but I interpret this to the editors whom I see much more frequently than the chairman.

'In fact, I see them socially, professionally and in every other way, and know them all, and they know me well. The point we are demurring at really is that as far as editorial policy is concerned we do not act as a committee but as a band of people in touch with each other, and who on the whole see eye to eye with each other.'

Lord Shawcross asked for further explanation. How, for example, did the *Mirror* formulate a policy on issues like the Common Market or the death penalty? Were the editors, he wanted to know, instructed as to the line they should follow. Cudlipp welcomed the opportunity of illustrating the two instances quoted by the chairman of the Royal Commission.

'A fortnight ago,' he said, '—the Common Market is a very good example—Mr. King thought it was time we began to explain the Common Market to the British public, which I set about doing with enormous zeal, as I am greatly in favour of the Common Market. Hence it is being explained, beginning last Thursday in the *Daily Herald*, and tomorrow in the *Daily Mirror*. From then on we do not have long conferences about it, because Cecil King has some faith in my intelligence, which I hope is justified, and he leaves it to me to carry on. I enthuse the editors on this issue, and they also by a happy coincidence are in favour of the Common Market. That is how it works in practice. But I should add this, that if the policy of the papers is, shall we say pro-Common Market, and a writer like Cassandra passionately felt that the Common Market would be disastrous for this country, he would not hesitate to say so.

'When Vicky drew cartoons for us, I can't remember a single occasion on which he agreed with the policy of the paper, and Cassandra might be miles away from it, but both are given freedom of action.'

The *Mirror* campaign in favour of the Common Market began in June, 1961, after King lunched with John Beavan, then editor of the *Daily Herald*, and a Cabinet Minister.

The idea of a united Europe had been stimulated by Churchill and his son-in-law Duncan Sandys at the Hague Conference in 1948, where a number of statesmen including Spaak and Robert Schumann decided to propose to their governments the setting up of a Council of Europe. Fundamentally, it was an attempt to re-form Western Europe in the face of Russian pressure. It was a political sequel to Churchill's Fulton speech with its recognition that an Iron Curtain divided Europe.

At the first meeting of the Council of Europe at Strasbourg in 1949, the delegates fell into two schools of thought—the federalists, who were eager to surrender their sovereignty to a European Government, and the functionalists, who, though eager for European cooperation, were not disposed to give up any substantial measure of national sovereignty. In the post-war lassitude, the federalists consisted primarily of the defeated and the disillusioned. The extreme nationalism of Nazism produced a revolution in favour of a European concept. In addition, the defeated felt that by combining their resources they would have a better chance of recovery in the post-war world. Though the French, Dutch and Belgians were nominal victors, they too had endured defeat and occupation. They wanted to be linked in institutions which would transcend national frontiers, and make territorial wars and disputes over natural resources bisected by political frontiers a thing of the past.

Britain was a victorious power, and the Labour Government in the euphoria of its election victory was not disposed to surrender any measure of sovereignty which might prevent the domestic planning necessary for the fulfilment of its programme. Despite Bevin's anxiety to consolidate the power of the West, he remained deeply attached to the idea of an independent Britain planning its own destiny. Attlee was fundamentally a Little Englander who gave the justified appearance of disliking, though tolerating, foreigners. As for Morrison, who led the first delegation to Strasbourg, he characteristically was in favour of an empirical approach to questions of European unity, but only towards the end of his life did he become an enthusiast for the Common Market.

The Conservatives at Strasbourg, led by Winston Churchill and Harold Macmillan, advocated European unity, but were reluctant to define it. The Labour delegation, on the other hand, was constantly accused of 'dragging its feet,' a description which was only appropriate in the sense that it had the same reluctance to surrender British sovereignty in 1949 as the Conservative Party in power was to show in the 1950s.

The formation of the Coal and Steel Community and later of the European Atomic Energy Commission (Euratom) in the early 1950s proved that a number of European countries were prepared to advance, if necessary without Britain, towards the ideal of unity. But with the signing of the Treaty of Rome, the division in Europe was established in 1958 between those who chose to seek European cooperation through pragmatic means and the Six, who wanted to build a European Community with a Common Market, accepting the necessity of the surrender of national sovereignty which accompanied it. Harold Macmillan, though an enthusiast of European unity, declined to be hustled into joining the Common Market since

Britain's obligations towards the Commonwealth, and her pattern of trade with the Scandinavian countries in particular, hampered him.

Cecil King, with his belief in expansion and economic growth, was dedicated to the idea of the Common Market. Macmillan was his first target. The *Mirror* fired its opening shot with an attack on the government in 1961 for a conspiracy of silence, and declared that Britain must try and join.

'We're waiting, Mr. Macmillan,' it said ominously. 'Impatiently.'

On May 17th, the *Mirror* turned its attention to the Labour Party, accusing it of not giving the country a clear lead. 'Let's not have an Opposition that say Yes-No-Maybe,' it said.

Rather enjoying its jest, it described Macmillan as 'Macwonder of 1959, Macdither of 1961.'

One of Macmillan's difficulties, as the luncheon with the Cabinet Minister had made clear, was that the Cabinet was divided. In a front page headline entitled, 'Cold Feet in the Cabinet,' the *Mirror* accused him of jeopardising Britain's economic and political future because of internal Tory Party politics. The problem of the Common Market had to be explained, and for many weeks the *Mirror* presented an a analysis of 'What the Common Market Means to 52 million Britons.' On the 27th June, in a double page spread it set out arguments in terms of employment under the heading, 'You and Your Job.' After a month of egging on the Government, the *Mirror* welcomed what it called 'A Historic Announcement by Mr. Macmillan that Britain Will Try to Join the European Common Market.' Seven months later, on March 5th, 1962, when the negotiations began between Britain and the Six, the *Mirror* decided to supplement its earlier analysis with what it called 'A new *Mirror* service to readers.' It invited its readers to send their questions to a new department, 'You and the Common Market,' which would handle the readers' queries.

Sidney Jacobson was in charge of the service, and day after day answered questions like, 'Will Germany be the dominant power politically?', 'If I took a job in a Common Market country would I still have to pay British income tax and National Health contributions?', 'What about language?', and 'What about conscription?'

As the Brussels talks proceeded, the *Mirror* gave its full support to Edward Heath, then Lord Privy Seal, in his efforts to obtain British membership of the Market. It also kept up its arguments and explanations into 1962. On June 25th, it began to publish daily six successive pages of interpretation about the Common Market Six, with titles like, 'Le Miroir du Jour'. On Italy it took a somewhat more romantic view. 'It's love in the sun, with Romeo winning all the time,' it declared. When it came to Germany, the *Mirror*'s title was, 'Der Tagespiegel,' with the headline, 'Work is Secret of German Recovery Miracle.'

The *Mirror* couldn't bring itself to back the entire Macmillan government, but to Heath, commuting between Brussels and London, it gave its unqualified support.

'The *Daily Mirror*,' it said on August 1st, 1962, 'wishes Ted Heath luck in the last round-up.'

At this time it set out the press line-up both for and against the Common Market. Supporting the Market were the *Daily Herald*, *Daily Mail*, *Daily Mirror*, *Daily Sketch*, *Daily Telegraph*, *Sunday Pictorial*, *Sunday Telegraph*, *Sunday Times*, *Guardian*, *Observer*, *People* and *Times*. Against was the Beaverbrook Press. Abandoning the old Fleet Street maxim that dog doesn't eat dog, it attacked Beaverbrook for his claim that the Commonwealth was ranged alongside him in opposing the Common Market.

'Lord Beaverbrook,' it said, 'was the first and greatest of the Empire Crusaders. Since he has not the slightest intention of departing from this earth he may well be the last of the Empire Crusaders, for he has never grasped the evolution of the Commonwealth of the twentieth century.

'No one questions his sincerity. But he should know, at 83, that in a debate of this magnitude the bogus claim is a dubious ally.'

At this time King was meeting Hugh Gaitskell, the Labour leader, and looking to him for support of Labour's entry into the Market. Although both men were Wykehamists, and thus might have been expected to have a natural affinity, King, consistent and unshakeable in his intellectual convictions, had little sympathy with some of Gaitskell's ambivalent postures.

In October, Gaitskell delivered a ninety-minute speech to the Labour Party Conference at Brighton on the subject of whether Britain should enter the Common Market. In its initial enthusiasm, and before Gaitskell had spoken the *Mirror* described his speech as marking a turning-point in British history, and announced its intention to publish his long speech in full. Balancing the argument in what it called 'The Great Common Market Debate,' it decided that it would publish Macmillan's speech on the same subject at the Tory

Party Conference, so that, as it put it, 'First Gaitskell, then Macmillan—*Daily Mirror* Readers are to get the Lot.'

After publishing Gaitskell's speech, the *Mirror* gave its verdict in sorrow and some anger. On its front page it published an article, 'The Man Who Must Think Again.'

'The *Daily Mirror* is a fair newspaper,' it said. 'At any rate, it strives to be.

'It has printed every word of Mr. Hugh Gaitskell's Common Market speech so that the largest audience in the land—the *Mirror*'s 14,000,000 readers—could study it, consider it and (if they so wished) swallow it.

'Accustomed as we are to sword-swallowing on this newspaper, the *Mirror* confines its praise on this occasion strictly to Mr. Gaitskell's memorable feat as a marathon orator.

'A conference stimulant falls far short of the statesmanship Mr. Gaitskell has consistently displayed on other major issues.

'The yardstick is: what did Gaitskell set out to achieve, and what in fact did he achieve?

'His objects were:

'To unite the Labour Party;

'To appease the Left Wing;

'To consolidate his leadership;

'To manoeuvre into a position from which he could win the next Election;

'And, while achieving all this, to pronounce a solemn judgment on Britain's future in this challenging century.

'He was over-ambitious; he failed in his mission.'

The editorial ended with a threat.

'Until this concept is corrected a General Election on the Common Market issue would imperil Labour's victory.

'An Election in which Labour threatened to repudiate the Common Market legislation of the present Government would be polling-booth poison and would lose Mr. Gaitskell yet more of his friends.'

At this stage, the *Mirror* fell into a difficulty. Hostile as it was to Macmillan, it couldn't help acknowledging that the Tory Party was more active than the Labour Party in the urgency with which it wanted to join the Common Market. At the same time, it didn't want Macmillan to be identified with the achievement of having taken Britain into the Common Market when that objective could more usefully be achieved by the Labour Party, thus supplementing its otherwise far more progressive policy.

'Mr. Macmillan,' said the *Mirror*, 'would be imprudent if he thought that the whole of the British nation could be railroaded into the Common Market merely because such a success would be useful to him in the next General Election.'

But soon the hopes of the *Mirror*, Macmillan and all of the Labour Party who wished well for the Common Market, were dashed when on January 30th, 1963, General de Gaulle, as the *Mirror* put it, 'sabotaged Britain's efforts to join the European Common Market.' The *Mirror*'s prophetic comment was, 'All Over? History Will Wait!'

Cecil King remained ardent in his enthusiasm for the Common Market, and after the Brussels breakdown ensured that the issue was kept alive in the public mind. At the 1966 election, the *Mirror* was to have a second chance. History would wait. But the *Mirror* wanted it to wait as short a time as possible.

CHAPTER X

Labour's Voices

IN 1949, Hugh Cudlipp had invited Richard Crossman, M.P. for Coventry East, to write a weekly column for the *Sunday Pictorial* from which he moved in 1954 to the *Mirror*.

The élan of the Labour victory had already dwindled. Accustomed to Opposition, the Labour Left had difficulty in settling down under the conformist leadership of Attlee, Morrison and Bevin. The 1945 Keep Left movement of which Crossman was one of the leaders began to revolve around Aneurin Bevan, who inside the Government seemed to keep alive his Left-Wing fervour and fighting past.

Lord Beaverbrook, impressed by Crossman's critical posture, not least his Amendment on foreign affairs to the King's Speech in 1947, wanted him to write for the *Daily Express*. But the *Mirror* group got in first, thus beginning a collaboration which was to last for ten years.

A Wykehamist like Cecil King, with a similar family background (his father was a judge), analytical, iconoclastic, and challenging received ideas, Crossman was a Bevanite on a paper which gave general support to the established leadership. Earlier, he had joined John Strachey in complaining that the Labour Party lacked books—that is to say, a theoretical basis for its policies. In default of books, Crossman gave the Party his column.

He was not, of course, a beginner in public affairs. As a leading figure in Psychological Warfare at SHAEF, he had studied and applied the art of persuasion. As a don at New College and a WEA lecturer, he had already proved his interest in teaching and popularizing. His chief asset was energy, combined with a talent for exposition; what he lacked, as many of his colleagues felt, was political tact. 'He is the cow,' a lobby correspondent said, 'who kicks over the pail of milk after filling it.'

Hitherto, Crossman's journalistic experience had been limited to the assistant editorship of the *New Statesman*. Now he had to find a language suited not to a semi-intellectual weekly but to a popular paper, often read hurriedly in a tea-break in factories. As a teacher used to simplification, Crossman quickly found the appropriate style—short paragraphs and simple questions followed by blunt answers. It was the *Mirror* style.

Among the Labour rank and file, Crossman's column was widely read; it certainly contributed to his annual re-election to the Labour Party Executive. It provided basic information and ready-made thinking. To the Left, but not too far—controversial, but not too bitter—intellectual, but not remote—Crossman was a theorist of a British reforming movement, classless and egalitarian yet not indifferent to its international affiliations, whuch was to become the basis of the Labour Government in 1964.

*

In 1945, the Labour Party was still bound to its Socialist ideology. 'This is D-day for the New Britain,' said Major John Freeman, splendid in uniform as he moved the Motion on the Address at the opening of the first post-war Parliament. The new Labour M.P.s, many of them still in uniform themselves, spilled over on to the benches opposite, submerging the Liberal remnant. George Griffiths, an elderly coal-miner Member, rose to his feet singing the Red Flag, and all the Government supporters joined in the tune, though it was noticeable that many of the new Members didn't know the words. There had, in fact, been a substantial influx of M.P.s on the Labour side whose socialism meant a desire for social change, and who, after being adopted in haste for some apparently hopeless seat, had been swept into Parliament by the great Labour tide.

Attlee gave them a special welcome. The new middleclass Members expressed for him the way in which the Labour Party was being transformed from a working-class party into a national party. Under his patronage, men like David Rees-Williams, Aidan Crawley, Evelyn King, Ivor Bulwer-Thomas and Hartley Shawcross rapidly achieved office in the Party they were shortly to renounce.

From the pinnacle of victory, the prospect before the Labour Government glittered bravely. The majority was irresistible. 'We are the masters now,' said Hartley Shawcross. He meant it, and he was right. The Welfare State was about to be translated from White Papers into legislation. The centres of power, like coal and transport, were to be nationalized. Anything in the Party programme that could be done by legislation would be done.

But there were matters that lay beyond legislation, chief among them the exhaustion of war from which Britain could recover only by aid and determination. After the stress of war where the enemy could be seen, the effort needed for peace against intangible enemies like deficits in the balance of payments was almost too strenuous. Cripps, offering a prescription of austerity to the nation, was as popular as a doctor prescribing a diet for a gourmet recovering from an operation. At the end of 1945, Britain wanted a spree; instead, it was offered a fast.

A host of post-war problems abroad burdened the Government. What should be done about Germany, India, Russia, Palestine? The country wanted to rest, but here were dangers which made it seem as if, even in Britain's foreign relations, its exertions would still have to continue.

The Tories for their part, unaccustomed to what they felt was the indignity of Opposition and unwilling to accept that the Labour Government was anything but an accidental interruption in the authority which belonged to them by natural right, attacked the Labour leaders both inside and outside of Parliament. The Tory press was particularly vindictive, constantly searching for sins and peccadilloes, especially those which might convict Labour Ministers of evading their own post-war regulations and restrictions. Attlee was determined that the Labour Government should be fit to join the Establishment, and in the career which was eventually to bring him the Garter he gave no mercy to those who fell below his standards. In 1948, at the time of the Lynskey Tribunal, John Belcher, an industrious and generally worthy Junior Minister, condemned for accepting some petty favours from Sidney Stanley, the contact man, appealed for grace. He got none. Sacked from his Ministry, he left Parliament, returned to his old job as a railway clerk and served honourably till his death in 1964.

Out of the Attlee Establishment with its conformist background sprang the defectors and the revisionists. But at the same time, the grass-roots tradition of the Left persisted, and later gave the Wilson Government its fundamental strength.

The Labour campaign of 1945 had been fought with the manifesto, 'Let's Face the Future,' a slogan which capitalized the energies and hopes of the generation of the 1930s. But the dropsical majority of

1945 induced a certain flabbiness. Herbert Morrison as Lord President was to spend a lot of his time devising forms of employment, chiefly in unheeded committee work, for his back benchers. As for the leadership, it was more concerned with retrospect than with facing the future. Its legislative programme of nationalization, the centre of its socialist heritage, was carried forward by the momentum of the past. So with its social legislation. The Welfare State was the legacy of the Beveridge Report. All these were, nonetheless, considerable achievements which transformed the general picture of Britain. Poverty in its extreme form was substantially reduced. The poor had opportunities of good health, once denied to them. Full employment became a national policy, and the many under-privileged were given their rights. New educational opportunities at the universities for the children of the working class created a twilight class of young men and women who, turning their backs on working class standards, found themselves *déclassés* in the new society and turned politically to the Right.

Relying on its fundamental and traditional thinking, the Labour Party between 1945 and 1950 failed to cater for the aspirations of an emergent youth to which the struggles and hardships of their fathers were beginning to be ancestral memories. Attlee, a colourless chairman, failed to contribute any new ideas to the Party's thinking after 1945. Fundamentally conservative in his outlook, he ignored the technocratic revolution which had been germinating during the war. In France, Jean Monnet had foreseen it, and the post-war French Governments, though not socialist, had gone ahead with their own brand of planning, allied to technological innovation, which was the beginning of France's post-war recovery. In Britain, on the other hand, the Labour leadership was tied to a self-satisfied preoccupation with economic Malthusianism of which Cripps was the chief exponent. After its first dynamic years, the Labour Government's theme was consolidation—another word for immobility.

In foreign affairs, too, Britain, victorious and at the apogee of its prestige, could have led Europe as well as the Commonwealth. But alternately introspective and retrospective, the Government approached its post-war problems with a mixture of apprehension and defiance. Attlee, who never quite got over the shock of finding himself Prime Minister, could smother opposition with his vast majority. As Disraeli said, 'A majority is the best repartee.' What he couldn't control was the rising public aversion from his Government's style.

The Labour Government represented in his person was drab. Cripps was respected by the nation but he bored it. Bevin was admired, even loved, but his massive incoherence failed to excite. Those who gave colour to the Party—men like Bevan and Foot—represented a Party faction and were treated as such by the hierarchy.

After a brief period of dejection, the Tory Party was beginning to make a comeback. Churchill at the first session of Parliament after 1945 said:

'A friend of mine, an officer, was in Zagreb when the results of the General Election came in. An old lady said to him, "Poor Mr. Churchill! I suppose now he will be shot." My friend was able to reassure her. He said the sentence might be mitigated to one of the various forms of hard labour which are always open to His Majesty's subjects.'

Yet it wasn't Churchill but Lord Woolton together with the Beaverbrook press who restored the Tory Party's fortunes. Lord Woolton recognized the axiom that the future always belongs to youth, and that youth is interested in fun. It was the principle which had given the *Mirror* its influence in the late 1930s and early '40s. Now it battled on in favour of youth, though shackled by its defence of Labour's unpopular attitudes. Woolton's Young Conservatives represented a mood rather than a policy. The butts of their satire were Strachey's groundnuts, Summerskill's margarine and Shinwell's power cuts. They weren't concerned with the origin of the heavy burden of post-war rehabilitation, the 'demob,' housing, the balance of payments, the American debt and food shortages. All they knew was that these problems existed under a Labour Government.

What the nation wanted between 1945 and 1950 was gaiety, relaxation, colour and glamour. The Beaverbrook press with great skill kept needling the Labour Party in its sore places. It emphasized grievances, aggravated resentment and laid hands in blessing on the Housewives' League, whose members constantly wagged their shopping baskets in the Government's face.

With public support dwindling more rapidly than the gold reserves, Attlee called a General Election for February 23rd, 1950.

From 1945 to 1950 the *Mirror* had remained optimistically faithful to the Labour Government. The obvious defections from the Labour Party, especially among the apolitical middle-classes who in 1945 had for the first time voted Labour, left the *Mirror* unmoved, and as the Election approached the paper became increasingly belligerent.

It gave prominence to a speech by Harold Wilson, then President of the Board of Trade, at Northwich, Cheshire, in which he said, 'What guarantee is there that if by some mischance the Tories were returned to power they would not produce some crisis, real or imaginary, as a result of which the social services would fall a victim?'

During the Election month, the *Mirror* presented the issues with a great appearance of objectivity, although on balance it weighted the case against the Tories. When Churchill promised to abolish petrol rationing, the *Mirror* called it contemptuously 'a stunt.' Memories of pre-war unemployment were still vivid enough among most working people for the *Mirror* to publish a full-page spread with pictures contrasting the dole queues of the thirties with the full employment of 1950. A picture of hungry children in the 1920s and well-fed infants in a day nursery underlined the message. It gave equal opportunity to the spokesmen of the three major parties to state their cases and added a pictorial roundup of views in which, as with Dr. Johnson's reporting of Parliament, the *Mirror* saw to it that their opponents had the worst of it.

But the climax of the *Mirror*'s campaign on behalf of the Labour Party came on February 21st in a leading article entitled 'Where We Stand.' Unlike 1945 when the paper merely supported the Labour Party by implication, it now backed the Labour Party unequivocally.

'The *Daily Mirror*,' it said, 'supports the Labour Party at the General Election. We have made this decision after full and careful consideration of the claims of all the parties. This has convinced us that the Labour Party's planning for recovery is needed for the safety of Britain as a whole.

'This is a critical moment in our history and the world's. It is not a time for starting to dither and go backwards; we must go forward determined to make secure the future of our great nation.

'Economic difficulties are bound to be ahead. We believe that the Labour Party is the only one which can deal with them.

'We support the Labour Party because it has kept its promises and earned our trust. Its policy has been one of fairness and humanity. We believe it is the only policy that can work. We must go forward with the people because in these days it is absolutely impossible to go forward without them.'

The following day, in a double spread, it urged the public to vote. The implication of it all was that in the interests of jobs, homes, families and country, the electorate should vote Labour.

The result of the Election was that Labour had a majority of five. No one can doubt but that the final heave of the *Mirror* in the last days of the campaign when support for Labour was running away like sand in an hour-glass made the difference between victory and defeat. The great majority of 1945 had disappeared in a wave of disillusion, cynicism and unfulfilled hopes. Churchill once said that the people voted not for benefits received but for benefits yet to come. So it was in 1950, when despite the achievements of the Labour Government in building the Welfare State, the electorate, looking for brightness, excitement and freedom from controls, turned its back on Labour's plans and intentions. Whatever the achievements of the Labour Government, their presentation had been grey; instead of offering the country the joy of a revolution, Attlee had merely presented it with what seemed a dismal series of restrictions. The *Mirror* itself had been decisive in winning the Election, but the public mood and the *Mirror*'s purpose had begun to separate.

For just over eighteen months the new Government struggled along, harried and harassed by the Tory Opposition, and keeping itself alive only at the cost of the health of its ageing Members, some of whose lives were undoubtedly shortened by the hardships of late nights and the arduousness of divisions which saw the sad progress through the Lobbies of the sick and the dying. By September 1951, it was clear that a General Election would have to take place in order to create a stable Government.

*

Once again the *Mirror* plunged to the aid of the Labour Party. But this time its impetus went ahead of its prudence. Eight months before the Election when Attlee visited America to discuss the atom bomb, the *Mirror* had asked, 'Whose finger do you want on the trigger when the world situation is so delicate?' The *Mirror* was much taken with this provocative question. Journalistically it was a compelling one, since every reader identified himself with the situation in which he was either at the receiving or the delivering end of a bullet. It created anxieties to which the least imaginative person could not fail to respond. As the Election approached, the *Mirror* reverted to the question in an editorial entitled 'Whose Finger?'

'Mr. Churchill,' it said, 'has referred at Loughton, Essex, to our much-quoted question, "Whose finger do you want on the trigger?"

'It is altogether too convenient for Conservative speakers to pretend that what they have to answer is a crude charge that they are warmongers. There are considerations of the utmost seriousness that should not escape attention.

'We do not of course imagine that anyone would want to pull the trigger, but in spite of our esteem for Mr. Churchill we must point out that there are forces at work in the world which he dangerously misunderstands. His attitude over India alone made this startlingly clear. If his finger had then been on the trigger the result would have been national suicide. There is no room to doubt that confidence would be so shaken by the return of Mr. Churchill to leadership of Britain that it would imperil the only links that exist between Asia and the Western world.

'Mr. Churchill suggested that we need not worry—because only Russia or America was in a position to pull the trigger. But we do worry, precisely because he can make such statements. They make our hair stand on end. The Tory leader's actual words were these:

' "It will not be a British finger that will pull the trigger of a third world war. It may be a Russian finger or an American finger, or a United Nations Organization finger, but it cannot be a British finger. Although we should certainly be involved in a struggle between the Soviet Empire and the free world, the control and decision and the timing of that terrible event would not rest with us." '

Churchill was deeply disturbed by what he regarded as an innuendo about his own concern for peace. But the *Mirror* kept hammering away with the question, 'Whose Finger on the Trigger?' On October 23rd it carried eight letters under that heading, all with the implication that the country would be safer with Labour's finger on the atomic trigger. The following day, it again repeated the slogan, 'Whose Finger on the Trigger?' with a selection of photographs of people interviewed, all of whom indicated that they would vote for Attlee's finger on the trigger.

On Election Day, the *Mirror* came out with an alarming cartoon of a menacing pistol with trigger cocked, and the headline, 'Today Your Finger is on the Trigger', with a caption 'Vote for the Party you can really trust. The *Daily Mirror* believes that Party is Labour.'

But this time the *Mirror* was unable to move the electorate from its hostility to the Labour Party which had been gradually hardening during the year. The Tories won the Election by sixteen seats. The *Mirror*, like the Labour Party was defeated. And there was more to come. Churchill took the view that the slogan, 'Whose Finger on the

Trigger?' implied that he himself was a warmonger. He issued a writ against the *Mirror* for libel. The *Mirror* resisted. The question was far too general to be libellous. Churchill returned to the attack, changing his ground. A fortnight earlier, the *Mirror* had published an off-the-record and unattributable statement by Robert Schumann, the French Foreign Minister, that Churchill had advocated a preventive war against Russia. Eventually, with Sir Hartley Shawcross briefed by the *Mirror* for its defence, the paper, unable to call Schumann as a witness, settled the matter out of court. It paid the new Prime Minister his costs and a £1,500 contribution to the Church Army Charitable Homes for Elderly People.

Churchill had reason to be pleased. He had won the Election, rebutted an attack, and opened up a new vista which was to lead to thirteen years of Conservative rule endorsed by the Elections of 1955 and 1959.

II

The chief disadvantage of the Labour Government in its six years of rule was a lack of self-criticism. Despite its bloated majority, it treated dissent as disloyalty. The result was that it remained as insensitive to legitimate criticism as it was inured to many of the unfair attacks of which it had been the subject in the Tory press. On the whole, though, Attlee was less amenable to criticism inside the Labour Party than he was to criticism from outside.

In the 1950's, Crossman's chief disadvantage was a tendency to inconvenient criticism. This earned him the reputation in trade union circles close to Ernie Bevin of being an intellectual—as one critic said, 'He'd rather hear a lecture on Paradise than actually go there.' It was a misjudgment. Crossman was by inclination, and to some extent by experience, a man of action interested in the practice of power. He refused—and this was a bold attitude in the climate of the Parliamentary Labour Party in the 1950s—to accept the idea that a man who had once used a pick-axe was necessarily better than a man who had only used his brains.

And so, on July 5th, 1957, he wrote a column with the title, 'The Unions Must Send Better Men to Parliament.' Sir Tom Williamson, chairman of the T.U.C., had made a speech calling for more trade union M.P.s. The origin of the article was a row which had broken out over the choice of a Swansea lawyer, John Morris, as the candidate for the safe bye-election seat at Aberavon in preference to a steelworker.

Crossman wrote in his column that a proper balance should be struck between the industrial (trade union) and political (intellectual) Wings of the Labour Party. Then he added a caveat.

'It is not merely the number of trade union candidates adopted by constituency that has declined, but their quality as well.

'It is this decline in quality that is gravely affecting the Parliamentary Labour Party.

'Of the ninety-seven sponsored trade union M.P.s in Parliament today, only four—Mr. James Griffiths (Miners), Mr. Aneurin Bevan (Miners), Mr. George Brown (Transport Workers) and Mr. Alfred Robens (Shopworkers)—suggest themselves for key jobs.

'In contrast, Mr. Attlee in 1945 was able to allot eight important ministries to sponsored trade unionists. Here is the list:

'Ernest Bevin at the Foreign Office (Transport Workers); James Griffiths at National Insurance (Miners); Tom Williamson at Agriculture (Miners); Aneurin Bevan at Health (Miners); John Lawson at the War Office (Miners); Ben Smith at Food (Transport Workers); George Isaacs at Labour (Printers); Ellen Wilkinson at the Ministry of Education (Shop Workers).

'The truth is that the trade unions are no longer sending even their second best men into politics. They are desperately short of talent to man the key positions in the unions.'

These were deadly words which caused an unrestrained fury in the Parliamentary Party, especially in the Tea-Room where the trade unionists in the afternoons would reflectively puff their pipes, and weigh up opinions and men. Some of them lacked formal education, but all of them, self-taught like Aneurin Bevan himself, had had long experience of work, committees and people.

Among them, Bill Blyton, a Durham miner, now Lord Blyton, and Charles Pannell, a Cockney extrovert, later Minister of Works and a close adherent of Gaitskell, were specially indignant at Crossman's statement.

On Wednesday morning after the usual Party meeting, Crossman received a message from George Brown, Chairman of the Trade Union Group, asking him to meet its executive. They met in the Tea-Room—Brown, Crossman, a Whip (Ernest Popplewell), of the N.U.R., and one other. The executive asked for an apology for the slur on their competence. Four out of ninety-seven, indeed! They wanted an apology in print, and Crossman after some discussion agreed, subject to an appropriate formula.

The next day the *Daily Herald*, followed at the week-end by the *Sunday Express*, published a story that the executive of the Trade Union Group had exacted an apology from Crossman, who had then tried to explain himself away in the *Mirror*.

The result of the Trade Union Group meeting that followed was a decision to report Crossman to the Executive, one of the Labour Party's severest forms of reprimand. More than that, at the Durham Miners' Gala Bill Blyton fiercely denounced Crossman in person.

At this period the Tory press was looking for every chance to deepen the fratricidal skirmishes in the Labour Party between Bevanites and others. The mischief between Crossman and the Trade Union Group delighted them. They didn't have to look very hard for details because a steady flow of leaks from the Group and the National Executive brought them news from the front.

At the meeting of the National Executive, according to press reports, there was a move by Miss Margaret Herbison who was in the chair to postpone the business of censuring Crossman in the light of a procedural wrangle between Bevan and Gaitskell as to whether the letter from the Trade Union Group should be 'received.' But Crossman moved that it should be taken under 'any other business'. Eventually the National Executive resolved the matter by taking note of the Trade Union Group's letter and deprecating a continuation of the dispute. The battle was over, but its effect was a shot across the bows of the trade unions, reminding them of their responsibilities, and a counter-shot across the bows of the intellectuals, reminding them where they draw their strength.

The Trade Union Group of the Parliamentary Labour Party is, indeed, a body of men fiercely attached to the ethical basis of socialism. As representatives of the founding fathers of the British Labour Party, they feel themselves to be the keepers of the flame, possessed of a *gravitas* lacking in some volatile intellectuals, and spurning their pretensions. Before the war, Aneurin Bevan's chief defect in Ernest Bevin's eyes was his flirtation with the Beaverbrook champagne circuit. Journalism was one of the dangerous occupations for a Socialist, since he was exposed to the temptation of capitalist employers and the corruption of a capitalist press.

*

Crossman was the first of the journalist-M.P.s to feel the hot breath of the Group's censure. It was felt again when in 1962 George Brown was asked by one of his colleagues at a meeting of the Trade Union Group about the truth of a report in the *Daily Express* that he had been employed by the *Mirror* as an industrial and trade union adviser for a number of years. Many of those present expected an instant denial. Although the article was headed 'Journalist,' Brown had never engaged professionally in journalism except to write occasional pieces as many Members do.

Brown replied simply that the report was true. He had, in fact, been employed by the *Mirror* in those capacities with a small retainer fee since 1953. There were some grumbles from those present, but the matter would have ended there were it not for the fact that some Members asked whether it was appropriate for Brown, while Deputy Leader of the Parliamentary Labour Party, to serve a paper whose interests might be in conflict with the Party's particular policy. In particular, Brown's critics referred to the *Mirror*'s holdings in commercial television, which Socialists like Christopher Mayhew wanted to reform. The mutterings grew till the point where Gaitskell as Leader of the Party and Cecil King as chairman of the company had to take notice of the innuendoes which were circulating.

Hugh Cudlipp decided that the *Mirror* should set out its own case and on 31st July, 1962, wrote the following article:

'*The Daily Mirror and Independent Television*

There have been rumours and hostile innuendoes about the *Daily Mirror*'s interests in commercial television, its relations with the Labour Party and in particular with Mr. George Brown, that Party's Deputy Leader.

This statement sets out THE FACTS:

1. The *Daily Mirror* and the *Sunday Pictorial* have interests in the commercial TV programme company, Associated TeleVision Ltd., and two of its directors serve on the board of that company.

This information has been public knowledge since 1956 and has been stated in the *Daily Mirror*.

2. In its issue of July 29 the *Sunday Telegraph* published these paragraphs in a news story on page one:

"Mr. Mayhew wants the Labour Party to come out in favour of the Pilkington Committee's proposals to reform commercial television. He is particularly keen on the proposal to take control of advertising and programme planning out of the hands of the companies and give it to the Independent Television Authority.

"The Shadow Cabinet is determined to sit on the fence over this and wait and see what the Government's proposals are. They are clearly afraid of incurring unpopularity with commercial television viewers.

"But many Socialists suspect there is another reason: pressure from the *Mirror* group of newspapers which has a big stake in commercial television.

"Apart from the *Daily Mirror* the *Mirror* group owns the other main Left-Wing national newspapers, the *Daily Herald* and the *Sunday Pictorial.*

"It is thought that Mr. Gaitskell and his colleagues are reluctant to risk antagonising their principal Press supporters by coming out in favour of a move that would hit the *Mirror* group profits."

THE FACTS:

On no single occasion has any representative of the *Daily Mirror* group exerted pressure, or endeavoured to exert pressure, or contemplated exerting pressure on any member of the Labour Party National Executive in relation to the Pilkington Report—or on any other topic of national significance.

3. The *Daily Express* yesterday published the following paragraph:

Journalist

The *Daily Express* understands that Mr. George Brown, Deputy Leader of the Labour Party, has been industrial adviser to the *Daily Mirror* for many years past.

THE FACTS

Correct. Mr. Brown has been an industrial and trade union adviser to this newspaper since 1953—long before he was appointed Deputy Leader.

The *Daily Mirror* takes advice from many sources and in many spheres of public interest.

So does every intelligent newspaper.

So should the *Daily Express.* It would be a more reliable newspaper if it did.

Two subjects on which the *Daily Express* urgently needs advice—and informed advice—are the Common Market and Independent Television.

4. Commenting on the *Daily Mirror*'s criticisms of the Pilkington

Report in the *New Statesman* of July 6, Francis Williams wrote:

"... the *Mirror* found no space to mention, either in its two-page leader or its double-page report, the fact that it and its associates hold between them 26 per cent of the voting shares in Associated TeleVision. ... An odd omission, surely."

THE FACTS:

Rubbish, Baron Williams.

The *Mirror*'s two-page leader emphatically states:

'Sir Robert Renwick, Bt., K.B.E., Chairman of Associated TeleVision Ltd., IN WHICH THE *MIRROR* GROUP OF NEWSPAPERS IS INTERESTED. . . .'

The *New Statesman* corrected the error in its following issue.

The *Daily Mirror* will be happy to clear up any future rumours (malicious or otherwise), innuendoes (hostile or mischievous), and will be particularly happy to answer downright lies.

Television writers who work for the *Mirror*—and its associated newspapers and magazines—are, of course, completely free to criticize or praise television programmes regardless of their source and entirely in accordance with their personal views.'

*

This retort direct was never published. On the same day, King, Brown and Gaitskell lunched together in the chairman's office and considered the tactics of the matter. Brown was in favour of publishing the article as it stood. Gaitskell and King were, wisely as events proved at the time, against it. Their reasons were that to offer a defence of one's integrity when it should never have been called in question would merely enlarge the opportunities of unjustified attack. 'Let it die a natural death,' Gaitskell argued. The issue soon faded from discussion.

But an interesting point had been raised. To what extent is a newspaper justified in appointing M.P.s who are not professional journalists to act as political or industrial advisers? At what point does patronage become inadmissible? They were questions which could be extended into the whole field of the consultative function of M.P.s to private commercial interests. The answer to these questions remains the common-sense one. As in the relations between George Brown and the *Mirror*, the deciding factor must be the integrity of the participants. In this, neither the *Mirror* nor Brown had anything to conceal. Brown's own potential dilemma as an adviser to the *Mirror* was never more manifest than at the beginning of 1961

VISITING THE MIRROR: (LEFT TO RIGHT) RT. HON. HAROLD WILSON, M.P., CECIL KING, MR. J. STONE (FATHER OF THE 'CHAPEL'), HUGH CUDLIPP

SYDNEY JACOBSON, FORMER POLITICAL EDITOR OF THE MIRROR, AND JACK NENER, EDITOR FROM 1953–1961

HUGH CUDLIPP, CHAIRMAN OF DAILY MIRROR NEWSPAPERS, RT. HON. HAROLD WILSON, LEADER OF THE OPPOSITION, AND SIR ALEC DOUGLAS HOME, THEN PRIME MINISTER, AT THE NEWSPAPER FUND'S CENTENARY DINNER, 1964

when the *Mirror* made its first offer to take over Odhams against strong competition from Roy Thomson, who was particularly anxious to get hold of a Fleet Street daily in the form of the *Daily Herald*, a newspaper with a splendid Socialist tradition and a long history of financial failure. John Beavan, then its editor, was just celebrating the paper's fiftieth birthday with the words, 'The *Daily Herald* is turning a dangerous corner.' An agreement for a merger between Thomson and Odhams offered attractive prospects.

'This is a marriage of convenience,' said Thomson on television, 'a truly 50–50 partnership, an equally divided board and no chairman's casting vote.'

Cecil King, who a week earlier had begun negotiations with Sir Christopher Chancellor, then general manager of Reuters and chairman of Odhams board, for a *Mirror* merger with Odhams, was piqued by this irruption by Thomson into his deal, and set about thwarting him. He promptly put in a counter-bid which the *Mirror*'s city editor, Derek Dale, summed up:

'The terms of the *Mirror* offer are more favourable to shareholders in Odhams than the proposed deal with Thomson. The *Mirror* group is offering nine new Ordinary shares for every two in the Odhams company. At last night's closing price of 12*s*. 3*d*. for *Mirror* shares on the Stock Exchange the offer values each Odhams share at 55*s*. 1½*d*. This compares with a price for Odhams shares of 40*s*. on Wednesday evening after the deal with the Thomson interests was announced.

'In a statement issued last night the *Mirror* board said it is convinced that a merger with Odhams outweighs any possible advantages of the proposed link with Thomson. The key to the deal is the big saving in expenses which the merger will effect on the magazine sides—where the two groups overlap. The *Mirror* believes the savings would be of benefit to both companies.

'Even if the proposed merger with the Thomson interests goes through, it is still the *Mirror*'s intention to go through with the bid. Except that it would then sell off the Thomson interests—including the stake in the Scottish Television Group.

'The *Mirror* board also announced last night its intention to give full voting rights to all the Company's Ordinary shares. In future it will be one Ordinary share one vote. This step will be very popular in the City where recently there has been growing criticism of the non-voting shares.'

But what interested the Labour Movement was the future of the

Daily Herald, its ewe-lamb and mascot. Not everyone read the *Herald*; it was bought out of loyalty; but that it should disappear was inconceivable. The *Mirror*, therefore, gave this assurance:

'1. The Board of the *Daily Mirror* recognizes that the *Daily Herald* plays an important political role in the life of the country. Nothing in the offer should be construed as implying that the *Daily Herald* will be any less free to press the Labour view than it is at present.

2. All possible steps will be taken to make the future of the *Daily Herald* more secure and ensure its continuance and development.

3. The *Daily Herald* will remain in solid support of the Labour Party as a serious political journal.'

The *Mirror*'s bid was financially a strong one. Politically, the *Daily Worker* summed it up by saying, 'Choosing between King and Thomson is like choosing between prussic acid and arsenic.'

King, meanwhile, was playing it cool. In a letter to Chancellor dated January 27th, he said, 'In view of the great attraction to your Ordinary stockholders of our offer, I assume that the proposed merger with Thomson Newspapers will not now proceed.'

With the *Mirror*'s hat now tossed into the ring, Cecil King had to take on four groups of opponents—the Labour politicians who were worried about the *Herald*, the Liberals anxious about monopolies in the newspaper industry, the newspaper men anxious about their jobs, and N. M. Rothschild's, the bankers acting for Odhams.

The complicating factor on the political front was that the T.U.C owned 49 per cent of the *Herald*'s shares. Few Socialists could view with equanimity the idea of the *Herald* falling into the hands of Roy Thomson, whose political neutrality was markedly Tory despite the fact that he had often described his journalistic function as making money. In Parliament, Sir Leslie Plummer gave the first alarm. Thomson, he said, was a Tory. If the *Herald* didn't make a profit, Thomson would close it down.

On Saturday, January 28th, a key luncheon took place at the Garrick with many of the cast assembled—Hugh Gaitskell, George Brown, Roy Thomson, Sir Christopher Chancellor, Charles Shard and H. L. Gibson, joint managing directors of Odhams, John Beavan, Stuart Campbell, the editor of *The People*, and George Woodcock of the T.U.C.

Woodcock said little at the luncheon; the T.U.C. had yet to know Thomson's conditions for keeping the *Herald* going.

Between Gaitskell and Brown there was a difference of sympathy. Gaitskell, though faithfully backed by the *Mirror* during the battles with Aneurin Bevan, was, on the whole, averse to the *Mirror* deal. Brown, on the other hand, was disinclined to sell the *Herald* to a Tory whom he had met for the first time, whereas, of course, he had been closely connected with the *Mirror* since 1953 and had faith in its radical trend.

Stuart Campbell had been editor of the *Sunday Pictorial* when Cudlipp was in the forces, and had left the group after a disagreement with Cecil King. At the luncheon, he expressed himself in tough terms against the deal. A fortnight later, he reinforced his views with a pungent editorial, 'About the grab for Odhams Press.'

'Fifteen thousand shareholders,' he said, 'are being asked today to sell *The People*—and everything else published by Odhams Press—to a great publishing combine, the *Daily Mirror*. . . . Now why? Not I assure you because the *Mirror* covets the success of *The People* or wants to run the *Daily Herald*, now the only popular radical daily newspaper left in Britain. Because if indeed the *Daily Mirror* does induce the Odhams shareholders to accept its offer it has announced that it will try to sell both papers. To sell them to anyone, just as a grocer sells a packet of tea across the counter to make a profit.

'What on earth then has caused this giant to launch its sudden takeover offer? I will tell you. It is a simple case of a concern that failed in one field setting out on a plundering raid on another firm that has succeeded in it.

'. . . Defeat was something the *Daily Mirror* could not tolerate. It decided to hit back—by resorting to power capitalism of the most naked kind.

'. . . This act of piracy should fail because . . . it will cause heartbreak to Odhams' 14,000 workers, many of whom have given their lives to the business and all of whom through their unions have protested against it—and *Mirror* workers joined in the protest.

'. . . I have the feeling that those 15,000 shareholders . . . will see us through this crisis. By throwing away the piece of paper that invites them to sell out to the monopoly tycoons.

'This act of piracy should fail, because it will not give shareholders the windfall some people imagine. . . . We hate the idea of this great newspaper being sold over our heads like an old car in a junk yard.'

That was, indeed, the feeling among many journalists and politicians. Brown and Gaitskell, on the other hand, wanted less emotion and more detailed probing. They issued a statement to the Press Association after the Garrick luncheon, calling for 'an immediate enquiry into the whole situation.' In the meantime Cudlipp had written to Gaitskell and King to Woodcock repeating their assurances about the *Daily Herald*.

In the House of Commons itself, the respective supporters of the *Mirror*'s bid and the Thomson-Odhams merger had begun to lobby. The chief anxiety of the *Mirror*'s opponents was about monopoly and the danger of the *Herald* being extinguished. In face of this rising criticism, Cudlipp wrote an article signed by King as chairman of the company, which read:

'What will be the position and future of the *Daily Herald* as the Labour newspaper if the *Daily Mirror* group gains control? Parliament and the public are entitled to know the answer directly from me as Chairman of the *Daily Mirror* board.

'The *Daily Mirror* has been for many years an independent newspaper of the Left. It has supported the Labour Party in every General Election since 1945. The *Daily Herald* has an even closer relationship with the Labour cause. Forty-nine per cent of the shares in the *Daily Herald* (1929) Ltd., are owned by the Trades Union Congress. It is, in a special sense, Labour's official newspaper and must remain so. But the *Daily Herald*, losing a tremendous sum of money every year, is in danger.

'So that no misapprehension might wrongly arise, the Board of the *Daily Mirror* today issues this public pledge.

'Our objective—as already stated—is solely to secure the advantages which should accrue from closer cooperation between the two groups' respective magazine interests. If as the final outcome of the present situation, the *Mirror* company also finds itself in control of the *Daily Herald*, the future of that newspaper as a separate entity will be fought for with the utmost energy.

'The leaders of the Labour Party and of the T.U.C. will be consulted. Indeed, letters expressing our desire for consultations were despatched on Saturday.

'It is also our desire that Mr. John Beavan, who has done so much to improve the *Herald* will continue his work as Editor.

'The *Daily Herald*, evolving its new personality, is not a competitor of the *Mirror*. We have never in the past contemplated an amalgamation between the two newspapers, and are not contemplating an amalgamation now.

'The Board of the *Daily Mirror* group announces that no amalgamation of the *Daily Herald* and *Daily Mirror* will ever take place during the period of the *Mirror* group's control of Odhams.

'It is my belief that the *Daily Herald* will be in a stronger position to fight for its continuance and development as a unit of a larger group with increased resources.'

This explanation was all the more necessary because a rumour had become widespread that the *Mirror* had only decided to back the Labour Party in the General Election of 1959 (where it was trounced) by a majority of one director's vote. This was untrue. But it influenced Labour opinion in the House.

On January 30th, King and Cudlipp met Gaitskell and George Brown in Gaitskell's room at the House of Commons. Gaitskell was in one of the stubborn moods which overcame him when he had a conviction of rectitude. Cudlipp put the familiar arguments that the *Mirror* was a paper of the Left, that King had proved his loyalty to radical ideas while Thomson was clearly a Tory. Gaitskell, on the other hand, kept reverting to the improvements in the *Herald* under Chancellor's sponsorship; there was also a long-term plan for the paper which offered good prospects. King, himself, was only willing to look two years ahead in his plans for the *Herald*.

This did nothing to cheer Gaitskell. Nearly a year later he summed up his views for Cudlipp's book, *At Your Peril*, in these words:

'Odhams had loyally supported the *Daily Herald* for a great many years and lost a substantial amount of money in the process. They therefore seemed to me to deserve the loyalty of the Party in return; moreover Sir Christopher Chancellor, in particular, had brought about a remarkable improvement in the *Daily Herald* in a very short time. Things were going well, far-reaching assurances had been given and there seemed to me no advantage in disturbing these developments. Quite independently of the particular case, many members of the Party, including myself, disliked the further concentration of the national daily press which the take-over bid involved. To this must be added the point that at first all that Mr. King was prepared to offer so far as the *Herald* was concerned was a two-year guarantee (of existence). It was much less satisfactory than the promise that Odhams had given a little time before. My anxieties were increased by the impression which had been created that the chairman of the *Mirror* board was not very enthusiastic about taking over the *Daily Herald* and would have been glad, had an opportunity arisen, to have got rid of it. At the same time, let me firmly place on record that in the event these anxieties were not justified, largely owing to the guarantee subsequently given to the T.U.C.'

Cudlipp saw that with Gaitskell's pull, the tide was beginning to flow against the *Mirror*. He therefore proposed to the Board—and his idea was accepted—that the *Mirror* would run the *Herald* for a minimum of seven years. This was psychologically the turning-point in the struggle. The Labour Movement felt that it had security of tenure in the *Herald*—though later events were to prove otherwise. Cousins and Woodcock were both persuaded that King was a better bet than Thomson.

In the House of Commons the Prime Minister, Harold Macmillan, under the impetus of the struggle and the collapse of the *News Chronicle* was to announce the setting up of another Press Commission. But for the rest, the struggle now became a simple financial one, ending in the surrender by Odhams to the *Mirror* in March, and the statement on April 20th by Sir Christopher Chancellor.

'At a Board meeting of the *Daily Herald* (1929) Ltd. held today Sir Christopher Chancellor resigned from the chairmanship of the company and from his seat on the Board and proposed Mr. Hugh Cudlipp, joint managing director of the *Daily Mirror*, as his successor. Mr. George Woodcock, vice-chairman, seconded Sir Christopher's proposal and Mr. Cudlipp was unanimously elected chairman.

'Sir Christopher said, "I am glad Mr. Hugh Cudlipp is taking over the chairmanship of the *Daily Herald*. This is a logical step. Mr. Cecil King, chairman of the *Daily Mirror* which now owns Odhams Press, has confirmed and strengthened his earlier assurances about the future of the *Daily Herald*, the new agreement with the T.U.C. last August is being ratified, and Mr. John Beavan, who has already done so much to improve the paper since his appointment last October, is continuing as editor. I believe the *Daily Herald* has a good prospect of becoming a successful and influential newspaper which will play an important part in our national life." '

Some time later the *Herald* became the *Sun*. John Beavan joined the *Mirror* as its political adviser, while by a process of cross-fertilization Sidney Jacobson of the *Mirror* joined the *Sun* as its editor.

The *Herald* died; but not because the *Mirror* took it over. It withered away because it didn't have enough readers. And it lacked readers because it was dull.

CHAPTER XI

King, the Left and the Press

1951, 1955, 1959, 1964, 1966—at each General Election the *Mirror* under King's direction gave the Labour Party its support. Nor did the rivalry of television lessen its impact on a mass readership which liked to take its time over its pictures. The early fears of newspaper proprietors that TV would undermine their advertising revenue and circulation weren't fulfilled. And besides, with a customary foresight, King had acquired a television interest for the *Mirror* in ATV.

Gaitskell, in his prim, academic detachment, had failed to recognize the full influence of the *Mirror* on the new working classes in the Welfare State. Carefully supporting himself on the hierarchy of the trade unions, the revisionists of the Labour Party and its solid centre, stable rather than dynamic, he refused to recognize, despite his personally good relations with the *Mirror*'s journalistic staff, the paper's influence on working-class attitudes.

The *Mirror* itself had gone through an a-political phase after 1951, when the momentum of post-war recovery and the arrival of the Affluent Society had made politics seem an irrelevance to the general public. Suez and the Common Market arguments were lightning storms illuminating a damp plain of indifference. But at the end of the Macmillan Age, in which the counterpart of a complacent materialism was the Profumo Affair, there arose a national self-doubt—not a total self-criticism but rather a national introspection. It is true that, measured in economists' terms of growth and consumption, or in café-society terms of conspicuous wealth, the nation had 'never had it so good.' The City pages of newspapers were read as never before. Yet the fateful slogan was paralleled by a rise in violence, crime, and an elevation of get-rich-quick-values which in turn produced a smouldering public resentment. Criticisms of this social decline could only express itself through a rejection of the Tory Government. The *Mirror* in the 1964 Election backed Harold Wilson and the Labour Party.

King liked Wilson; he liked his professionalism and his pragmatism; and the two men had frequently met in the chairman's room in the *Mirror* building, where they discussed Labour's plans. King had often urged through the *Mirror* the need for younger men to replace the tired and aged. In Wilson, he saw a political representative of a new and energetic generation in search of change.

As a paper which had often defined itself of the Left, it seemed natural to some—so it had seemed to Gaitskell—that the *Mirror* would automatically support the Labour Party. Later events were to show that this wasn't so.

In King's estimate, the Left was a state of mind, independent, liberal, critical, socially compassionate and tolerant of human behaviour—except perhaps of humbug. He never took the view that to support the Left meant the total unselective support of radical attitudes. For example, he personally disagreed with the long and successful campaign of the *Mirror* against capital punishment. The paper's policy on this subject, begun by Cecil Thomas, the editor, in 1947 with Cassandra's vigorous support, had run counter to public opinion from the very start. But to Thomas and his colleagues it was a moral issue, and King respected their views.

'It is an important matter,' said the *Mirror* on April 14th, 1948, 'on which millions of people feel deeply, for upon it will ultimately depend the whole ethical and humanitarian trend of criminal justice in these supposedly enlightened times.'

King has said, 'I personally didn't agree with the End Hanging campaign of the *Mirror*, but I allowed the overwhelming consensus of office opinion to prevail.'

The *Mirror* took its own poll on the public's attitude to hanging. Of 39,666 readers who gave an opinion, 25,845 were opposed to hanging. But by 1962, the public opinion polls showed that the country as a whole was strongly in favour of retaining capital punishment. The *Mirror* stuck to its anti-hanging theme, nevertheless. In 1965 hanging was abolished, and the courageous pioneering of the *Mirror* endorsed by Parliament. King's acquiescence in the *Mirror*'s policy was his tribute to the integrity of his colleagues which had helped to reshape public opinion.

How powerful is the press in shaping public opinion? This is a question which newspaper proprietors and writers must constantly ask themselves. Nor is there any scientific way of answering it. Sociological surveys and opinion polls usually require of readers in this connection a fallible act of memory which vitiates their purpose. Sociology itself is the art of social assessment, not a science. Yet no one could reasonably argue that the press by its daily effect does not mould public attitudes, of which political attitudes can be among the most important.

Gaitskell was reluctant to acknowledge the influence of the *Mirror*. Wilson, on the other hand, expressed his gratitude openly to King for the help which the *Mirror* had given. Without it, it seems certain that the tiny Labour majority of 1964 would have been replaced by a minority.

King didn't back the Labour Party merely out of friendship for its leaders. With his liberal mind, he was constantly preoccupied with the responsibility of the press, whether in politics or, in the widest sense, in morals. Newspapers, he believed, should be concerned with morals; but should not be moralists.

'It is no accident,' he wrote in the *20th Century* magazine in spring, 1963, 'that the expansion of newspapers has coincided with the discovery of a social conscience by the public at large. In spite of the increase in some kinds of crime and bewildering changes in standards of sexual morality, we have as a nation become a good deal more responsible in our outlook. In the course of this century we have ceased to take violence for granted in our daily lives. We are shocked by cruelty to children and animals. Intolerance of minorities is less common. We are far less casual in our attitude towards suffering and collectively feel a need to act in the face of social problems. In the same period the number of national newspapers sold every day in this country has increased from about ¾ million to 15 million. This enormous addiction to newspaper reading has not caused these changes. But newspapers have helped to create a social atmosphere in which change has become possible.'

Millions, he pointed out, who would read nothing else, read newspapers. At one time, it was the practice of newspapers to dogmatize. The new semi-literate readership of the first twenty years of this century had an inordinate respect for the mystique of the written word, and the result was that a few individuals could at climacteric moments manipulate the political thinking of millions. The *Mirror*'s strength was that it asked as many questions as it offered answers. It provoked its readers to think.

'The popular press,' King said, 'has taught ordinary people to question and to make up their own minds. They are still not very good at it. They still come to decisions emotionally rather than by reason, but they are immeasurably better informed.'

King always defended the press against the charge that with its reporting of sex and crime it encouraged a decline in sexual morality and promoted a rise in crime. Newspapers, in his view, were more a reflection of society's concerns than initiators of public attitudes. In the case of crime, for example, King argued, however questionably, that crime vicariously enjoyed in print is a substitute for crime itself.

With an Olympian serenity, he believed that the function of a newspaper was to reflect the balance of forces in our society. Throughout his journalistic career, he has regarded censorship as an evil. Who are the censors? They are those who want to conceal the news for good or ill from the citizen. Concealment, King said, is always in somebody's interest, apparently for the best reasons, but the press is invariably right to resist such pressures. Like his uncle before him, King fought against censorship, and his emotional reaction to it was reinforced by his clash with Churchill during the war. The fight against the censor went on in the seventeenth and eighteenth centuries, but it was only in 1854 that *The Times* could boast, 'We hold ourselves responsible to the people of England for the accuracy and fitness of that which we think proper to publish.' Since that time, in King's view, subtle censorship has eroded this right. King claimed in the ninth Annual Report of the General Council of the Press that:

'The British press is, in fact, censored. Not directly; not openly by decree. But by the arbitrary operation of a series of loosely drawn laws which make it hazardous in the extreme for newspapers to comment or even report on a number of issues of vital public importance.'

What King had in mind were primarily the Official Secrets Acts and the laws against libel. To this he also added his concern about the abuse of Parliamentary privilege and the law against contempt of court, whose weight the *Mirror* itself had felt in the case of its editor Sylvester Bolam. He has called the law of libel a nightmare to editors and working journalists.

'No editor,' he said, 'when he goes home to bed, can be sure his paper does not contain some unwitting libel. In the face of the grossly excessive damages awarded by juries, the press is inhibited from its duty of public and critical comment.'

It is censorship which distorts news and may cause a malaise in our society, not publication.

In the matter of sexual morality, the critics of the press are more often than not those who believe that while sexual immorality is acceptable behind the *huis clos* of the upper classes, it is somehow or other unsuitable for the rest.

'The sexual morality of Victorian England,' said King, 'was very much a class matter. The upper classes and masses were pretty promiscuous; middle-class women were not. Their world was kept stable by the high incidence of prostitution. In the mid-twentieth century we are less hypocritical and we know far more about how people actually behave.'

But what of the press in this? King has doubted whether newspapers have much effect on sexual morals. Chastity, in fact, is one of the recommendations both of women's magazines and of most newspapers. What he has recognized above all is that in our society human relationships, not only those of sex, have moved towards a greater sense of mutual responsibility. The Victorians in the forties of the last century could remain unmoved for the most part by the death of a million Irish during the potato famine. We in our day have until recently been relatively indifferent to the hunger of the under-developed members of the world.

Yet nowadays, despite the fact that we live in an acquisitive society, newspapers have helped by the social content of their reporting to make the British people conscious of their responsibility not only for each other but for mankind too. It is not an accident that King should have interested himself personally in his West African newspapers. Contemplative by nature, he sought to surround himself with vivid, outgoing men, and among the Africans he found, paradoxically, an affinity and a companionship which is part of his world view.

Hugh Cudlipp has said, 'Nigeria's *Daily Times*, Ghana's *Daily Graphic* and Sierra Leone's *Daily Mail* are as important to King as the *Mirror* and the *Pictorial*.'

But King's anti-racialism didn't prevent him from endorsing in 1964 the Labour Government's policy on immigration which was designed to adjust the rate of immigration to the country's power to absorb and integrate.

King's constant theme has been that newspapers must use power with responsibility. A second—and related—theme has been that the common-sense of the people should be trusted. That is not to say that the people can't lose its common-sense and indulge in a fit of hysteria. At that point, King would say, it's the duty of the press to recommend reason and restraint.

The *Mirror* has always been fond of the word 'brash' to describe its approach to life. Yet in its thirty-year history under Bartholomew and King, it has constantly urged caution and prudence—caution in the use of sanctions, caution in the face of Hitler's promises, and caution at the time of Suez. This statesmanship, which many politicians might envy, has been accompanied by a dynamism which calls for boldness—boldness in denouncing fascism when a deferential Right Wing press was genuflecting towards it, boldness in prosecuting the war, and boldness in urging Britain's entry into the Common Market.

In the General Election of 1966, King continued to press Harold Wilson to declare himself and the Labour Party in favour of Britain's entry into the Common Market. In the seventeen months of Labour Government, during which he had accepted a directorship of the Bank of England, King had become steadily more convinced that Britain's survival depended on her entry into Europe. He linked that conviction with his belief in the country's need to modernize its institutions. And from his own experience of negotiation with the trade unions, he regarded reform of the trade unions as the most pressing of these changes.

Shortly after the 1964 Election, King made it clear to Wilson that the *Mirror* would maintain its critical independence of the Government, and every now and again a monitory leader gave a hard pull on the bridle. As the 1966 Election approached, the *Mirror* appeared with a powerful front-page leader entitled, 'Watch it, Harold!' It was a warning in the classic Northcliffian manner. It was an exhortation to the Prime Minister to keep in front of him the ideas of modernization, the Common Market, trade union reform and youth in government.

If ideology had been all, this might have put the *Mirror* in a fix. These were, indeed, the central planks in the programme of the Tory leader, Ted Heath. During the opening days of the Election, the *Mirror*'s sharp strictures on some of the older Labour Ministers might have led the unsophisticated to believe that Cecil King might have swung his support to the Tories. But to any student of the *Mirror*'s style, it was clear that the *Mirror*'s underlying sympathy, later expressed in categorical terms, was with Labour.

Labour could have won the 1966 Election without the *Mirror*'s help, though not necessarily in face of the *Mirror*'s opposition. But the 1966 Election was fundamentally a popular endorsement of the 1964 Election when the *Mirror* had made a major contribution to Labour's victory. In that sense, the *Mirror* could rightly claim to have laid the foundation of Labour's 1966 victory in 1964.

The banner of the *Mirror* in 1966 remained the banner of the group of talented and vigorous men who arrived in the 1930s—King, Cudlipp and Connor. The escutcheon was Youth. They first raised their flag among a young working class and made the *Mirror* in that decade the most popular newspaper in the world among readers below the age of forty-five. The question remains.

Can the *Mirror* retain the impetus of its youth? Can it still blow battle bugles for the young? King, who called for a sweep-out from the boardrooms of the old fuddy-duddies, has shown that even as the young men of the thirties mature through middle-age, the theme of the *Mirror* remains the theme of youth.

King in his study has the complete works of Benjamin Disraeli, the Tory radical, the visionary realist. His favourite among them, *Coningsby*, the best of Disraeli's political novels, ends with a challenge to the young.

'They stand now on the threshold of public life. They are in the leash, but in a moment they will be slipped. What will be their fate? Will they maintain in august assemblies and high places the great truths which, in study and in solitude, they have embraced? Or will their courage exhaust itself in the struggle, their enthusiasms evaporate before hollow-hearted ridicule, their generous impulses yield with a vulgar catastrophe to the tawdry temptations of a low ambition? Will their skilled intelligence subside into being the adroit tool of a corrupt party? Will Vanity confound their fortunes, or Jealousy wither their sympathies? Or will they remain brave, single and true; refuse to bow before shadows and worship phrases; sensible of the greatness of their position, recognize the greatness of their duties; denounce to a perplexed and disheartened world the frigid theories of a generalizing age that have destroyed the individuality of man; and restore the happiness of their country by believing in their own energies, and dare to be great?'

'Dare to be great'—it is Cecil King's own invocation to Britain, the unwritten epigraph of the modern *Mirror*.

APPENDIX I

From the 'Mirror', April 1st, 1966

THE INSIDE PAGE

Looking back today on fifty years of Election mornings-after.

14TH DECEMBER 1918

RESULT: Lloyd George Coalition, 478 seats. Others, 229. POLL: 58·9 per cent.

WAR-TIME Premier Lloyd George and his coalition swept the country on the platform of 'Punish the Kaiser! Make Germany pay! Bring the soldiers home!'

'The result,' said the *Mirror*, 'shows the confidence of the people in the man who won the war.'

The *Mirror* had been less than subtle in its Election-eve advice to readers:

'Don't forget to vote.

'Vote for the right man or woman (Coalition).'

Readers were further instructed:

'Mark your cross in the blank space against the name of your candidate; not against the **OTHER** candidate, under the impression that it's a black mark against him.'

The *Mirror* may have felt this elementary advice was necessary.

It was the first time in British history that women were allowed to vote—as long as they were thirty years and over.

A miserable day for Asquith, Liberal veteran and an ex-premier.

He lost his seat at East Fife after thirty-two years.

Labour's golden boy Ramsay MacDonald lost by 14,000 votes at Leicester.

15TH NOVEMBER 1922

**RESULT: Tories, 345 seats. Labour, 142. Others, 128.
POLL: 71·3 per cent.**

LLOYD GEORGE ousted. 'Terrible unemployment, loss of trade and staggering taxation' were the cause, said the *Mirror*.

Winston Churchill, defeated as a Liberal at Dundee, strongly denied he was in tears at the result.

The first Communist ever elected to Parliament—Newbold, at Motherwell—wired the news to Moscow.

Despite Labour's great gain in seats (from 63 to 142), their leader, Arthur Henderson, was defeated at Widnes.

6TH DECEMBER 1923

RESULT: Tories, 258 seats. Labour, 191. Liberals, 159. Others, 7. POLL: 70·8 per cent.

STANLEY BALDWIN following Bonar Law's death, was Prime Minister by then.

His post-election comment was a classic understatement:

'I think, from the look of things, I am going to have rather a difficult time.'

It took a week to prove him right.

His Government was defeated by a combined Labour-Liberal vote and Ramsay MacDonald, as leader of the next biggest party formed the first Labour Government.

29TH OCTOBER 1924

RESULT: Tories, 419 seats. Labour, 151. Liberals, 40. Others, 5. POLL: 76·6 per cent.

THE *Daily Mirror* of the day declared: 'The country's crushing verdict on Socialism and Red intrigues.'

For the Liberals—down to forty seats from 159—it marked their end as a major party.

Ramsay MacDonald's morning-after comment: 'The Labour Party is up against a maximum reactionary movement.'

30TH MAY 1929

RESULT: Labour, 288 seats. Tories, 260. Liberals, 59. Others, 8. POLL: 76·1 per cent.

IT WAS dubbed 'The Flapper Election'—for at last the vote was given to girls of twenty-one.

The *Mirror*'s Election day advice to flappers: 'WOMEN'S DUTY TO VOTE TODAY TO KEEP SOCIALISTS OUT.'

Ramsay MacDonald, who became Labour Premier for the second time in seven years, adopted a cautious outlook:

'I have been sceptical of reducing within a year the figures of unemployment (1,230,000) to normality.'

The Mirror's post-Election comment:

'Ought we to call this a plunge in the dark?

'Ought it not, after all, to be more accurately named a leap with the eyes open—to suicide?'

The Flapper Election achieved one thing.

The first woman Cabinet Minister, Margaret Bondfield, Minister of Labour.

27TH OCTOBER 1931

RESULT: National Government, 554 seats. Labour, 52. Others, 9. POLL: 76·3 per cent.

A FAMILIAR ring about Ramsay MacDonald's (now National Premier) morning-after promises:

To restore world confidence in the pound. Balance Britain's trade. Resist inflation.

An unhappy aftermath for J. H. Thomas, who followed MacDonald into the National ranks.

The National Union of Railwaymen, furious that their ex-secretary should take office in a non-Labour Government, refused him a union pension.

Thomas retorted: 'They can deprive me of my pension but not my soul or independence.'

Wry, morning-after comment from the *Mirror*:

'The Lloyd George Liberals at the moment are in the ludicrous position of being able to ride to Westminster on a tandem bicycle. They number only two.'

14TH NOVEMBER 1935

RESULT: National, 432 seats. Labour, 154. Liberals, 20. Others, 9. POLL: 71·2 per cent.

PRIME MINISTER Stanley Baldwin declared: 'A splendid result.

'The country has expressed decisively its confidence in our will and ability to continue our work for national restoration and world peace.'

Unemployment: two million.

Ramsay MacDonald lost Seaham, Durham, to Labour's Emmanuel Shinwell. By 20,498 votes.

'I'm not surprised,' said MacDonald.

5TH JULY 1945

RESULT: Labour, 393 seats. Tories, 213. Liberals, 12. Others, 22. POLL: 72·7 per cent.

LABOUR LANDSLIDE. The *Mirror* had pursued one of its most effective campaigns: 'Vote for Them!'

It urged the women at home to vote for the thousands of men still fighting overseas who were denied a vote.

A vote, the *Mirror* declared, which has been 'filched from them for Party purposes.'

Wild, cheering erupted from Transport House the Labour H.Q. as results came in.

In contrast, reported the *Mirror*, 'the scenes at the Conservative Party H.Q. were reminiscent of the funeral of a millionaire at which all the mourners have just learned that they were left out of the will.

'Grief, anger and despair were obvious everywhere.'

Clement Attlee, the new Premier, said: 'This is the first time in the history of this country that Labour has ever had a clear majority.

'It will enable us to implement the policy of the Socialist Party.'

Winston Churchill declared: 'I regret that I have not been permitted to finish the work against Japan.

'For this, however, all plans and preparations have been made.

'It only remains for me to express to the British people for whom I have acted in these perilous years my profound gratitude for the unflinching, unswerving support which they have given me during my task.'

23RD FEBRUARY 1950

RESULT: Labour, 315 seats, Tories, 298, Liberals, 9. Others, 3. POLL: 84 per cent. (highest since 1910).

TWO MORNING-AFTER COMMENTS with a 1964 ring about them. . . .

Surviving a near dead-heat, Premier Attlee said gravely:

'It is the duty of the present administration to continue in office.

'The King's Government must be carried on.'

Lady Megan Lloyd George, surveying the Liberals' nine seats:

'I think the Liberal Party is going to play a very important part in the new government.'

The Liberals had lost 300 deposits.

The Communists lost their only two seats.

The *Mirror*'s post-mortem; 'The mood of the country has never been more thoughtful.'

25TH OCTOBER 1951

RESULT: Tories, 321 seats. Labour, 295. Liberals, 6. Others, 3. POLL: 82·5 per cent.

AT SEVENTY-SIX Winston Churchill became the oldest Prime Minister since Gladstone.

It was also the first time the British public had elected him Premier.

With characteristic pugnacity Churchill told his Party:

'There lie before us hard times. I have no hesitation in saying I have seen worse and had to face worse.

'But I don't doubt that we shall come through.'

Mr. Attlee gave a clipped verdict on Labour's defeat:

'Our loss of seats has been due to the fact that when it came to it more Liberals were Conservative than Labour.'

The *Mirror*, who backed Labour, agreed:

'It is the Liberals who have gone Tory.

'There is no sign of loss of confidence in Labour.'

26TH MAY 1955

RESULT: Tories, 344 seats. Labour, 277. Liberals, 6. Others, 3. POLL: 76·7 per cent.

THE *Mirror* conducted the inquest:

'Labour lost because its leaders are too old, too tired, too weak.'

8TH OCTOBER 1959

RESULT: Tories, 365 seats. Labour, 258. Liberals, 6. Others, 1. POLL: 78·8 per cent.

THE TORIES become the first Government this century to increase its majority in two successive elections.

Returned as Premier Harold Macmillan said blandly:

'It has gone off rather well.'

APPENDIX I

15TH OCTOBER 1964

RESULT: Labour, 317 seats. Tories, 303. Liberals, 9. Others, 1 (the Speaker). POLL: 77·1 per cent.

AT 48, Harold Wilson became the youngest Prime Minister of the century.

Of his tiny majority, he said:

'I want to make it quite clear that this will not affect our ability to govern.'

APPENDIX II

The 'Mirror' on Winston Churchill and Lord Moran, May 24th, 1966

THE PERPETUAL LOVE-HATE affair between politicians and the Press is often passionate, sometimes spiteful, invariably uneasy.

Never was this historic relationship more strained than between Sir Winston Churchill and the *Daily Mirror*.

The true depth of feeling between Downing Street and the offices of the *Mirror* is disclosed in the remarkable memoirs* of Lord Moran, Churchill's physician and friend.

Explosive

In his copious bedside jottings (300,000 words, 3¼lb. net weight) Moran kept a fascinating record of Churchill's views on the *Mirror*.

They were generally explosive.

Moran reports that when Churchill picked up the morning papers, he generally turned to the *Mirror* or the *Daily Worker*.

'Perhaps he means to get the worst over first,' wrote the omnipresent physician.

What particularly stung Churchill over his breakfast table?

Moran's entry for August 17th, 1953:

'Have you read the *Daily Mirror*?' he asked, and rang for a secretary.

As it was handed to me, I read the big headlines on the front page: 'What is the truth about Churchill's illness?'

Stroke

The *New York Herald Tribune*, according to the *Mirror*, had stated that the P.M. had had a stroke in the last week in June, and that although he had made a near-miraculous recovery, those in the best position to judge did not believe he would ever again be able to assume active day-to-day leadership of his country.

* *Winston Churchill: The Struggle for Survival, 1940–1965* by Lord Moran (Constable 1966).

'Is there any reason,' the *Mirror* went on, 'why the British people should not be told the facts about the health of their Prime Minister?

'Is there any reason why they should always be the last to learn what is going on in their country?

'Must they always be driven to pick up their information at second hand from tittle-tattle abroad? . . .'

'Five million people read that,' the P.M. said grimly. 'It's rubbish, of course, but it won't help at Margate' (the Tory Party Conference).

Serious

On March 7th, 1953, William Connor ("Cassandra") wrote a brilliant and biting epitaph on Stalin.

Moran recorded at the time:

'He (Churchill) is much incensed by the *Daily Mirror*'s remarks about Stalin and describes it as "dancing on his tomb."

'The *Mirror*, for its part, complains of Mr. Churchill's crocodile tears.'

Five months later Churchill showed Moran a copy of a monthly magazine called *History Today* (circulation 30,000).

'It is written by young historians for serious people,' Churchill said.

'This is the more serious side of the nation. I find all this very encouraging.

'It would appear that not everyone in England reads the *Daily Mirror*.'

Churchill returned to the attack on November 24th, 1953.

Moran wrote:

As I entered the P.M.'s room this morning he threw away the *Daily Mirror* with a gesture of disgust.

'They want Prince Charles to mix with working people.'

Subdued

'I suppose they would have a ballot, and each day the successful twelve would come to the Palace.

'I wish we could buy that rag; it is doing so much harm.'

I picked up the *Mirror* while he got on with his breakfast. 'Why not open the Palace to the people?' was the heading.

It was this that raised his ire—there was nothing about Prince Charles.

'Poor Queen,' Winston muttered over his breakfast, 'she will be asked to do so much.'

On January 26th, 1954, Moran wrote:

Winston is very subdued this morning. 'I wish I had more energy. Can't you do anything for me? I must do something for my living.

'The *Mirror* is suggesting I am past it and that I ought to resign. Read it,' he growled, passing me the paper.

'Why do I waste my time over this rag? I am being bloody tame.

'I defer too much to other people's opinions.'

But there was worse to come from another (an unexpected) quarter.

On February 4th, 1954, Churchill showed Moran a cartoon in *Punch.*

It depicted Churchill in a state of advanced senility.

'There's malice in it,' said Churchill.

'The *Mirror* has had nothing so hostile.

'Look at my hands—I have beautiful hands.'

On April 1st, 1954, Moran offers his own critical assessment of the Mirror:

My cook from Ayrshire takes her political views from the *Mirror*, and when it is particularly venomous about Mr. Churchill she brings me her copy.

(*By 'venomous' Moran presumably was irked because the 'Mirror' was telling the nation the truth about Churchill's state of health.*)

It was half-past nine by Big Ben as I made for No. 10 to see for myself whether the *Daily Mirror*'s attack had got under his skin.

When I went upstairs, his valet said he had not gone to bed until one o'clock and was still asleep.

Outside his bedroom there was a pile of morning papers.

I settled down to get the hang of things.

On the back page under the caption, 'What America says about Churchill now,' the *Mirror* quoted the *New York Times*:

'For the first time since Parliament reconvened last autumn, Sir Winston appeared unsure of himself and tired.

'This wasn't the Churchill of two years ago and was only the shadow of the great figure of 1940.

'In his replies to questions, Sir Winston contradicted himself.'

I turned to the leader in the *Daily Mirror*, 'Twilight of a Giant,' to find what the Editor was about.

He dotted the i's and crossed the t's.

Statue

On September 10th, 1954, Churchill showed Moran a page he had torn out of the *Mirror*.

It carried a picture of Nye Bevan standing before a statue of Lenin taken during a Labour Party delegation's visit to Russia and China.

'That might be useful to the Party Office as propaganda,' said Churchill.

'It shows the fellow is a Communist.'

In November, 1954, the *Mirror*, along with other papers, was attacking Churchill for disclosing that he had been prepared to use Germans against the Soviet Union at the end of the war if the Russian advance had continued across Europe.

(*On November 30th, Churchill's 80th birthday, the 'Mirror' declared a truce and produced a souvenir issue.*)

Slip

Moran quotes Churchill on his birthday eve:

'If my slip had done harm with the Russians I may pull out sooner that I intended. Take my pulse, Charles.'

It was 82.

When I had reassured him, he brightened up a little.

'The *Daily Mirror* has declared a truce for tomorrow.

'They have sent £1,000 to my birthday fund.

'I am to be given a cheque for £140,000 tomorrow.

'All this leaves me very humble: it is more than I deserve.'

There are many other mentions of the 'Mirror' in Lord Moran's brilliant diagnosis.

And no doubt there will be as many more mentions of Moran in the 'Mirror'—and in other newspapers which were treated by Winston with silent respect, but certainly with public indifference.

APPENDIX III

Editors of the 'Daily Mirror'

1904–1907	Hamilton Fyfe
1907–1915	Alexander Kenealy
1915–1920	Ed Flynn
1920–1931	Alexander Campbell
1931–1934	L. D. Brownlee
1934–1948	Cecil Thomas
1948–1953	Sylvester Bolam
1953–1961	Jack Nener
1961–	L. A. Lee Howard

Bibliography

Publish and Be Damned. Hugh Cudlipp (Dakers, 1953)
At Your Peril. Hugh Cudlipp (Weidenfeld & Nicolson, 1962)
The Romance of the Daily Mirror (Daily Mirror Newspapers, 1924)
Street of Ink. H. Simonis (Cassell, 1917)
Sixty Years of Fleet Street. Hamilton Fyfe (W. H. Allen, 1949)
Northcliffe. Pound and Harmsworth (Cassell, 1959)
Certain People of Importance. A. G. Gardiner (Jonathan Cape, 1926)
The Press in England. K. von Stutterheim (trans. W. H. Johnston) (Allen & Unwin, 1934)
British Newspapers and Their Controllers. Viscount Camrose (Cassell, 1947)
Newspaper Lords in British Politics. C. J. Hambro (Macdonald, 1958)
History of The Times, 1912–1948 (Pt. II, Chaps. XIII–XXIV). (*The Times*, 1952)
English History, 1914–1945. A. J. P. Taylor (Clarendon Press, 1965)
The Appeasers. Gilbert and Gott (Weidenfeld & Nicolson, 1963)
The Age of Illusion. Ronald Blythe (Hamish Hamilton, 1963
The Baldwin Age. Ed. John Raymond (Eyre & Spottiswode, 1960)
A King's Story. The Duke of Windsor (Cassell, 1951)
Call Back Yesterday, Memoirs 1887–1931. Lord Dalton (Muller, 1953)
The Fateful Years. 1931–45. Lord Dalton (Muller, 1957)
High Tide and After. Lord Dalton (Muller, 1960)
Diary with Letters. Thomas Jones (Oxford University Press, 1954)
Private Papers of Hore-Belisha. A. J. Minney (Collins, 1960)
Beveridge and His Plan. Lady Beveridge (Hodder & Stoughton, 1954)
The British General Election of 1945. McCallum and Readman (Frank Cass, 1964)
The Age of Austerity. Ed. Sissons and French (Hodder & Stoughton, 1963)

The Fifties. John Montgomery (Allen & Unwin, 1965)
Herbert Morrison: A Pictorial Biography. (Lincolns-Prager, 1950)
An Autobiography. Lord Morrison (Odhams, 1960)
As It Happened. Earl Attlee (Heinemann, 1954)
Full Circle. Lord Avon (Cassell, 1960)
This Great Journey. Jennie Lee (MacGibbon & Kee, 1963)
Winston Churchill: The Struggle for Survival, 1940–1965. Lord Moran (Constable, 1966)
Dangerous Estate. Lord Francis Williams (Longmans, Green, 1957)
The Press and Its Readers. Mass Observation Report (Arts & Technics, 1949)
What I Said About the Press. Randolph Churchill (Weidenfeld & Nicolson, 1957)
The Sugar Pill. T. S. Matthews (Gollancz, 1957)

Parliamentary Debates (Hansard), 1904–1964 (H.M.S.O.)
Dod's Parliamentary Companion, 1940–1964
20th Century (Spring, 1963), pp. 98–102
The Press and the People. 9th Annual Report of the General Council of the Press
Royal Commission on the Press, 1961
The files of the *Daily Mirror*, *Sunday Pictorial* and *Sunday Mirror*

I would also like to thank the publishers of the following books for permission to quote from them:

Northcliffe (Cassell); *History of The Times* (The Times); *English History, 1914–1945* (Clarendon Press, Oxford); *A King's Story* (Cassell); *This Great Journey* (MacGibbon & Kee); *Winston Churchill: The Struggle for Survival* (Constable).

Index

Notes

Topics which cannot be given separate headings are grouped under the entry, '*Daily Mirror*'.

Foundataion dates of newpapers and journals, when known, are shown in brackets after their names.

'(Ed.)' after a name means 'Editor of the *Daily Mirror*'.